SISTERS IN THE LIFE

SISTERS
IN THE LIFE

A HISTORY OF OUT AFRICAN AMERICAN LESBIAN MEDIA-MAKING

Yvonne Welbon & Alexandra Juhasz, editors

Duke University Press • Durham and London • 2018

Library of Congress Cataloging-in-Publication Data
Names: Welbon, Yvonne, [date] editor. | Juhasz, Alexandra, editor.
Title: Sisters in the life : a history of out African American lesbian media-
making / Yvonne Welbon and Alexandra Juhasz, Editors.
Description: Durham : Duke University Press, 2018. | Series: A camera obscura
book | Includes bibliographical references and index.
Identifiers: LCCN 2017040717 (print)
LCCN 2018000303 (ebook)
ISBN 9780822371854 (ebook)
ISBN 9780822370710 (hardcover : alk. paper)
ISBN 9780822370864 (pbk. : alk. paper)
Subjects: LCSH: African American lesbians in motion pictures. | Lesbianism
in motion pictures. | Lesbian motion picture producers and directors—
United States. | Lesbians, Black—In motion pictures.
Classification: LCC PN1995.9.L48 (ebook) | LCC PN1995.9.L48 S57 2018 (print)
| DDC 791.43/653—dc23
LC record available at https://lccn.loc.gov/2017040717

Cover art: (*from top*) Dee Rees directing *Pariah* (photo by Jenny Baptiste,
© Focus Features/Courtesy Everett Collection); Shine Louise Houston
directing *Crash Pad Series* (photo by Tristan Crane for CrashPadSeries.com);
Tina Mabry on the set of *Queen of the South* (photo by John Brawley).

Contents

ALEXANDRA JUHASZ

Preface

To Be Transparent: Seeing Directions and
Connections in Black Lesbian Film

> To be transparent, I write these words as a deeply invested beneficiary and longtime fan. . . . Yvonne Welbon, the editor and initiator of this book, and other contributors have participated in the[se] activities . . . and this is as it should be. The future of Black lesbian filmmaking is not something about which we can be objective; it is something we do. It *is* our lives, and it saves our lives. It is our tangible practice for representing and creating the world.
> **—Alexis Pauline Gumbs**

For a number of reasons, this collection ends but also begins with Gumbs's words from "Creating the World Anew: Black Lesbian Legacies and Queer Film Futures." I like the circularity. This construction replicates a number of the preoccupations and commitments expressed throughout this collection and as a form clarifies the unique and complex contributions of black lesbians to American film history and politics, committed as these artists and films are to nonlinear or nontraditional arrangements for time and place, media, and human connection. Although the anthology is organized historically, the delicate tissues that link authors, filmmakers, films, and their audiences become apparent in this anthology's totality as a powerful, exploding constellation of directions and connections defining the subject at hand: an impressive body of films made by and for a tightly knit community characterized by care, protest, and possibility. As Yvonne Welbon explains in her introduction and elsewhere across the volume, this relatively small group of artists has produced a disproportionate number of films within the canons of African American, women's, and queer cinema, and yet they go underrecognized.

Hence this effort; hence so many efforts like it, all built from a small community with important support structures, according to Pamela Jennings in her video interview with Welbon, made for the transmedial segment of this project and included in this volume. And yet, as Gumbs suggests, this tradition *is* known well, and often deeply and dearly, to itself. The intentional knowing, making, sharing, producing, and loving of the black lesbian film community is what allows for its productivity, permanence, and power.

In this vibrant community, artists, activists, and scholars make multi-directional and -dimensional connections of care and creativity to support each other and their work across time and space and in many relations to each other. The loosely chronological structure of the anthology barrels over how this art and these artists circulate. For instance, many of the filmmakers discussed here (as well as their respected critics) make work and community across all of the history marked out in the anthology's title. And there is no one simple or standard trajectory from the anthology's start in 1986 to the present. Rather contributors' movements (and the black lesbian film movement's linked trajectories) are spatial, formal, economic, and cultural: from city to city, job to job, girlfriend to girlfriend, 16mm to digital, digital to analogue. Time flows accordingly. While Gumbs ends by looking forward, and I begin by looking back at her, other authors name influences from moments in American history considerably before there was ever a possibility for the "out black lesbian filmmaking" that flourishes in the 1990s. For instance, Karin Wimbley looks to the antebellum Mammy figure when writing about Cheryl Dunye's *The Watermelon Woman* (1996), and Marlon Rachquel Moore turns back to Nina Simone's civil rights protest music to better frame Tina Mabry's *Mississippi Damned* (2009).

Just so, in these pages, you will find the names of black (queer) artists who lived and worked before there was this (and other) movements to join. In no particular order we hear of Audre Lorde, Storme, James Baldwin, Josephine Baker, Marcus Garvey, Zora Neale Hurston, Hattie McDaniel, Ella Fitzgerald, Nina Simone, Alice Walker, bell hooks, Patricia Hill Collins, and many others. Several of the films share this legacy project as well (I think of "Cheryl" in *The Watermelon Woman*, a film that I produced, as she holds up to the camera stills of her black female and lesbian foremothers, or of the Fae Richards archive we faked with the photographer Zoe Leonard so that "Cheryl" could find and hold images of the lesbian precedents she knew had come before her, including the character I played for these photos, the film director Martha Page, who was modeled on Dorothy Arzner). Welbon's media work also shares this project (*The Cinematic Jazz of Julie Dash* [1992], *Living with Pride: Ruth Ellis @ 100* [1999]), one of finding, naming, celebrating, and sharing those who came before, those who fought and paved the many ways. But not only names return, and no path for black lesbians is simple given the many structural obstacles and possible openings along the way. Jennifer DeClue writes about the "circuitous route of presenting black butch" in the films of Dee Rees, moving, as the films and Rees do, through the many connected spheres of New and even Old Queer Cinema, queer film festivals, and mainstream cinema circuits. Imagining even more paths of connection, Roya Rastegar delineates how "the embodied, participatory relationships incited by [Shari] Frilot's curatorial approaches reframe linear relationships between the spectator and the screen and generate new dynamics that require people's collective presence to experience cinema."

Rastegar's thinking about Frilot's work, like Gumbs's opening words and my recirculation of all of these critical ideas of assembly, also marks the critic's and historian's role in these colliding orbits of black lesbian (self-) representation. In our writing we contribute to the world-making project initiated by filmmakers—or was this initiated by relationships? or community? curating? sex? or political exigency?—by placing their images into the traditions and frameworks of scholarly, historical, and teachable analysis. Here you will see black lesbian films situated within long traditions of African American expatriatism and the Black Atlantic (according to Devorah Heitner discussing Welbon's autobiographical film, *Remembering Wei-Yi Fang, Remembering Myself* [1995]), or artistic movements such as the New Black Cinema, Third Cinema, Black Arts Movement, and the LA Rebellion (in relation to the oeuvre of Michelle Parkerson, the pornography of Shine Louise Houston, or the project to teach filmmaking explained by Gumbs in her essay on the Queer Women of Color Media Arts Project and Black Feminist Film School). Some of the work is framed disciplinarily, for instance when Kara Keeling looks at Pamela Jennings's work through science, technology, and society's interests in "computational-based creative expression," or when Candace Moore uses production studies to understand how the work of four producers and three producer-collaborators creates some of the necessary scaffolding for this tradition. Of course, there are many, varied, and sometimes even competing institutional frameworks that support the work, for instance, Indiewood and the New Queer Cinema (for Frilot, Dunye, Rees, and Angela Robinson) and institutionalized Black Feminism for others, some of whom helped to "institutionalize" it, some who learn later from and grow its legacies (the queer porn of Houston or the current organizing of Queer Women of Color Media Arts Project). Meanwhile, it is the significance of the black church that frames other projects. While Jennifer Brody notes that Coquie Hughes is inspired by religion, Tiny Mabry and Rees make their out black lesbian films through an intense reckoning with the cruel force of religion.

But "us" and "them"—we faithful and they sinners, we critics and they filmmakers—like all the relations discussed thus far, is not a neat or even particularly useful structure for understanding this community. This is because many of the critics writing here are also filmmakers, the filmmakers we write about are curators, and all of this work focuses on people, images, and ideas that are also always circulating. Like me: I write this preface and was also interviewed by Candace Moore as one of the producers in the tradition she studies and details in her contribution. Here's where the "to be transparent" part circles back in: in being transparent I can begin to better explain my own circulation across this anthology and history, and better yet, I can introduce and frame Yvonne's. For, to be transparent, Yvonne and I—comparable to the relationships of so many authors in this collection—have worked together, eaten together, celebrated and championed together in uncountable and varied ways across the twenty-five-plus-year history that is the subject of this book, which is the living and loving that make this book: a community that creates its own art, infrastructure, "scholarly proof" (or "materials to teach," as Yvonne calls it), databases, and archives—and their analyses—not only because no one else would (although this is one of our motivating political critiques), not only because we can do it better, but because the doing of it "*is* our lives, and it saves our lives," as Gumbs suggests. And no one demonstrates this particular manifestation of power—making one's life as one makes one's work and history and community—as profoundly and consistently as does Welbon, who has devoted her career to Sisters in the Cinema: finding, archiving, making, circulating, teaching, and understanding the work of African American women's media expression. Her voice, influence, and passion—as director, producer, curator, historian, teacher, mentor, friend, and editor of this collection—bubble up again and again across the anthology (as is true for many of the participants) because hers is the force of will that built this particular transmedia project, as she has so many others, for and within the community she documents and so conjures into being and history.

Interestingly, the transparent telling of the community's making (and remaking) of itself is inextricably connected to the story of the films' making (how else could it have gotten done given the lack of support elsewhere!) and also to the films' narratives, which is to say that many of these films are about both the making of this community and the making of these films (see the essays on the self-reflexive work of Hughes, Houston, and Dunye, for instance). "The network among ourselves is born from necessity and proximity. Many of us are closely connected to alternative media networks, know each other from our fields of activism, and have maintained those relationships," explained Jocelyn Taylor in 1997 in a dialogue among black queer filmmakers, "Narrating Our History," selections of which are reprinted here. In 1997, already engaged in this project of self-reflexive self-naming and self-historicizing (at the very moment when the possibility for this tradition comes into being, as the tradition begins because the community makes it so), Taylor and others come together, document the moment, and circulate it.

Our anthology begins with two reprints: "Birth of a Notion" by Michelle Parkerson from 1991–93 and "Narrating Our History: A Dialogue among Queer Media Artists from the African Diaspora" (with an update by one of its original authors, Thomas Allen Harris). But neither of these efforts was really the beginning, as many of them attested to then. While Parkerson looks to the "flurry of black gay male visibility" as a critical bellwether of things that will (and indeed did) come—*Tongues Untied* (Marlon Riggs, 1989), *Looking for Langston* (Isaac Julien, 1989), *Paris Is Burning* (Jennie Livingston, 1990)—Dawn Suggs says, "My first exposure to queer works of color was at the screening of Parkerson's *Stormé* [1991] in 1989." "Thomas Allen Harris and Cheryl Dunye organized the first panel of black gay and lesbian artists that I know of," says Welbon as she thinks back to the first national Gay and Lesbian Studies Conference in 1991.[1] Panels, friendships, activism, partnerships, one-night stands—or was it the civil rights or feminist or LGBTQ movement? As I've been insisting, this history isn't lived or told with neat causality. What I can verify is that I knew Jocelyn, Isaac, Jennie, Yvonne, and Dawn at that time. We were all friends or colleagues, lovers or ex-lovers, or at the very least passionate associates.

Jocelyn affirms and questions the role of these associations in "Narrating Our History": "If we're all friends writing our own history, well . . . it's been done before. History is not absolute truth, it's merely a documentation of selective memories and events." And again, she's right, at least in that circular way that I suggest is moving us forward. We've done it all before: narrated our histories in rings of care, taken care of ourselves for ourselves, made our own histories for each other and then for history and others. And yet two expansions, not repetitions, seem useful here. First, over time those artist-friendship-activist circles and their conversations *change*: new people join, either unaware of the earlier conversations or not able to have joined them in the first place; people die and others are born; relationships change: lovers and partners and even producers become ex; knowledge and audiences develop; the rules of entry and belonging shift, as do the names we call ourselves; American (and international) culture opens new possibilities for people of color and queers as it closes others. Second, technologies of transmission and connection grow. In the short time span of this history, "filmmaking" has taken up any number of media, from celluloid to video to digital, and that alters black lesbian product as much as process. This project, which is transmedial in form—holding this book, and a film, website, and archive—could not have been generated in these many forms when this history began and could never have delivered so much to so many.[2] For instance, "Narrating Our History" was published in the anthology *XII Black International Cinema* in Germany in 1997. This rather difficult-to-access document of a selective conversation among friends is much easier to access here in its book form, and even easier still when it manifests in this project's online format. Thus, circling back to it via new (and old) media formats serves new uses for the audiences who access it here for the first (or second) time. While documents may stay the same (and a good many are gathered here, and there's even more in the online archive), our needs, audiences, and uses for them change.

Continuing to cite Taylor, and persisting in being transparent, I attest that our engagements with that particular past dialogue (and the other histories and historical documents shared in this collection) will be no more "objective" or "impartial" than have been any of the critics, filmmakers, or activists engaged by this project because to read or write here is to become part of the tangible process of representing and creating the world of black lesbian filmmaking whether you are friend, lover, ally, student, or even, dare I say, a black lesbian yourself. We do not shy away from our closeness to the objects, people, politics, identities, or analyses at hand. How could we? Why would we? This collection is one part of a greater, growing, and powerful process of transparent, attached community expression, production, and care, the one responsible for the impressive, inspirational body of film and history under consideration.

And, to be clear, I am not a black lesbian, although my roles in this history are many: as friend, lover, coparent, film producer, actor, scholar, coeditor, and collaborator. Here I raise two more concerns, amply covered in the pages that follow. The first, a definition of *black lesbian*: Who is one? What might this phrase mean? Across these pages you will find that this term and its constituent communities, practices, and issues are used differently, are understood variously, are mobilized toward multiple ends. Authors write about films that are "queer despite [their] lack of explicitness about gayness" (Heitner on Welbon's *Remembering Wei-Yi Fang*), and how, according to Keeling, "to the extent *black lesbian* does not appear in her work, despite, perhaps, our desire to find it there, [Pamela] Jennings challenges us to generate other logics and language for what does appear there, prompting us to create concepts for whatever we can perceive in her work." Rastegar explains that, for Frilot, "the goal was not to simply include people of color in the paradigm of gay and lesbian identity but to reconceptualize sexuality entirely so that race, identity, nationality" could be constituent. Houston is interested in black female masculinity and often casts white men in her porn.

Here black lesbians are held to old and new logics, languages, and reconceptualizations, but what you won't find, perhaps surprisingly, is much drama or anxiety about this particular naming project. Instead each author, and the filmmaker she focuses on, finds a place of comfort from which to speak about, within, and for this community (in its exploding expansiveness and powerful encompassing), and then she gets to work. While the project of defining terms, and the communities and politics that they in turn delineate, is a worthy one, as well as one that takes up a significant amount of time within queer, feminist, and critical race theory and activism more broadly, it simply doesn't end up being the primary concern of the authors here. Perhaps that's because preoccupations with naming would get in the way of the task at hand (looking closely at a film and filmmaker), or perhaps authors felt that Yvonne invited them to write, and she had already selected the list of qualified artists from which they could then choose to write, and *Yvonne* called these artists "black lesbians," so, so be it. But maybe it's because so many of the films and filmmakers within this tradition have done this work already. The situated, contested, communal making and remaking of names, identities, and connections happen in the films, by and for the community. Houston, explains L. H. Stallings, "instead of replacing one configuration of realness with another . . . simply advises that all impetuses to realness are someone's fabrication. Is it real black or real lesbian if it is directed and produced by someone who is not black or lesbian?" Or, according to Candace Moore (quoting Louise Wallenberg), in her study of women who have worked as producers of black lesbian cinema, "such media challenges the construct of an 'essential black queer subject,' figuring her instead 'in the spaces *between* different communities—at the intersections of power relations determined by race, class, gender and sexuality.'"

Of course the second clear concern raised by my admission that I am not a black lesbian is about the place in this effort, community, and field for white women, women of color who are not African American, men, and queer or trans people who do not identify as lesbians or women. Again, perhaps surprisingly, this does not seem to be much of a concern for those who write here (black lesbians and not). Frilot, quoted in Rastegar, explains how a quite capacious understanding of community organizes her curatorial work of black queer cinema, in this case for MIX 1996: "The blackness of the 'black' folk who have made these pieces and who are presented within them tends to be a fairly slippery, perhaps even incoherent phenomenon. Male/Female, Latin/Anglo, Dark/Not-So-Dark, Queer/Not-So-Queer, the identities represented within Victoria MIX are necessarily strung together loosely, a fact that is exacerbated by the resistance to traditional narrative found within many of the works."

While a resistance to narrative and other traditional forms defines Frilot's work in supporting and building a black lesbian film community and its media legacy, in these pages you will also find films and filmmakers who fit more clearly within more hegemonic generic traditions. Here you will find analysis of filmmakers sometimes working within the heart of the studio or television systems (Robinson, Rees, and sometimes Dunye) and on its very many generic edges (Hughes in online video, Houston in porn, Jennings in computational media, for instance). But this very binary of mainstream and alternative forms is also challenged by Patty White writing on Robinson: "The opposition between mainstream and independent may be an economic one, but it may no longer be as potent an aesthetic or political one, and not only because studio classics divisions have created something called Indiewood." And then, of course, there's Michelle Parkerson, who at the beginning of this tradition made her career by creating what were "traditional" (albeit some of the first) documentaries about black women's and black lesbian life (. . . *But Then, She's Betty Carter* [1980] and *Stormé: The Lady of the Jewel Box* [1987]). Various filmmakers move from margins to centers and perhaps back to margins again (Dunye is an obvious example, as she made a Hollywood studio movie in the 1990s only to then make another experimental feature in 2010, *The Owls*, that I also produced, then radical porn [*Mommy Is Coming*, 2012], and then, wow, in 2014 a new short, *Black Is*

Blue; back to where she started, but this time focusing on a black trans man and not [herself] a black lesbian); filmmakers move from production to curation and sometimes back to production (Frilot comes to mind), or from directing to writing to producing to directing (see Welbon!); artists range across media and platforms (from video to digital, from film to video, from video to 16mm), as they become available, as media helps to expand access and audience; some fluctuate between creating urgent, radical media and a negotiation with a "mainstream" industry that seeks to profit from marginal identities and media production (Robinson, Rees, Mabry, Dunye).

Given this variety and multiplicity, the many merits of black lesbian filmmaking and its history and analysis are of considerable importance for a wide variety of scholarly fields, most obviously those of queer, feminist, black, and ethnic filmmaking, but also indie and American cinema and the many disciplinary studies of social and cultural movements for civil rights and justice. In "Narrating Our History," Raúl Ferrera-Balanquet explains: "The two books about queer cinema don't say anything about our works, our critical writings, our friendships, and all the history we have gone through together"—a statement that proves true for all those other kinds of cinema books, I'm afraid. For it is only we who want to and then can transparently explain the deep connections that allow for unsupported, unacknowledged, underappreciated work to be made and seen, and also then to be so damn strong. Authors here attest to how it was always another member of this community who inspired one filmmaker to pick up a camera for the first time, or who showed her the right inspirational images, or who got her a gig, or who wrote that first article about her. It was we lesbians and queers who made posters for each other, carried cables, and together made meals and archives. Of course culture, politics, identities, and technologies have shifted (often because we engaged in activism and filmmaking!) over these twenty-five years. Some members of this community no longer, or never, identified as women or lesbian, for example. Our community responds to and makes such changes. The evidence of these challenges and dynamic relations—to each other, to other activist and artistic communities, and more broadly to American and world culture—is the very subject of the films that are analyzed in the following pages. These films hold black lesbians' thoughts and images about civil rights, black feminism, neoliberalism, queer and trans politics, the trans- and multinational, American history, aging, religion, pornography, and so much more. This is why Welbon begins each of the anthology's two sections with a brief overview of the historical, political, representational, and technological landscape (as these are of particular impact on black lesbian media-making). Here she creates a broader contextual analysis for this formative movement by highlighting the relationships among media technologies, access, media production, and the formation of an out African American lesbian community.

In the essays, interviews, biographies, critical analyses, and loving homages that follow, I hope you will see some of what has been so inspiring and feeding for me and for others in this community. While at times, and in various essays, the place of this work and also its makers can feel utterly vulnerable, precarious, and sometimes unsafe, in that same time, and essay, we also learn how solid, sustaining, and supportive can be the community and the media work that it generates so as to unmask and unmake oppression. Individuals, communities, and our political needs and demands change, but the films stay the same: marking where we've been, what we thought, who we knew, what mattered once. This scholarly anthology uses the films to name and sustain a dynamic history, community, and politics for black lesbians in America.

But I've been trying to emphasize throughout that this is not a traditional scholarly anthology, not because the scholarship isn't traditional but because this is no traditional tradition. Here you will find the requisite footnoted essays, as well as elegant interviews and authorized reprints. But we also provide transcripts from Yvonne's interviews with two of the filmmakers (Jennings and Hughes) because, as of yet, the scholarly writing about them is limited. We include their words to facilitate and inspire that communal (self)production definitive of the work. In 1990 Parkerson observed that, as black gay male and lesbian cinema expanded, "a wellspring of critical analysis and theoretical study has concurrently evolved." Hence, more than a quarter-century later, this volume attests to a critical mass. But there's always more work to be done. Our readers will become the community's new critics and filmmakers. You are welcome to join our authors as they speak with transparency, circularity, and pride, just as do the films considered, by naming their place within, their connections among, and their right to the tradition of out black lesbian filmmaking that Welbon so generously set into radical motion with her life's work. With transparent connection, Gumbs follows, continues, and moves forward: "If we say that Black lesbian feminist filmmaking and Black queer filmmaking are rooted in the lived experiences and organizing culture of Black lesbians, that means not only do the films we make draw resources (audiences, actors, crew, funding) from Black lesbians and the organizations that we have created, but they also replenish the soil by bringing people together, increasing visibility, and providing a vehicle for necessary conversations in our community."

Let the conversations begin!

Notes

1 Raúl Ferrera-Balanquet et al., "Narrating Our History: A Dialogue among Queer Media Artists from the African Diaspora," in *XII Black International Cinema Anthology* (Berlin, 1997), 136.

2 Please see www.sistersinthelife.com for more resources, information, objects, and writing from the Sisters in the Life project.

YVONNE WELBON

Introduction

The Sisters in the Life Archive Project

Since the 1922 theatrical release of Tressie Souders's *A Woman's Error*, approximately one hundred feature films have been directed by African American women.[1] Almost one-third of those films were directed by black lesbians. Statistically about 4 percent of the adult American population is likely to identify as lesbian, gay, bisexual, or transgender, but over 30 percent of the feature films have been directed by this minority population.[2]

While production budgets and audience reach vary widely, the black women who have directed the most feature films are almost all black lesbians. Coquie Hughes has directed eight features. Cheryl Dunye has directed six feature films. Shine Louise Houston has directed five feature films. Tied for fourth place with four features each are their straight counterparts Kasi Lemmons and Ava DuVernay. Black lesbian directors have also eclipsed their straight counterparts in other areas of filmmaking. In 1974 Michelle Parkerson became the first African American woman to win a student Academy Award for *Sojourn* (1973), a film she codirected with Jimi Lyons Jr., a fellow Temple University student. The first black woman to be nominated for a nonstudent Academy Award for directing is also a black lesbian. Dianne Houston was nominated for her short film *Tuesday Morning Ride*, starring Ruby Dee and Bill Cobb, in 1996. The highest grossing Hollywood studio film directed by a black woman was directed by a black lesbian. Angela Robinson's Disney film *Herbie Fully Loaded* (2005), starring Lindsay Lohan, grossed over $144 million worldwide. At the time Robinson had also directed the film with the largest Hollywood studio budget: $50 million for the same film.[3] In 2017, out lesbian Lena Waite made Emmy history as the first black woman to win for writing for a comedy series—*Master of None*.

Why are black lesbians having a markedly different experience in the film industry than their straight sisters? Why are films directed by African American lesbians disproportionately represented? While there may be a simple answer or multiple answers, it remains difficult to say at this time. African American women directors in general and black lesbian directors in particular are an understudied group of artists. It is the goal of the Sisters in the Life (SITL) transmedia project to begin a discourse and increase the knowledge base about this little-known and overlooked group of directors by providing a wide range of primary and secondary resources. SITL is part of a larger project called Sisters in Cinema that seeks to promote all African American women media makers.[4] The components of the SITL project include this book of essays and interviews written by media scholars; a feature-length documentary film; a resource-rich evolving website with filmmaker and scholar interviews, clips of films, historical timelines, and bibliographic data (www.sistersinthelife.com); and an archive of media and ephemera that may be housed at the UCLA Film and Television Archive's Outfest Legacy Project and also made accessible, in part, online and through a select number of public libraries. The SITL project will provide resources to a public interested in learning more about black women filmmakers.

Project Origins

I can trace the roots of this project back to my undergraduate days at Vassar College. In 1983 I registered for a class called Women in Latin American History. As a child of an immigrant tracing my roots to Honduras, Nicaragua, and Costa Rica, I was excited to finally have an opportunity to learn about my family history in an academic setting.

On the first day of class we reviewed the syllabus. My family wasn't there. I learned that we would basically spend the semester studying Mexican nuns of European descent. "Where are the black women?" I asked. My professor explained that there was little material on black women in Latin America that could be incorporated into our course. She said she was aware of the absence and had included *Child of the Dark*, the diary of an Afro-Brazilian woman, in our readings even though Brazil wasn't part of Spanish-speaking Latin America as we were studying it.

Throughout the semester I searched for scholarly proof of our existence. My professor was right. I found little that could be incorporated into a college course. If I had not been in the class, would the other students have learned there was a history of black women in Latin America that we were not studying? The experience demonstrated on so many levels how what is taught has tremendous power to shape historical scholarship and our understanding of ourselves and of the world we live in. It also drove home the point that without materials to teach, entire populations would continue to be understudied, or possibly not studied at all, inadvertently rendering them invisible.

Almost a decade later, while working on my MFA in film and video and later on my doctoral dissertation focused on the history of African American women feature filmmakers, I found myself in a similar place. Once again I was trying to learn about a history in academia and discovering that it was not being taught there. While there were definitely texts in print about African American film in general, the book-length texts usually mentioned black women's involvement in cinema in front of the camera, not behind. In those pre-Internet days, I began to spend a lot of time in libraries searching through texts and journals and microfilm to find black women media makers. Slowly I began to find articles about African American women's media production, and I began to build a database of the filmmakers and their films.

In order to develop my research for this project I had to first find the work of black lesbian artists. To this end I became a board member of Women in the Director's Chair (WIDC) and served for over three years (1991–94). During that time the WIDC Film and Video Festival received between three hundred and six hundred submissions of new works by women annually. I also joined the film and video committee of the Chicago-based African American Women in the Arts (AAWA) Conference and served for three years (1991–93). At that time AAWA held the only African American women's film competition in the country and had received close to one hundred submissions. As an advisory board member (1992–93) and a volunteer (1995) for the Chicago International Lesbian and Gay Film and Video Festival, I found another excellent resource for uncovering black lesbian work.

Excited by what I was seeing, I began to independently curate programs for Chicago Filmmakers, a nonprofit media arts center. I also began to write articles on black women media makers for the *Independent* and on lesbian film and video for the *Windy City Times*, a Chicago-based gay and lesbian news weekly. All of these actions gave me "official" reasons to see most of the new work being made by black women filmmakers at the time and created opportunities for me to meet many of the media makers both in person and on the phone.

As a filmmaker I was able to meet my peers at conferences and festivals. The first organized panel of black gay and lesbian video artists I attended convened at the Gay and Lesbian Studies Conference at Rutgers University in 1991. The lesbians on the panel included Michelle Parkerson, Cheryl Dunye, Dawn Suggs, and me. In attendance were Jacqueline Woodson and Jocelyn Taylor. "Sistah Said What?," a panel discussion among lesbian film and video makers of color, took place at the 1993 San Francisco Lesbian and Gay Film Festival. The black lesbian panelists included Aarin Burch, Shari Frilot, Dawn Suggs, and me. The independent curator Margaret R. Daniel, founder of the Women of Color Film Festival, and the filmmaker H. Lenn Keller, both black lesbians, were also in attendance. Other festivals, conferences, and university gatherings brought us together. The largest gathering of black lesbian media artists met at the Black Nations/Queer Nations conference in New York in 1995.

Through these events we were all able to establish friendships and working relationships. As a result the black lesbian community of film and video artists became a tight-knit network between 1986 and 1995. We stayed in touch via letters, postcards, phone, fax, and email. I was able to explore the personal media archives of my new friends. We worked on each other's projects, read each other's scripts, screened each other's rough cuts, and sometimes even cried on each other's shoulders. My curiosity sent me on a journey that has now spanned over twenty years—a search for my sisters in cinema.[5]

What began as a simple database became three distinct and interconnected projects: a website, a feature documentary, and my doctoral dissertation. All three projects share the name *Sisters in Cinema*. In doing the work and through my new and growing friendships with my peers, I amassed what is perhaps one of the largest archives of African American women's media production in the country. Stored in boxes and on a wide range of digital storage devices, the archive includes over one hundred hours of videotaped interviews and transcripts; over one hundred films, videotapes, and DVDs directed by African American women; and over one hundred boxes of related artifacts that include correspondence, posters, photos, rough cuts, festival programs, box office reports, trailers, journal articles, buttons, T-shirts, and a wide range of other ephemera and memorabilia. The Sisters in the Life archive has become a fourth interconnected project and is one component of the larger Sisters in Cinema archive project.

According to the historian Mary Ritter Beard, "Without knowledge of women in history as actual history, dead women are sheer ghosts to living women and to men."[6] With her goal of including women in what is understood as history, Beard stressed the importance of the archive as a repository of the documents that could do just that.[7] The Sisters in the Life archive gathers essays, video and print interviews, films and multimedia, posters, scripts, buttons, postcards—a treasure trove of proof of the existence of black lesbian media makers and our work—and organizes it in a range of accessible ways. In building the archive I have saved everything. And I have searched for more, filling box after box. I have worked with others to gather and to create primary and secondary sources. What I've learned on this journey that began in my class at Vassar is that without documents there is no history. And without a documented history it is as if some people don't exist—and that goes for both the living and the dead.

All the Women Are White, All the Blacks Are Men, but Some of Us Are Invisible

According to the French historian Pierre Nora, we live in a time when it is imperative "to keep everything, to preserve every indicator of memory . . . to produce archives." He believes the responsibility of "remembering" has been delegated to the archive and "requires every social group to redefine its identity through the revitalization of its own history."[8] This process makes "everyone his own historian" and privileges memory, which for Nora is already history. But what I learned in working on the archive project is that it doesn't matter what I think is important. I learned that my desire to produce any kind of archive, be it a website or a documentary or my doctoral dissertation, to remember our history is not enough alone to make sure that black women are included in cinema history—especially when we are socially, and as a result culturally, invisible.

In 2010 two researchers, Amanda Sesko and Monica Biernat, concluded that, based on their studies, black women were indeed socially invisible. The researchers did "not mean to suggest Black women literally go unnoticed and unheard, that their presence is undetectable. Rather, they are treated as interchangeable and indistinguishable from each other, and in this sense are less 'visible' compared to other groups." In addition they found that black women were not being correctly credited for their contributions. Rather their contributions were attributed to white women or black men. Why? They found that gender is usually associated with white women and race is usually associated with black men. Black women are left in between and therefore experience "a qualitatively different form of discrimination in which their non-prototypicality contributes to their not being recognized or correctly credited for their contributions."[9]

The researchers reference bell hooks's introduction to *Ain't I a Woman? Black Women and Feminism*: "No other group in America has so had their identity socialized out of existence as have black women." States hooks, "We are rarely recognized as a group separate and distinct from black men, or as a present part of the larger group 'women' in this culture. When black people are talked about the focus tends to be on black men; and when women are talked about the focus tends to be on white women."[10] Parallels can be drawn in studies of women filmmakers focused on white women and African American filmmaking centered on black men.[11]

Sisters in the Life, the Book

I, like so many others, have chosen this moment in time to remember a period that began in the mid-1980s that has been termed New Queer Cinema. This period has been marked by the creation of a number of archival documents. In 2013 B. Ruby Rich marked the history of the term she coined with the publication of her book, *New Queer Cinema: The Director's Cut*. The Winter 2014 issue of *Cinema Journal: The Journal of the Society for Cinema and Media Studies* looked at this recent history of queer cinema. And a number of films were released commemorating the twenty-fifth anniversary of ACT UP. The archival footage used extensively within the films was made possible, in part, by queer media makers documenting our lives with new media technologies that put the power of media production into the hands of ordinary people. While these are just a few examples of how New Queer Cinema has been recently archived, what is consistent is the demonstration of the power of the archive to privilege certain histories and marginalize others.

In the ACT UP films our activist history is remembered as largely white and male. In the publications the diversity emphasis has shifted to "global versus American and multicultural." While Rich does offer a short essay on Dunye's *The Watermelon Woman* (1996) and discusses the work of Dee Rees, Angela Robinson, and Michelle Parkerson, the space devoted to the works of black lesbian media makers totals only a few pages of the 322-page volume.

When studying New Queer Cinema, there is little indication that over thirty feature films and over two hundred shorts and multimedia works were directed by over one hundred out black lesbian media makers.[12] Given that there were only a handful of films directed by out black lesbians in the 1980s and the notable experiences of black lesbian media makers described at the beginning of this essay, it seemed appropriate to also look back at this period with a focus on this work and to create a media archive project that attempts to document a phenomenon in media representation.

So, to begin to write black lesbian women into media history, why not begin with a book? And, remembering my experience at Vassar, an academic peer-reviewed anthology to boot. I enlisted the assistance of a number of scholars to write essays for the book and Alexandra Juhasz, a film scholar and media maker, to serve as my coeditor. I provided the scholars with a list of filmmakers and subjects to choose from, and they decided on the shape their essays would take. I provided a list of the 130-plus media titles in my database at the time and enlisted their assistance in further developing the list.

The book is divided into two sections. The first section covers the period from 1986 to 1995. The 1986 video *Women in Love: Bonding Strategies of Black Lesbians* by Sylvia Rhue is described by Jenni Olson, author of the *Ultimate Guide to Lesbian and Gay Film and Video*, as the first film by an out black lesbian about black lesbians.[13] The film was screened at the 1987 Los Angeles International Gay and Lesbian Film/Video Festival and marks the beginning of what this survey considers the history of out black lesbian media-making.[14] The works created during this time were experimental films, short narratives, documentaries, computer-generated media, and installation pieces. There were approximately twenty-five artists working during this period, together producing over seventy-five media productions. In this section the focus is on five of the twenty-five artists.

The second period covers from 1996 to 2016. The division is marked by the theatrical release of the first feature film directed by an out African American lesbian, Dunye's *The Watermelon Woman*. A feature film is a dramatic narrative that is about seventy minutes or longer. Through a combination of theatrical and ancillary distribution, feature films generally tend to reach a larger audience than short films and documentaries. The marketing and publicity generated by the theatrical release of a feature film often bring the director into the public spotlight, creating name recognition and situating the film and filmmaker within popular culture. The first narrative feature with a theatrical release marked a new phase in out black lesbian media-making, creating the possibility for our work to reach a national and international stage.

Sisters in the Life is the first book of its kind to offer a comprehensive overview of an understudied history of out black lesbian media-making. To be clear, there are a few books that reference some of the makers included in this volume.[15] Media makers such as Dunye and I have chapters dedicated to our work in a few texts. Other filmmakers, such as Rees, Shine Louise Houston, Robinson, and Tina Mabry, are sometimes mentioned in collective thematic paragraphs or have small sections dedicated to them in overviews. Most of the media makers included in this book have been the subject of essays and journal articles.

History Is Not Absolute Truth

"Archives—as records—wield power over the shape and direction of historical scholarship, collective memory, and national identity, over how we know ourselves as individuals, groups and societies."[16] It is the archive that solidifies our history and determines in our present what will be known about our past. Who decides what to record, preserve, and, as a consequence, privilege? While historically marginalized or minority groups may desire an archive, it is ultimately the archivists, those who control the archive, who determine what will be considered worthy of preservation.

In 1996 queer media makers Raúl Ferrera-Balanquet and Thomas Allen Harris created an archive project called "Narrating Our History: A Dialogue among Queer Media Artists from the African Diaspora."[17] The dialogue was published in *XII Black International Cinema Anthology* in Berlin in 1997 and provides a rich history of a community of media makers who were also curators and writers and collaborators. The project asks the contributors to remember a history that was still undocumented within queer cinema history and African diaspora film history. For Ferrera-Balanquet, documenting our own history played an important role in filling the gaps. "I have seen how 'queer cinema' has become so commercialized, and also how the white queer media makers have capitalized the audience and watered down the real issues affecting us. The two books about queer cinema don't say anything about our works, our critical writings, our friendships and all the history we have gone through together." The media maker Jocelyn Taylor says, "History is not absolute truth, it's merely a documentation of selective memories and events. Even straightforward testimony has gaps and is misleading and irresponsible at times in relationship to truth." So this current telling of our history is in line with Taylor's concerns. It is selective at best and offers a particular perspective.

In "Narrating Our History," the only curation was the initial set of questions asked. Each media maker was able to respond without any editing, mediation, or censoring. In *Sisters in the Life*, with the exception of two selections from my own interviews with filmmakers, the media makers are written about by film scholars. In some cases the writers interviewed the filmmakers, but for the most part the reader will have little access to the primary data the filmmakers provided the writer for her essay. To lessen this "power over the documentary record, and by extension over the collective memory" of this underrepresented group of media makers "and indeed over their representation and integration into the metanarratives of history," the SITL archive project extends beyond this book of scholarly essays.[18]

With the Sisters in the Life archive project, the revitalization of our history is fraught with challenges I did not foresee. The fact that I am asking some media makers to recall what happened decades ago is problematic. In some cases the media makers simply don't remember the details. Questions about where their film screened or how it was received are documented more easily with festival catalogues and film reviews. In some cases the filmmakers were not involved with the distribution of their films, and the results of my research were sometimes news to them. The most surprising outcome was the number of women who did not understand why I would want to interview them or include them in the archive project. They did not see the value of their contributions to our collective history. For Nora the responsibility of remembering has been delegated to the archive: "The less memory is experienced from the inside the more it exists only through its exterior scaffolding and outward signs. . . . Even as traditional memory disappears, we feel obliged assiduously to collect remains, testimonies, documents, images, speeches, any visible signs of what has been, as if this burgeoning dossier were to be called upon to furnish some proof to who knows what tribunal of history."[19] If this is indeed the case, I want to have my hand, and my community's, in the archive's construction and dissemination.

In Jamika Ajalon's 1997 short experimental film *Memory Tracks*, a young woman chases a past represented by a 1960s woman activist who comes to her "as a reflection." As she quickly moves through city streets to a rhythmic beat ("Where the revolution at? Where the revolution at?"), she spots her reflection looking at her through the lens of a Super-8 film camera. They both run. But instead of catching the revolutionary, she finds the camera. When the young woman looks through the camera lens she is able to travel down "memory tracks" and connect with her revolutionary past. The film ends with the two doing a sort of mirror dance, facing each other, slowly following each other's moves. Then they both turn and stare directly at us, breaking the fourth wall and acknowledging our presence as spectators. In

Intro.1 *Memory Tracks,* directed by Jamika Ajalon, 1997.

that moment they see us, and we, no longer enmeshed in the fiction, see them. In that moment they are not invisible. In that moment it is clear "where the revolution at."

Notes

1 "Film Company Expanding," *Billboard*, January 28, 1922, 104.

2 Experien Simmons, "The 2012 LGBT Report: Demographic Spotlight," accessed August 24, 2017, http://www.experian.com/assets/simmons-research/white-papers /simmons-2012-lgbt-demographic-report.pdf.

3 DuVernay's 2018 release, *A Wrinkle in Time*, budgeted at $100 million, is now the largest budgeted film directed by an African American woman.

4 In the 1986 black gay anthology *In the Life*, the editor, Joseph Beam, defines *in the life* as a term that describes "the gay life." I am using this phrase in this essay with the term *sisters* to describe African American homosexual, lesbian, queer, bisexual, same-gender-loving women. While many of the women self-identified as lesbians and out at the time their work was created and originally distributed, today some artists no longer identify themselves with any of these terms.

The Sisters in the Life archive project has received support from two Mellon Fellowships: the Future of Minority Studies Postdoctoral Mentoring Fellowship, under the guidance of William A. "Sandy" Darity Jr. at Duke University, and the Humanities Writ Large Visiting Faculty Fellowship at Duke University. In addition, support was provided by Bennett College for Women. The project requires additional funding and support to be fully realized.

5 For an overview of the research process and methodology, see the introduction in Yvonne Welbon, "Sisters in Cinema: Case Studies of Three First-Time Achieve-

ments Made by African American Women Feature Film Directors in the 1990s," PhD diss., Northwestern University, 2001.

6 Mary Ritter Beard, "The Historical Approach to Learning about Women," speech given at Radcliffe College, May 22, 1944, Mary Ritter Beard Papers, A-9, Schlesinger Library, Radcliffe College, Cambridge, Massachusetts.

7 Anke Voss-Hubbard, " 'No Document—No History': Mary Ritter Beard and the Early History of Women's Archives," *American Archivist* 58.1 (1995): 16–30.

8 Pierre Nora, "Between Memory and History: Les Lieux de Memoire [1984]," *Representations* 26 (1989): 14–15. The title of this section is a reference to the collection of essays edited by Gloria T. Hull, Patricia Bell Scott, and Barbara Smith, *All the Women Are White, All the Blacks Are Men, but Some of Us Are Brave: Black Women's Studies* (Old Westbury, CT: Feminist Press, 1981), which calls for an inclusion of black women in both women's studies and black studies.

9 A. K. Sesko and M. Biernat, "Prototypes of Race and Gender: The Invisibility of Black Women," *Journal of Experimental Social Psychology* 46 (2010): 360.

10 Sesko and Biernat, "Prototypes of Race and Gender," 360.

11 Examples include, but are not limited to, Mary G. Hurd, *Women Directors and Their Films* (Santa Barbara, CA: Praeger, 2017); Jan Lisa Huttner, *Penny's Picks: 50 Movies by Women Filmmakers 2002–2011* (New York: FF2 Media, 2011); Jean Petrolle and Virginia Wexman, eds., *Women and Experimental Filmmaking* (Urbana: University of Illinois Press, 2005); James Quinn, *This Much Is True: 14 Directors on Documentary Filmmaking* (London: Bloomsbury, 2013); and Jeremy Geltzer, *A Separate Cinema: 50 Years of Independent African American Filmmaking* (Burbank, CA: The Hollywood Press, 2014).

12 Works produced as part of the San Francisco–based Queer Women of Color Media Arts Project (QWOCMAP) are not included in these figures. While there are an additional seventy-five titles that were produced through the workshops by over eighty-five black lesbian media makers between 2006 and 2013, only the films produced as part of QWOCMAP that have been programmed and screened outside of QWOCMAP festivals have been included in these figures.

13 Jenni Olson, personal interview, June 29, 2009.

14 The 1973 student Academy Award–winning short, *Sojourn* by Michelle Parkerson (and Jimi Lyons), is thought to be the first film directed by an out black lesbian filmmaker. In the 1980s Parkerson directed . . . *But Then, She's Betty Carter* (1980) and produced *Gotta Make This Journey* (1983), about the a cappella women's group Sweet Honey and the Rock. In her early films Parkerson did not focus her lens specifically on black lesbians.

15 These titles include JoAnne C. Juett and David M. Jones, eds., *Coming Out to the Mainstream: New Queer Cinema in the 21st Century* (Newcastle: Cambridge Scholars, 2010); Alexandra Juhasz and Jesse Lerner, eds., *F Is for Phony: Fake Documentary and Truth's Undoing* (Visible Evidence; Minneapolis: University of Minnesota Press, 2006); E. Patrick Johnson and Mae G. Henderson, eds., *Black Queer Studies: A Critical Anthology* (Durham, NC: Duke University Press, 2005);

Michele Aaron, ed., *New Queer Cinema: A Critical Reader* (New Brunswick, NJ: Rutgers University Press, 2004); Alexandra Juhasz, *Women of Vision: Histories in Feminist Film and Video* (Visible Evidence; Minneapolis: University of Minnesota Press, 2001); Alison Darren, *Lesbian Film Guide* (Sexual Politics; London: Cassell, 2000); Phyllis R. Klotman and Janet K. Cutler, eds., *Struggles for Representation: African American Documentary Film and Video* (Bloomington: Indiana University Press, 1999); Judith M. Redding and Victoria A. Brownworth, *Film Fatales: Independent Women Directors* (Seattle: Seal Press, 1997); Gwendolyn Audrey Foster, *Women Filmmakers of the African and Asian Diaspora: Decolonizing the Gaze, Locating Subjectivity* (Carbondale: Southern Illinois University Press, 1997); Chris Holmlund and Cynthia Fuchs, eds., *Between the Sheets, in the Streets: Queer, Lesbian, Gay Documentary* (Visible Evidence; Minneapolis: University of Minnesota Press, 1997); Jacqueline Bobo, ed., *Black Women Film and Video Artists* (AFI Film Readers; New York: Routledge, 1998).

16 Joan M. Schwartz and Terry Cook, "Archives, Records, and Power: The Making of Modern Memory," *Archival Science* 2 (2002): 2.

17 Raúl Ferrera-Balanquet et al., "Narrating Our History: A Dialogue among Queer Media Artists from the African Diaspora," in *XII Black International Cinema Anthology* (Berlin, 1997).

18 Schwartz and Cook, "Archives, Records, and Power," 17.

19 Nora, "Between Memory and History," 13–14.

PART I • 1986–1995

The emergence of out black lesbian media-making is closely tied to what the filmmaker and scholar Clyde Taylor termed in 1983 as New Black Cinema, a movement unified in its "determined resistance to the film ideology of Hollywood." This movement linked filmmakers through a cultural kinship, resulting in the production of a diverse body of work driven by "aesthetic individualism, cultural integrity, or political relevance." For Taylor New Black Cinema "was born out of the black arts movement of the 1960s, out of the same concerns with a self-determining black cultural identity."[1]

Spike Lee is one director who helped define New Black Cinema. His 1986 film, *She's Gotta Have It*, sparked the black independent cinema movement that marked the end of the twentieth century. While Lee was being lauded for the "realness" in his portrayal of the black community, for many black lesbians, Opal Gilstrap, the stereotypical black lesbian in the film, lacked cultural integrity. She was not reflective of the worlds they knew, and yet there she was, the only media representation of a black lesbian that most movie viewers had ever seen. The black lesbian filmmaker Cheryl Dunye was in the audience at a Spike Lee lecture when he was asked about his black lesbian misrepresentation.[2] His reply, "[Let her] create her own images if she wanted different representations." Dunye and the first wave of out black lesbian media makers were inspired by Lee's comment and his ever growing body of work. Together they created the first media images of black lesbians by black lesbians that were truly reflective of our diverse lives and communities.

"As race, sexuality, and gender emerge as popular themes in the media, I have come to realize that I can no longer accept the lack of and misrepresentation of black lesbians in films and videos," said Dunye.[3] That same sentiment is what inspired Sylvia Rhue to make her first film. After spending long hours watching films as a requirement for her doctorate in human sexuality, she decided that she could do a better job. Her 1986 video, *Women in Love: Bonding*

I.1 *Women in Love: Bonding Strategies of Black Lesbians*, directed by Sylvia Rhue, 1986.

Strategies of Black Lesbians, is described by Jenni Olson, author of the *Ultimate Guide to Lesbian and Gay Film and Video*, as the first film by an out black lesbian about black lesbians.[4] The film was screened at the 1987 Los Angeles International Gay and Lesbian Film/Video Festival and marks the beginning of what this survey considers the history of out black lesbian media-making.

Part I, "1986–1995," begins with "Birth of a Notion: Toward Black, Gay, and Lesbian Imagery in Film and Video" by Michelle Parkerson.[5] For many black lesbian media makers, Parkerson was our Spike Lee. She was the first black lesbian filmmaker and sometimes also the first black woman filmmaker that we knew. She was an out black lesbian and she was making movies and had been doing so for a long time. Because of her, so many of us believed that we too could become filmmakers.

In her essay she writes that "a new generation of gay and lesbian filmmakers of color has begun to produce imagery countering the invisibility and social stigmas." One reason for this emergence was the advent of low-cost media-making technologies and media arts centers that rented production and postproduction equipment to independent filmmakers at affordable prices. Parkerson began her career when independent media makers used

16mm film to make their movies. At roughly $400 per produced ten minutes of editable 16mm footage, the cost of production made filmmaking unattainable for many. With the introduction of new video formats that included VHS ($2 per editable sixty minutes to two hours of footage), Hi-8 ($8–10/hour), and pixel vision, which was shot on an audiocassette tape ($1/hour), media-making became something almost anyone could participate in.

At the end of her essay, Parkerson asks black filmmakers, "How can we broaden gay and lesbian experience and imagery beyond 'the celluloid closet'? How will we construct an ethnocentric, diverse nation of lovers? How will we undertake this birth of a notion?" In the chapters that follow her questions are answered in various ways.

The first response is a rich oral history of LGBT media makers, writers, and curators of the African diaspora captured in 1995. Thomas Allen Harris and Raúl Ferrera-Balanquet were concerned that our history wasn't being documented as part of Queer Cinema history and saw this dialogue as a "point of departure in the development of the narrative of our history."[6] For the organizers it was important that the history be recorded as a conversation "due to the oral traditions of our cultures." They asked that participants, including myself, respond in a conversational voice reflective of dialogue. While the project was shared with over a dozen media makers, with a request to extend the invitation to others, ten participated, five women and five men. "Narrating Our History" is a collection of thoughts, reflections, and remembrances that recount the collective and individual histories experienced by a group of avant-garde queer film- and video-makers from the African diaspora.[7]

The dialogue sets the tone for this book in our attempts to create an archive of varied and surprising items. In the dialogue we hear directly from five of the twenty-five artists that make up the first wave of out black lesbian media makers: Shari Frilot, Leah Gilliam, Dawn Suggs, Jocelyn Taylor, and me. Together we reference half a dozen others: Cheryl Dunye, Jacqueline Woodson, Aarin Burch, Vejan Lee Smith, and Michelle Parkerson. The dialogue tells the story of a movement that included queer men and women and so many others. It provides what I believe to be one of the best documents available that captures the birth of black queer media-making.

Part I continues with five selections focused on media makers that provide a broad and varied history of the period via a range of terrains. Kara Keeling's "Construction of Computation and Desire" introduces my interview with Pamela Jennings. I first encountered Jennings's work in an experimental documentary class while I was an MFA student at the School of the Art Institute of Chicago. She was a student too, breaking new ground with her quick embrace of emerging technologies. The introduction and the interview provide a portrait of an artist engaged with a range of technological innovations. Jennings begins as a photographer, moves to video, and finds a home in computational media. Keeling describes Jennings's works as "characterized by a spirit of scientific experimentation with the artistic possibilities of today's technologically mediated world." Jennings is viewed from three angles. Keeling provides a framework for viewing the artist. My interview with Jennings allows her to tell the story of her journey that includes stops in New York City, Alberta, Canada, and the IBM Almaden Research Center in San Jose. And Jennings's "the book of ruins and desire" offers documentation of her interactive mechatronic sculpture that no longer exists.

Roya Rastegar's essay on Shari Frilot, "A Cosmic Demonstration of Shari Frilot's Curatorial Practice," explores exhibition and how the work of an artist reaches an audience. Rastegar offers a comprehensive overview of the artistic and curatorial career of one of the first out black lesbian media makers. While Jennings's interest in science is as an artistic practice, Frilot explores scientific themes in her work that is never explicitly queer. Part I ends with Devorah Heitner's "Identity and Performance in Yvonne Welbon's *Remembering Wei-Yi Fang, Remembering Myself: An Autobiography.*"

Circling back to Parkerson's question of broadening gay and lesbian imagery and experience, it is important to note there were other out black lesbians who directed their first films during this period who do not have individual chapters in this volume. They include Anne Marie "Jade" Bryan, who directed *Cutting the Edge of a Free Bird*, the first film by an out deaf black lesbian, and Dianne Houston, who was nominated for an Academy Award for her short film *Tuesday Morning Ride* (1995). Other women who emerged during this period include Jamika Ajalon, Aarin Burch, Leah Gilliam, C. A. Griffith, Melanie Hope, Natalie Hutchinson, H. Lenn Keller, Gail Lloyd, Mary Morten, Cyrille Phipps, Aishah Shahidah Simmons, Vejan Lee Smith, Christina Springer, Dawn Suggs, Jocelyn Taylor, Jacqueline Woodson, and Stephanie Wynne. Together they produced approximately seventy-five films. Their short experimental, documentary, and narrative films varied greatly, from Phipps's *Our House: Gays and Lesbians in the Hood* (1993) to Burch's autobiographical *Spin Cycle* (1991), to Wynne's comedic short *Never Say Never* (1995), about a straight woman who swears she could never love another woman but ends up changing her mind, and Gilliam's *Sapphire and the Slave Girl* (1995), a video that investigates racial passing, cross-dressing, taboo sexualities, and other transgressions of identity and location. Their work helped to expand what Parkerson saw as the "birth of a notion" to an explosion of media of black lesbian self-representation unlike any in cinema history.

Notes

A complete filmography and selected interviews and short films from out black lesbian media makers are available online at www.sistersinthelife.com.

1 Clyde Taylor, "New U.S. Black Cinema," *Jump Cut: A Review of Contemporary Media*, no. 28 (April 1983): 46–48.
2 Cheryl Miller, "In the Life: New Works by Black Lesbian Filmmakers," *Hot Wire* 8.3 (1992): 38.
3 Cheryl Dunye, "Building Subjects," *Movement Research*, no. 4 (Winter/Spring 1992): 18.
4 Jenni Olson, personal interview, June 29, 2009.
5 This essay was originally published in the *Advocate* 570 (February 12, 1991). It was expanded and republished in *Queer Looks*, edited by Martha Gever, Pratibha Parmar, and John Greyson (New York: Routledge, 1993).
6 Fax from Raúl Ferrera-Balanquet, November 16, 1995.
7 Raúl Ferrera-Balanquet et al., "Narrating Our History: A Dialogue among Queer Media Artists from the African Diaspora," in *XII Black International Cinema Anthology* (Berlin, 1997), 135.

Birth of a Notion
Toward Black, Gay, and Lesbian Imagery
in Film and Video

In mainstream media, gays and lesbians of color are either woefully present or predictably absent. The litany of black gay and lesbian characters in Hollywood films and network television reads like its own form of blackface.

They range from the burly, black "bulldagger" as whorehouse madam in the 1933 film *The Emperor Jones* (starring Paul Robeson) to the predatory lesbian vamp in Spike Lee's 1983 *She's Gotta Have It*; from Eddie Murphy's ultracamp Miss Thing hairdresser on NBC's *Saturday Night Live* to the snap! queen duo on Fox TV's *In Living Color*.

These relentless stereotypes are part of a continuum of silence and mockery and denial surrounding lesbians and gay men within our own African American community—a community that is, of course, one of the largest consumers of Hollywood and network entertainment. With no other screen alternatives, audiences believe this is who we are.

In reducing our lives and complexity to caricature, such program formulas, capitalizing on homophobia and racism, produce big profits for mainstream media. The constricted images of black gays and lesbians are the same appropriated to all nonwhites in film and video: enemies, entertainment, or exotica.

Recently a new generation of gay and lesbian filmmakers of color has begun to produce imagery countering the invisibility and social stigmas. These filmmakers are using media to reverse decades of misrepresentation, replacing negative myths with whole and humane depictions. The films and videos currently being produced *by* black gays and lesbians *about* black gays and lesbians—this birth of a notion—represent the opening of a dialogue,

1.1 Robert Reid-Pharr, Michelle Parkerson, and Cheryl Dunye, date unknown. Photo by Yvonne Welbon.

overdue and unflinching. From the United Kingdom, witness Isaac Julien's lush cinematic meditation, *Looking for Langston* (1989), and here in the United States, Marlon Riggs's *Tongues Untied* (1989). Both feature the incisive poetry of Essex Hemphill and the music of Blackberri. These groundbreaking black gay directors expand the discourse on race and homoerotic desire in their current works: Julien's ebullient *Young Soul Rebels* (1991) and Riggs's video shorts, *Affirmations* (1990) and *Anthem* (1991).

Among younger generations of black gay men and lesbians, the films and videos of Dawn Suggs, Thomas Harris, Sylvia Rhue, Cheryl Dunye, Jacqueline Woodson, Jack Waters, Aarin Burch, Jocelyn Taylor, and Yvonne Welbon are emerging. Their works challenge the boundaries of experimental, auto-biographical, and documentary genres. They offer innovative production styles in presenting visions of being "in the life." These productions are also changing the complexion of AIDS media—exploring the devastation and celebrating the courage of a community disproportionately ravaged by the epidemic. These film- and video makers are the first wave of a developing black gay and lesbian film movement. Now a legacy begins.

Several other films by white producers and directors have investigated black gay life: Shirley Clarke's 1967 experimental study of a black hustler, *Portrait of Jason*, and the Greta Schiller and Andrea Weiss documentary, *Tiny and Ruby: Hell-Divin' Women*. This 1987 film highlights the lesbian flamboyance of Tiny Davis, former trumpeter extraordinaire for the International Sweethearts of Rhythm jazz band, and is narrated by the African American lesbian poet Cheryl Clarke. More recently Jennie Livingston's remarkable, controversial, 1990 documentary, *Paris Is Burning*, explores the world of vogueing balls created by young black and Latino street queens in New York City.

As the body of black gay and lesbian film expands, a wellspring of critical analysis and theoretical study has concurrently evolved, validating this birth of a notion. Scholars in lesbian and gay studies, film theorists, and cultural activists have proclaimed, in articles and new publications, the significance of this first wave of black gay and lesbian media (particularly the works of Riggs and Julien) in illuminating the transgressive territory of identity and gay representation. Many of these critics are themselves black gay men and lesbians. In the United Kingdom are the filmmaker Pratibha Parmar and the critics Kobena Mercer and Stuart Hall. In the United States the writings of Marlon Riggs, Thomas Harris, Essex Hemphill, and bell hooks (who is not gay) have been influential and provocative.

Indicative of the growing visibility and accessibility of gay film, a media conference in New York was dedicated to investigating the concept of queer aesthetics unique to lesbian and gay imagery. The most compelling and contentious moments of that 1989 "How Do I Look?" conference were stimulated by discussions of race and representation in the works of Julien and other black gay artists, as well as white gay artists such as Robert Mapplethorpe who were perceived as commodifying black male sexuality.

In tandem with increased production has been an upsurge in the marketing of black gay and lesbian films and videos. Among distributors who have been particularly responsive to the influx of work by African American lesbians and gays are Women Make Movies (the largest distributor of feminist media with a long-standing focus on lesbian issues), Third World Newsreel (targeting the new wave of films and videos by gays and lesbians of color), and Frameline (a lesbian and gay arts organization that supports the distribution and exhibition of films and videos).

In the 1980s and early 1990s Hollywood negotiated easy heterosexist niches for homosexuality on the silver screen, allowing for the commercial success and mainstream acceptance of films such as *Personal Best* (1982), *Desert Hearts* (1985), and *Longtime Companion* (1990). These were palatable categorizations reducing gay experience to lifestyle comedies, sexual preference soaps, and AIDS dramas.

1.2 From *A Litany for Survival: The Life and Work of Audre Lorde,* directed by Ada Gay Griffin and Michelle Parkerson, 1995.

Then, at the top of the 1990s came three films that complicated the issue of homosexuality with affirmations of blackness and differences of race politics. These films imposed diversity upon the lily-white, largely male stereotype of gay experience.

The censorship surrounding the controversial PBS broadcast of *Tongues Untied* brought to public attention the realities and intersection of race and sexuality. *Looking for Langston*, flagrantly breaking the complicity of silence surrounding the homosexuality of the black poet-icon Langston Hughes, swiftly drew condemnation from many in the straight black community and a lawsuit from the Hughes estate. *Paris Is Burning* emerged from subculture success on the gay and lesbian film festival circuit to become the U.S. box office surprise of 1990. All three programs garnered critical acclaim, awards, and enthusiastic international audiences. They catalyzed national debates about freedom of expression and brought to many their first awareness of a black gay community.

But where in the current flurry of black gay male visibility on screen are the black lesbian movies—our own "evidence of being"? The question that remains for us, as we turn the century, is not so much "How do I look?"

as "Where am I?" Lack of viable economic support, limited exhibition and distribution, and, indeed, a real and pervasive racist and sexist bias within our own gay and lesbian community all contribute to the marginalization of black lesbian productions.

Yet the short films and videos of Cheryl Dunye, Dawn Suggs, and Aarin Burch, among others (including my own 1987 film, *Stormé: The Lady of the Jewel Box*), have reached the screen in the face of tremendous odds, against a rising reentrenchment of censorship. These black lesbian film- and video makers embody the cinematic tenet of persistence of vision.

A Litany for Survival: The Life and Work of Audre Lorde is hopefully the seed of a trend toward full-length documentary and dramatic productions concerning black lesbian life and history. This documentary feature engages the work and perspectives of the late African American feminist poet and the context of her life as a lesbian of color in America. Using Lorde's words and images as its core, the film is referenced with scenes of her literary and political activities and commentary by her family members, contemporaries, students, and others affected by the emergence of an international, lesbian, feminist agenda among women of color.

The recent phenomenon of progressive black gay and lesbian imagery will not continue without growing numbers of openly gay and lesbian African American filmmakers producing works that address ethnicity and sexuality as equally critical identities. Black gay and lesbian filmmakers face sexism and homophobia within the black independent cinema movement, as well as racism in the feminist film community and the whitewash pervasive in gay and lesbian media. Historically we have been locked out of the Hollywood and television industries. But such challenges inspire me to make the movies that *Desert Hearts* and *She Must Be Seeing Things* (1987) are not: films that are lesbian-specific but, just as important, race-conscious.

As black filmmakers, how can we broaden gay and lesbian experience and imagery beyond "the celluloid closet"? How will we construct an ethnocentric, diverse nation of lovers? How will we undertake this birth of a notion?

Perhaps, twenty-four frames at a time.

Note

Essay © Michelle Parkerson. Edited versions originally published in *Advocate*, no. 570 (February 12, 1991) and in *Queer Looks: Perspectives on Lesbian and Gay Film and Video*, edited by Martha Gever, Pratibha Parmar, and John Greyson (New York: Routledge, 1993).

Narrating Our History

An Introduction

Around 1994 or 1995 I came across a call for articles for an anthology to be published by the *XII Black International Cinema*, documenting ten years of the festival and associated activities, 1986–95. The request asked for articles and film lists from an international and intercultural group of scholars and filmmakers, and I thought this was an opportunity to document the exciting and pioneering work that was being done by a community of emerging Black lesbian and gay film- and video makers at the time. It was the early 1990s and the height of the culture wars in the United States that were fueled in part by the urgency of the AIDS epidemic, the legacy of feminist scholarship, and the success of the global anti-apartheid movement. Activists and artists such as Marlon Riggs, Anita Hill, Audre Lorde, bell hooks, and Essex Hemphill were making the personal political by untying their tongues to speak truth to power and thereby shift the culture. This was happening in the realms of film, art, television, politics, the academy, and conferences, and it was also coinciding with a critical mass of Black LGBT media makers, artists, and activists who were meeting in these same spaces and were recognizing the commonality of our shared experiences while at the same time celebrating and supporting one another's work across differences of gender, nationality, location, and experience.

The Afro-Cuban video maker and scholar Raúl Ferrera-Balanquet and I decided to respond to the call together and reached out to the community of LGBT makers we knew to see if there was interest in generating a dialogue among this community so as to historicize our work. After receiving an enthusiastic response, we wrote the proposal, which was accepted by *Black*

International Cinema. I had met Raúl after reaching out to him about including his work in a video program titled *FIRE: Experimental Films and Videos
from the African Diaspora*, which I was curating with the filmmaker and artist Cheryl Dunye and the filmmaker Shari Frilot for the Experimental LGBT
Film Festival. *FIRE* was inspired in part by Isaac Julien's groundbreaking film,
Looking for Langston, which opened us up to looking at the suppressed and
hidden queer narratives of the Harlem Renaissance. We took the name of our
program, *FIRE*, from the 1926 Harlem Renaissance transgressive publication
of the same name, started by Wallace Thurman, Zora Neale Hurston, Aaron
Douglas, John P. Davis, Richard Bruce Nugent, Gwendolyn Bennett, Lewis
Grandison Alexander, Countee Cullen, and Langston Hughes.

Like the original *FIRE*, our program explored edgy issues in the Black community such as homosexuality, bisexuality, interracial relationships, promis-
cuity, prostitution, and color prejudice. Dunye and I had initially proposed
the program together as we were already collaborating on a number of projects and panels. Frilot and I were best friends and had also been collaborating, beginning with our work as producers for a public affairs show broadcast
on WNET/Thirteen, New York's flagship public television station. *FIRE* was
sold out, due in part to our outreach to LGBT communities on Christopher
Street and in bars, clubs, and elsewhere. It also cemented certain relationships.
We realized that we were in fact a movement that was creating change; we
could no longer be ignored or marginalized by mainstream queer or Black
festivals. At the same time we were mindful that because our work was not
being written about or referenced in connection to such movements as New
Queer Cinema, this meant we were being written out of the queer media narrative even as we were reshaping the landscape with our work and activism.

Like the Harlem Renaissance artists who gathered to produce *FIRE*, we
sensed that it was our responsibility to leave a trace of who we were and
what we were doing in the form of a publication. We reached out to all
the folks that we knew or had heard of through the network of LGBT media
makers—approximately twenty people, in New York, Los Angeles, Chicago,
Philadelphia. We had to find a way to create a dialogue based on the formal
and informal dialogues that we had been having. This was before the age
of the Internet, so our idea was to use what was then still a relatively new
technology—the fax machine—to create or re-create a dialogue among all
who were able to share their perspectives. To kick things off, we sent out a
series of questions to which we asked folks to respond. These questions
became the subject headings to create an outline and organize the published

discussion. Some people responded to specific questions; others responded in a more free-form way. Some answered many questions, and others answered only a few.

Once all the responses were in, we began the process of editing the piece, cutting and pasting fax paper—much like a paper edit of the documentary film I was making concurrently, VINTAGE *Families of Value*, which was also a series of conversations between lesbian and gay siblings. Our goal was to maximize the dialogue, making sure to leave their responses intact as well as trying to avoid unnecessary repetition, so that ultimately the whole would be larger than the sum of the parts. It was a delicate balance. As was true for VINTAGE, I was also interested in creating a collaborative approach to the creation of this document, and we fearlessly shared the different versions of the piece with the various contributors to get feedback and clarification. We had a quick turnaround; I remember taking copies of the transcript with me to edit during a trip to Brazil.

The piece was finally published in 1997 in Germany as part of Fountainhead's *XII Black International Cinema Anthology 1993–1997*. It was great to finally see the piece as well as the other articles in the anthology, which included "African Films: A Retrospective and Vision for the Future" as well as "Culture, Communication and Afrocentrism: Some Rhetorical Implications of a New World Order." We were in good company. In addition, our film and video titles were also included in the Black International Film List. Together this meant that we had inserted ourselves into an international discussion around African diasporic cinema. On the other hand, because the piece was published in a catalogue in Germany, it had limited distribution, especially within the USA. After it came out, we provided copies of the document to all the contributors and asked them to share it as widely as possible. As a creative nonfiction filmmaker, I am aware of the value of archive, both as something to be found, discovered, and preserved but also as something to be created— from scratch if necessary. With this project we sought to create an archive that could be dug up and republished and that could one day reach and inspire a wider audience. I am deeply gratified that that day is today.

Narrating Our History

Selections from a Dialogue among Queer Media
Artists from the African Diaspora

*"Narrating Our History" is a collection of thoughts, reflections, and remembrances
that recount the collective and individual histories experienced by a group of
avant-garde queer film- and video makers from the African diaspora. This is by no
means an official history but the beginnings of a dialogue around the past several years of making and exhibiting our work, curating and lecturing, panels and
festivals. The contributors to this dialogue represent a cross section of artists who
have been navigating various cultural, spiritual, and political spaces. Our works
encompass the geographical regions defined as the United States, Canada,
Central and South America, Africa, Asia, and Europe. Despite the respective
differences in our backgrounds and practices, much of our work engages the
subject of autobiography in its many and varied manifestations.*—RAÚL FERRERA-
BALANQUET AND THOMAS ALLEN HARRIS, EDITORS

Historical Recollections: How We Met at the Crossroads

JOCELYN TAYLOR: The first time I spoke in public about my work was during
the Los Angeles Lesbian and Gay Festival in 1990. Cheryl Dunye was the
only other woman of color on the panel. When I asked a question regarding
funding, I naïvely stated that funding was not a problem for me considering
the fact that my work at that time was of medium to low production quality.
I had minimal access to a low-end production facility, and my piece was only
five minutes long. I was alluding to the fact that it has been "easy" for me. I
was swept up into the politically correct chic of the queer festival. I have been
"discovered," as it were, as a new woman of color video maker. Every queer
festival was calling me about my little five-minute piece. I thought it had been

pretty simple to get a lot of exposure as a new maker. Being on a panel with Cheryl really opened my eyes to the hypocrisies existent within the queer festival circuit. Naturally we engaged in dialogue.

That was a historic moment for me. It was an entry into a burgeoning network of queers of color. Many encounters at many more festivals have occurred since then. The network has been solidified because we have sought each other out. Any unfamiliar name in a festival schedule for a program of black queers is taken note of and maybe even contacted by another black queer maker, programmer, academic, or writer. We all want to know what people are doing and how it may or may not be connected with what we're doing. Many of us wear more than one hat and function both as makers and writers or makers and programmers and further facilitate the network.

THOMAS ALLEN HARRIS: The festival circuit for experimental lesbian and gay film played a critical role in my development as an artist by providing me with a community of African diasporic artists who were attempting to create a new space within the American media landscape. In 1990 I had been asked by Martha Gever, the editor of the *Independent*, to review DCTV's *look-out festival* curated by Catherine (Saalfield) Gund. The seven days I spent at the festival represented a pivotal juncture in the formation of a very special community of media artists. In this festival I first saw the works of Dawn Suggs, Jocelyn Taylor, Richard Fung, Ming Yuan S. Ma, and Cheryl Dunye and began to dialogue with these artists both personally as well as through our work.

It was at subsequent meetings at different film and video festivals that we began to express our dissatisfaction with the way our respective work was ghettoized in mainstream lesbian and gay film festivals while at the same time was ignored by black festivals. In an effort to have more control over the context in which our work was screened—as well as reach our audiences— many of us began curating our own programs as well as panels. The results of our work changed the way lesbian and gay film festivals curated the work by lesbians and gays of color while at the same time established solid audiences for our work. It also served to bring us into contact with other African diasporic filmmakers from around the nation and the world.

YVONNE WELBON: Thomas Allen Harris and Cheryl Dunye organized the first panel of black gay and lesbian artists that I know of. It was at the Gay and Lesbian Studies conference at Rutgers University, Mason Gross School for the Arts in New Jersey in 1991. There I met a number of you for the first time. Those on the panel included Michelle Parkerson, Cheryl Dunye, Dawn Suggs, myself, Thomas Allen Harris, and Jack Waters. Both Jacqueline Woodson and Jocelyn Taylor were in attendance at the conference, and I got the chance to meet both of them for the first time too.

That conference was a jumping-off point for some of us. We would organize programs where we could, and invite each other. For instance, I was involved with the Women in the Director's Chair in Chicago and helped to organize a black lesbian program as part of the festival in 1992. We invited Dunye and Parkerson to come.

Aarin Burch was involved with Frameline Gay and Lesbian Film Festival in 1993, and she and Shari Frilot organized a panel where both Dawn and I were invited.

These invitations were not paying gigs, but they did provide airfare and the chance to spend hours upon hours with each other. And an opportunity to screen our work with each other. These meetings helped to build bonds between us.

RAÚL FERRERA-BALANQUET: In the summer of 1992 I went to the San Francisco Gay and Lesbian Film and Video Festival. David Olivares had curated the most complete Latino program to that date. I went there on my own. Bruce Karl Knapper hosted me. I met Thomas Allen Harris and Alfonzo Moret the opening night. The late Mark Finch asked me to participate in a panel called "True Colors" to talk about multiculturalism with Thomas and Alfonzo. Cheryl Dunye was there. I remember sitting at an outdoor café having breakfast with Thomas, Alfonzo, and Cheryl. She was talking about how we belonged to a NEW WAVE. We decided we were the New Wave. We were charting new ground in the history of media-making. One day we all met at Karl's house—Cheryl, Thomas, Alfonzo, Karl, and I. We cooked brunch, talked, videotaped, and processed a lot of stuff. That conversation strengthened our future network.

In July Thomas and I met in Los Angeles for the "Color Me Here" panel. The 1992 Gay and Lesbian Film Festival treated us badly. Dawn Suggs was ignored at the office. When I called they dismissed me because "on the phone I sounded like I was one of those Latinos from East Los Angeles." Alfonzo came from San Diego. We met Joe Castel, a Latino queer media maker and a schoolmate of mine from the University of Iowa. That time together was for processing and action. We wrote a flyer, and then that evening we passed it out to the audience. Our panel was great. But by that time we realized that a lot of gay and lesbian festivals were using us to get money and then the only thing they paid for was the plane ticket. It was true intellectual racism. Shari Frilot and Lyle Ashton Harris arrived the following week. We spent a whole day at the beach. Yemaya was blessing our friendship. The discussions were long. We had so much in common.

SHARI FRILOT: The first independent work I produced that found its way through the queer festival circuit was a twenty-minute video entitled *A Cosmic Demonstration of Sexuality* (1992). I had quit public television to produce it, and I spent nearly all of my savings doing so. Nevertheless, when the tape was solicited by Meena Nanji, who was a curator at the time for the 1992 Los Angeles Lesbian and Gay Film Festival, I managed to scrape together the funds to go and attend the premiere screening.

Going to that festival changed my life. That is where I met you, Raúl! That is where I also met filmmakers Tamara Murphy, Darisha Kyi, and Pratibha Parmar. I also saw my old friends, filmmakers Dawn Suggs, Thomas Allen Harris and his brother, photographer Lyle Ashton Harris. We spent time fawning over each other, exchanging ideas, and encouraging each other's work. We all took a fabulous trip to the beach: Lyle brought his camera and we all took photos of each other. It was a tremendous time and marked both the beginning and a solidifying of most of the important friendships and alliances I have today.

The 1992 Los Angeles Lesbian and Gay Film Festival also provided an immediate introduction to the shortcomings of the queer festival circuit for artists of color. The festival was held at the Director's Guild in Hollywood, which has two large theaters and one thirty-seat video. The majority of the works made by people of color were screened in the micro-theater to audiences, which were overwhelmingly white. Some of my filmmakers of color received poor treatment by the festival staff. As other queer festivals screened *A Cosmic Demonstration of Sexuality*, I found that the conditions I encountered in Los Angeles were systemic and were likely to be perpetuated since none of the directors of these festivals was from a community of color.

DAWN SUGGS: The first formal dialogue I attended for black queer filmmakers was the panel organized by Cheryl Dunye and Thomas Allen Harris as part of the Gay and Lesbian Studies conference at Rutgers University. The following year I attended the eleventh annual Los Angeles International Gay and

3.1 Shari Frilot and Dawn Suggs, Sistah Action panel, seventeenth San Francisco International Lesbian and Gay Film Festival, 1993.

Lesbian Film and Video Festival, where a group of us formed an informal Coalition of Film and Video Artists of Color and developed a flyer, which recounted and called attention to the discrimination against queers of color at the festival.

In 1992 I got together with the late Dellon Wilson, a veteran producer of social and cultural events for black lesbians in New York City, and founded Through Our Eyes, a program of black lesbian films and videos. This program offered a sampling of works by black lesbian filmmakers in a club setting followed by a discussion and reception. This small festival was one of several that sprang up nationally around this time in an effort to develop self-reliant networks for screening black lesbian work within black lesbian communities. The following year Shari Frilot codirected the festival with Dellon. The Through Our Eyes festival also sought to challenge the domination and appropriation of black lesbian films and stories mediated by a system of white patronage.

In 1993 Aarin Burch curated the "Sistah Action" program as part of the seventeenth San Francisco International Lesbian and Gay Festival. Aarin brought several black lesbian filmmakers to San Francisco and contributed to a dialogue of black lesbian filmmakers on the West Coast.

RFB: Then came the 1992 New York Experimental Lesbian and Gay Film Festival. I was invited by Cheryl Dunye and Thomas Allen Harris to be part of *FIRE!*, a program of queer media artists from the African diaspora. It was a sigh of relief. After years of being denied my African self because I spoke Spanish, my brothers and sisters now were seeing me as a true brother. That year Cheryl and Jocelyn organized Lookout, the DCTV lesbian and gay video festival. Ming-Yuen S. Ma and I were the guest artists. My sisters created a great program. Shari designed the poster.

In 1993 the newly created MIX had another program about the African diaspora, "Moto and the Human Touch," organized by Vejan Lee Smith and Thomas Allen Harris. Karl and Alfonso put on a great program for the festival. The discussion after the program was insightful. They really produced the type of audience response they expected. I wonder why MIX doesn't have after-screening discussion any more. That year MIX gave Thomas and me a birthday party.

In 1994 during the Society for Photographic Studies conference Thomas, Lyle Ashton Harris, Yvonne, Jocelyn, Coco Fusco, Zeinabu irene Davis, Ayana Udongo, Nereyda Garcia Ferraz, and myself got together in my apartment. The men cooked a meal of yams, collard greens, and chicken. We ate a lot and did a whole workshop—watching everybody's work and discussing critical issues within the works and works in progress. It was a special occasion.

The Black Nations/Queer Nations conference in March 1995 was a great meeting place. A lot of us were there. Cheryl, Jocelyn, Thomas, Dawn, Shari, Karl, Lyle, Kobena, Coco, Robert Reid-Pharr, Isaac, and myself, among a lot of great powerful warriors.

Also the Queer Conference at University of California at San Diego in January 1995 was a great encounter. Dawn, Robert, Lyle, Thomas, and myself got together at this conference.

LEAH GILLIAM: I've been trying to get it up to write something re: a collecting of queer black history but to say the least it's been, well, hard. Mostly because for the past month since MIX, I've been speechless. Now this is a term that is overused, I know, so I'll explain what I mean. What I can do: daily bullshit conversations with colleagues, walk the dog, worry about my fate, watch re-runs of the *Rockford Files* (as far as I'm concerned the opening sequence is a cinematic masterpiece), watch *What's Happening* and then *What's Happening Now*, which comes on right after and are also totally neglected according to my research in the annals of African diaspora history (They're based on Michael Schultz's 1975 film *Cooley High*, which brought black $$ and black teen fuck-ups to the silver screen. The *What's Happenings* give great 70s fashion black nerds and a star: Dee, the original mouth as weapon gun non-hieroglyph black body just what a downtrodden relief from the body I have me needs), reread Ntozake Shange's letter again where she squashes Greg

Tate for calling her/categorizing her/pinning her/taming her in the *Village Voice*, field a phone call where I'm asked to be on something or another and bring all of my black queer friends (if you knew me you'd be laughing now), surf the net and pretend to be a liberal white fag trapped in the netnoir chat room, diss my colleagues (powerless empowerment), and talk on the phone.

Wiring the Network

YW: This network is informal. We send each other tapes. We call each other up with questions. We send each other scripts. Sometimes we take suggestions and sometimes we don't.

I know when I wanted to make a black lesbian film short I called a few people for suggestions. I wanted the film to be more than me. I wanted the film to be of our community. And it was a conversation that I had with Jacqueline Woodson that inspired me to tell the story that I choose to tell in *Sisters in the Life: First Love* (1993). Jacqueline said, "We need coming-of-age stories." That was all I needed to hear.

One person, who I met at the Frameline Festival in 1993, is not a filmmaker but she is an important part of our black lesbian network. Margaret R. Daniel is the founder of the Women of Color Festival in Santa Cruz and an independent curator. She was an incredible help to me on my last film, *Remembering Wei-Yi Fang, Remembering Myself: An Autobiography* (1996). She read draft upon draft of my script, critiqued different edits of my tape, and basically wouldn't hesitate to tell me that I needed to work a little harder in some areas and that I had definitely made my point in other areas.

RFB: The network among ourselves takes place at these festivals and also during the phone conversations, letters, and postcards. When I made *Cities of Last,* Thomas Allen Harris provided me with footage. We have talked a lot on the phone about our projects. Shari and I are always calling each other and helping with projects. I feel that there is a community here with a lot of potential. Some of us have taken time to become real good friends, creating a space where we can talk about our emotional, psychological states, our desires, critique our works, and create fantasies about our plans for the future.

JT: The network among ourselves is born from necessity and proximity. Many of us are closely connected to alternative media networks, know each other from our fields of activism, and have maintained those relationships. We

3.2 *Sisters in the Life: First Love,* directed by Yvonne Welbon, 1993.

are friends who have started making work under similar circumstances for similar reasons. Here's a proximity example: makers whose work has evolved around questions of identity and/or sexuality have gravitated toward one another to talk about programming issues, give critique, and analyze style. (That actually includes most people we know.) We run into each other, touch base, maybe have dinner, then pass the word on to another maker at another event about what so-and-so is doing. Since many of us are busy representing black queer culture (if such a monolith does exist), it is necessary that we discuss the reception of our work by our various audiences.

TAH: Since the beginning I have always collaborated with colleagues directly or indirectly. This type of collaboration has been integral to my work. Shari was my associate producer on my first piece, *Splash* (1991), and Raúl introduced me to the concept of Esu—the subject of my third tape, *Heaven, Earth and Hell* (1993). Some of the early inspiration for VINTAGE was Jocelyn's *Father Knows Best* and Dawn Suggs's *Chasing the Moon* (1991). There has been constant feedback between myself and fellow filmmakers on all of my work. In 1991 Dawn, Vejan Smith, Reggie Woolery, Lorna Johnson, and I began a film and video workshop in Fort Greene, Brooklyn. In this workshop we got together every two to three weeks over the course of a year to show and discuss work. It was out of this workshop that I began producing VINTAGE—*Families of Value* (1995), a feature-length documentary film that looks at three African American families through the eyes of siblings who are lesbian and gay. VINTAGE is itself a collaborative project. The subjects of the film interviewed each other, operated the camera, and wrote the fantasy sequences in which they performed. This type of shared filmmaking parallels the working relationships I have had with a number of media makers over the past five years.

DS: The network among ourselves was initiated largely through our dialogues at festivals and university programs. My first exposure to queer works of color was at the screening of Parkerson's *Stormé* in 1989. Work as an assistant with Parkerson and Griffin on *A Litany for Survival* (1995) introduced me to a large community of lesbians of color filmmakers. Programming of black lesbian works by black lesbians over the past five years has helped develop an informal network of black lesbian filmmakers. I had many discussions with Ada Griffin of Third World Newsreel in 1991 regarding the need for more distribution of new works by queers of color. Around this time several queer filmmakers of color found Third World Newsreel to be more receptive and appreciative of our works than some of the distributors who had large collections of works by white queer artists.

I regard my friendships with other queer African American filmmakers as home base within a large film community. While some friendships are more active than others, I believe that all of us have expressed a willingness to assist each other in navigating and negotiating production and distribution. I find a few close friends, queer African American filmmakers, provide me with the strongest critical feedback on my work.

Documenting History

JT: The documentation of the growth and development of this network of queer black media folks would be a great project. As with any history, however, I would want to question who it would include. Our particular clique, perhaps? If we're all friends writing our own history, well . . . it's been done before. History is not absolute truth, it's merely a documentation of selective memories and events. Even straightforward testimony has gaps and is misleading and irresponsible at times in relation to the truth. I am freaking out now. Okay. History is fine. Nuff said.

SF: As a curator, I have not only witnessed a tremendous mushrooming of works produced by queer artists of color internationally, I am also noticing the influence these works are having on the development of the community of emerging media artists. The opportunity to historicize this important cultural phenomenon in the *Black International Cinema Anthology* is a vital one.

It will serve to preserve the dimensions of this important artistic movement by preventing them from being lost in the unconscious, if not outright racist and homophobic documentation of various, white-dominated venues and texts.

RFB: This is where the issue of documenting our history comes to play an important role. I have seen how "queer cinema" has become so commercialized, and also how the white queer media makers have capitalized the audiences and watered down the real issues affecting us. The two books about queer cinema don't say anything about our works, our critical writings, our friendships, and all the history we have gone through together. A lot of us have published in different and disparate venues—we should bring all of those critical writings together and produce a book.

Autobiography

RFB: The critical autobiography is an issue that must be examined in a large context. All of us have produced work from our experiences. I think that we are markers and makers of history, and our bodies represent a map that is in a constant dialogue. Like the African American slave narratives, we have turned the autobiography into a weapon to decolonize ourselves. I think that the economic means of production have obligated us to do autobiographical works also.

DS: I find traveling inward to be a very important part of the decolonization process. It has been a formidable struggle for me to trust my instincts and sensibilities, which counter the Hollywood standards within a film school that increasingly depends upon and gains viability within the Hollywood system. While the political and social climate had changed tremendously since the time of the "L.A. rebellion" of the seventies within UCLA's film school, the legacy was largely initiated through the works and efforts of many black filmmakers, including Billy Woodberry, Zeinabu irene Davis, Julie Dash, Charles Brunett, Haile Gerima, Carol Parrot Blue, Sharon Alile Larkin, Barbara McCullough, O. Funmilayo Makarah, Larry Clark, and many others.

I see third cinema as cinema that goes a step further than conventionally depicting the conditions of our existence. It proposes alternative ways of seeing things and aggressively counters the hegemony of dominant cultures.

YW: African Americans have always been interested in testifying and telling it like it is. I just wrote a paper on black lesbian film and video artists. My survey included twenty-one artists and sixty-eight short films, videos, and interactive computer media. I found out that virtually all of the artists had done some work in which they included themselves. I feel that this act closely parallels the choices African Americans made when they began to write slave narrative in the eighteenth century. It was so important for our ancestors to make themselves present in a world in which they were not considered human. It is still important. Ours is a political act of self-affirmation. We choose to make ourselves subject in a world that has always considered us an object, an other—rendering our once invisible selves visible.

TAH: The late twentieth-century, postcolonial autobiographical film and video works should be read not only in terms of content but also in terms of form: the narrative structure, the gaps, the language, repetition, and rhythm—all of which are imbued with an awareness of the risk as well as the empowerment involved in using this type of articulation. Such a reading is critical to the understanding of the new and emerging languages that we are creating within the medium of film and video.

Personally I employ autobiography within my work to critically engage questions of ethnicity, the body, sexuality, and location. Situating myself within an African American literary tradition of autobiography, I employ autobiographical strategies as a way to further explore postcolonial subjectivity and the construction of diasporic identities. Constructing self through various sites, including family, history, nation-states, and the psychic realms of fantasy, places such work within what Teshome Gabrial, author of *Third Cinema in the Third World*, refers to as an expression of a nomadic aesthetic, which he defines as one that "smashes down boundaries between documentary, ethnographic, travelogue, experimental and narrative fiction."

The act of self-construction is an autobiographical act. It is a place of comfort and a source of power. It is a personal, political, and liberatory action. I am speaking about an autobiography that continues to push beyond the boundaries of disclosure and self-explanation on the level of content. And there are risks. For example, history shows us that Zora Neale Hurston's autobiography, *Dust Tracks on a Road*, was sharply criticized for not disclosing enough of the particularities of her life. However, Hurston wanted to use her text to create or construct an intellectual self with controversial views on the national and international contemporary issues—a space that was not allowed her, a black woman folklorist, in the 1920s, 30s, and 40s. In fact whole chapters of the book were censored by her editor and publisher.

Production Values

YW: There is an urgency to create work. Sometimes that urgency takes precedence, leaving the production values of early black gay and lesbian work lacking. For the most part we are a young movement. Most of us have been producing works for one to five years. We need time to learn about our craft and about ourselves as artists. We need time to grow. And I have found that as we grow the production values of our work improve.

DS: Generally production values for a film or video refer to a film's slickness and seamlessness—its professional gloss. I'm interested in considering a film's aesthetic value based on its use of film language in a broad creative and artistic sense. Many black queer works have been made under severe technical restraints and limitations; nevertheless many achieve a lyricism and poignancy that films with "high production quality" in a traditional sense may not.

RFB: "The camera is my weapon and style is the immediate response to an aggression."

Production value is a hard topic among us. Let's face it. How many of us have gotten enough money to produce what we want or need? I produced because I have a network of friends who are constantly helping me to produce the work, and because I teach to get access to postproduction—not the best, but it helps. The grants I have gotten have been very small.

Technology is an issue since a lot of us don't have the time, the money, and the space to be trained in new technologies.

TAH: In my previous life I produced documentaries and public affairs programs for public television. I think that experience informed the way I think about image production. Although I shoot on hi-8mm and 8mm video and Super-8 mm film, I find ways to online on beta, which is still much cheaper than film. I keep cost down by shooting myself and collaborating with other artists, friends, as well as seeking out artist residencies that offer access to equipment and support, such as the Banff Center for the Arts in Canada and the Experimental Television Center in Oswego, New York. I have chosen to take a position as an assistant professor to have time and equipment to produce my work. Economically the production of work is still a difficult and challenging proposition.

JT: I've always thought that as it gets harder and harder to get money to make projects, more folks will choose to work collectively as a means to make work. I have a personal objective or mission, if you will. I would go as far as calling it an artistic vision. That vision is located in a desire to address the collective group. Actually it's a desire to fill a lack expressed by the collective. Though I separate myself out as an "artist," I belong to the collective as well. Making media toward a collective desire is like placing salve on a wound. Artists have the skill to heal very deep pain. The stuff of being an artist is also about embarking on a critical path for the sake of collective discussion and analyses.

Grassroots is the key word here. I've always stayed with a certain framework of immediacy, quickly piecing together inexpensive alternative resources, using minimal technology, background, and equipment. I've just started paying the people who work with me because I appreciate getting paid for working on other people's stuff myself. My production values have gotten increasingly better, aided by grants I've received in recent years.

Narrative Strategies

JT: We have, I believe, become disgruntled with well-known studied conventions of media-making and understanding. Constant exposure to mediocre modes of storytelling—after all, for the most part they are not our stories— have encouraged us to stretch the narrative to encompass both our story and our creativity. One question: Have we been afforded the opportunity to employ fantasy in our work? I've found that when I choose to conflate fantasy and desire, I get to the question of audience. Who is it? Non–folks of color so readily identify with the story of "identity," but when that identity is assumed and not coded as a marker within the work, white folks want to ask me why I have an all-black cast. They might even tell me they feel like they're "intruding" because I dare to show my fantasy to them rather than cloak it in a discussion of identity politics. They must "see" me. I'm tired of looking at them all the time.

Frankie & Jocie (1994) and *Father Knows Best* have specifically addressed the prevalence of homophobia in the black community. Neither of the pieces resolves.

TAH: In *VINTAGE* I introduce each of the subjects/characters of the film as starring in a show about them and us. Then I construct the narrative along the lines of a thematic dialogue (much like the one we are engaged in) between individuals and families. I allow the emotional arcs to emerge throughout the piece. Through the composition and juxtaposition of images that move between time, documentary, fiction, fantasy, and memory, I attempt to reveal a constructed whole through its elusive parts.

RFB: Narrative style is intriguing to me. There was a time when I wanted to do fiction based on my real experience and when I wanted to document my imagination. Then I was experimenting with form and I found out that the old modes of cinematic address were not satisfying my voice. That was the time when I started mixing everything and finding out how a hybrid text was the closer narrative style to my experience. Somehow the mixing of these styles reflects my mestizo self.

LG: What I can't do is work. I can't push my tape. Can't think. Can't fuck. Can't make money. In short, I can't help. It just seems too ironic furthering/teaching/theorizing the cause of experimental media and doing millions of bullshit gigs so I can afford the luxury of my indentured servitude. I've never been an optimistic person. I've always been completely cynical and negative, and now it seems to have caught up with me. The last time the credits rolled on my tape I realized that all but one of the funding sources had disappeared and the one remaining was the least supportive, most cheap, most "lift up the race," most queer-unfriendly one left. Within a historical trajectory I know things have been worse. More repressive, more insane, less coherent, and that I am but one more grumpy mongrel dog black riot artgirl raggedy poor white trash white girl friend having not happy to be queer not happy to be anything prozac-loving ritalin-needing thing who is not on the street not married not in advertising not waiting on my feature not someone i should meet and mostly not a fictional character.

DS: We are involved in the struggle to make film language accountable to our experiences. I constantly struggle with the narrative form, in an effort to represent my worldviews. One film that I directed, *She Left the Script Behind* (1993), went from a more conventional form of narration to an expressionistic montage. The transition in form represented my attempt to break with dominant film language in order to express the inner world of a black woman protagonist. Queer audiences, black and white, were generally receptive to this rupture in form; however, a violent kiss between two black women in one scene received strong criticism from some feminists and was met with hostility at a screening for a predominantly straight black audience. Such responses were a harsh reminder of the vulnerability we face and the responsibility we assume when we seek to challenge traditional conservative notions of sexual representations within our films.

YW: I create films and videos that are hybrid in form. All five of my films are documentaries. They all employed narrative and experimental techniques to tell the story. I have found that this form of storytelling makes the most sense to me. I don't feel that I have to adhere to formal definitions of "documentary." I believe that many of us feel that way. Our work is reflective of our place in society. We don't adhere to anyone's idea of what it is to be black, what it is to be female or male, what it is to be indefinable to others—we make sense to ourselves.

In *Sisters in the Life: First Love* I took the liberty of creating black lesbian home movies of childhood because I couldn't find any real ones. There were none of my life, but that didn't mean my life didn't happen. So I felt that creating the home movies after the fact was okay. Many viewers actually thought the home movies were real movies at first.

In *Remembering Wei-Yi Fang, Remembering Myself: An Autobiography* I offer cross-cultural stories of migration as I parallel my grandmother's movement from Honduras to America at the age of twenty-two, and my movement from America to Taiwan at the same age. I look at my Latin American heritage and the influence on my life of the six years that I lived in Taiwan. These things have shaped me just as growing up black in America has shaped me. In my film I stress the importance of claiming my past and present.

Exhibition

SF: In 1992 Thomas Allen Harris and I were approached by Sarah Schulman to direct the New York Lesbian and Gay Experimental Film Festival. Thomas was busy with his film *VINTAGE*, so I took the festival on with the Brazilian filmmaker Karim Ainouz. We changed the name of the festival to MIX: The New York Lesbian and Gay Film/Video Festival in the interest of expanding the focus of the festival to encompass the intersection of race, class, and ethnicity as well as gender and sexuality. Of the twenty programs we presented in MIX 93, seventeen contained *entirely* works by people of color. (So much for that old excuse "We don't program work by people of color because there is just not that much around"!) We were able to increase the number of works by people of color not by relying on the festival's mailing list but by aggressively scouting out works as well as working with guest curators of color who had entirely different networks than the festival had access to.

In 1993 we also founded, in conjunction with the Brazilian guest curators André Fischer and Suzy Cap, the first lesbian and gay festival in the history of Brazil, MIX Brasil: Festival das Manisfestações da Sexualidade (Festival of Sexual Manifestations). MIX Brasil tours São Paulo, Rio de Janeiro, Curitiba, Belo Horizonte, and Fortaleza every year. The festival also maintains the first gay computer network via the Bulletin Broadcasting System.

Now I direct MIX in New York and Suzy directs MIX Brasil. We are sister organizations that operate independently from each other but support one another by providing programming and advice. Together we are building a network of festivals that offers unprecedented exposure for queer work. Through the New York festival and our program with Free Speech TV, a national cable access program, the films and videos in MIX reach more than fifty million people across the United States. MIX Brasil reaches more than ten thousand people all over Brazil each year. And MIX has premiered more work by queer makers of color than any other festival in the world.

MIX has been an incredible opportunity to bring new voices to the media circuit, celebrate exceptional artists and their work, and bring together audiences of color to screen work intended especially for them. Film festivals are critically important in the process of building community and professional networks. They open doors of opportunity to media artists by bringing their work to the attention of other curators. The festival also brings artists together with their audiences, and thereby plays an important role in the critical dialogue of artist and media work.

RFB: MIX 94 and MIX 95 were points of reunion. MIX has become the place to show since Shari Frilot became the director. It is the largest experimental festival in the world and the space where I have been most comfortable premiering my work. Now MIX sees connections that go beyond ethnic backgrounds and puts together shows about our experiences. This year Brent Hill and I were in a program about traveling identities curated by Eve Oshi.

3.3 Yvonne Welbon, Thomas Allen Harris, Sandi DuBowski, and Shari Frilot at the Tribeca Film Festival, 2014. Photo by Steven Bognar.

DS: I am excited to see so many of us working in areas of exhibition and programming. I believe that many filmmakers involved in this dialogue, particularly Shari Frilot, have done critical work to develop new models of programming for works by queers of color. When I began frequenting queer film festivals in the late 1980s, I was appalled to see the sloppy and unapologetic manner in which works by queers of color, particularly African Americans, were programmed.

TAH: I've found that the curators who have been most receptive to my work—particularly my latest work—have been African diasporic. For instance, Cameron Bailey programmed *VINTAGE* in the first Planet African Program of the Toronto International Film Festival. Pearl Bowser was responsible for taking a group of us to the Festival del Art Negra in Brazil, and Shari Frilot opened this year's MIX Festival with my film. On the other hand, American and European festivals that do not have black representation on their curatorial board did not recognize the value of *VINTAGE* and did not invite me to screen my film at their festivals.

A Festival Director's Concern

SF: I have also learned many difficult things through my experience with MIX. I have witnessed that who gets shown in festivals and who gains entrée into the media circuit has so much to do with who you know and who is out there championing your work. I have seen too many victims of exclusion from those "in the know" networks. I have seen firsthand the hypocrisy of gay institutions that claim to be working for the good of the "community" but refuse to support organizations like MIX because they consider our interests too transgressive and abject.

Sadly I have seen artists of color who invest in the "politics of novelty"—of being the *only* one—to the extent that they do not reciprocate the support they receive from their communities to other individuals in those very communities. The political and economic pressure we face collectively as people of color makes this sort of cultural cannibalism both abominable and frighteningly insidious. It is difficult to call out perpetrators for fear of breaking the silent code of nationalist duty. At the same time, this tacit consent makes it as difficult to realize how we might be guilty of such perpetration as it is easy to become caught up in the illusion of rising to the nationalist call of "representing the community." But it seems that if you can't count to three in remembering the first and last names of the individuals in your community whom you helped this month in getting to where you are (members outside the community of color do not count!), then if I might invoke the words of Audre Lorde, "you are not doing your work!"

Note

The complete text of "Narrating Our History: A Dialogue among Queer Media Artists from the African Diaspora" is available online at www.sistersinthelife.com.

Construction of Computation and Desire
Introduction to Yvonne Welbon's Interview
with Pamela L. Jennings

Early in the following interview, Pamela Jennings explains to Yvonne Welbon that her work gradually expanded from an initial and abiding interest in street photography toward working with and through forms of computational media. Jennings equates her move toward what she describes as "computational-based creative expression" with her growing interest in multimedia throughout the early 1990s, and she uses the term *multimedia* as a way of marking her work in a variety of different media and her interest specifically in computational media because the formulation *computational media* was not available to her then. The compelling relationship Jennings narrates between her art and her knowledge of and interest in science and computation is a reminder that the activities involved in audiovisual media-making always entangle living beings with technology.

A multimedia artist exploring various possibilities for audiovisual expression, Jennings has had a remarkable career, characterized by a spirit of scientific experimentation with the artistic possibilities of today's technologically mediated world. From the seemingly low-tech pixel-vision documentary images of the 1989 ACT UP march on City Hall and the 1995 CD-ROM entitled *Solitaire: dream journal* to *the book of ruins and desire*, a "kinetic sculpture" Jennings completed in 1996, and CONSTRUKTS, her most recent project in computational media, Jennings's art evinces an interest in revealing the psychosocial dynamics of technological mediation. Like other artists experimenting with multimedia during the late 1980s and early 1990s, Jennings explored connections between embodiment, communication, identity, desire, and technology. *the book of ruins and desire*, for example, is described in this way in the PDF documentation of the project:

> The optimum environment for this kinetic sculpture is a darkened room. In the center of the room stands a simple table with the sculpture object on top. Murmuring from its proximity is a barely audible voice whispering "touch me." This is to draw the user closer to the object and give permission to touch the object. When the sculptural object registers the human touch the sound track changes from "touch me" to gentle breathing. The manipulator of the object, as the director of the experience, will proceed in composing his/her own collage of imagery and sound by turning the hinged pages.[1]

the book of ruins and desire is a multimedia project for which Jennings wrote code for a "fuzzy logic inference engine" that would enable users to manipulate the collage of images and sounds by turning the pages at different speeds. Building an interactive sculpture as a way to meditate on how CD-ROMs change the nature of books, Jennings uses computer code as an expressive creative medium through which to highlight some of the logics of "interactivity" available in digital media technologies in ways that position the user's body as central to those logics. By calling attention to the sticky matter of embodiment not only through the user's interactions with the sculpture but also through the sonic and visual experience of the embedded audiovisual media, Jennings's exploration of the interactive book form allows one to perceive blackness, gender, and sexuality as already caught within the transformations wrought by computational interactivity.[2] Erika Muhammad declares that Jennings's "use of iteration, serialism, open structures, fuzzy logic, language, desire, and interactive media proves to be a potent combination."[3] Given this, an analysis of Jennings's work can inform ongoing efforts in film and media studies to offer ways to think about the relationships among blackness, gender, sexuality, and formal logics of computational media.

In her groundbreaking 1995 book, *The War of Desire and Technology at the Close of the Mechanical Age*, Allucquère Rosanne Stone (Sandy Stone) explains that her own interest in and explorations of the social environment of cyberspace in the early 1990s were animated in part by her sense that "the kinds of interactions we can observe within spaces of prosthetic communication" are "emblematic of the current state of complex interaction between humans and machines." She asserts, "The identities that emerge from these interactions—fragmented, complex, diffracted through the lenses of technology, culture, and new technocultural formations—seem to me to be, for better or worse, more visible as the critters we ourselves are in process of becoming."[4] Seen in the context of the artistic and scholarly explorations of identity and sociality with and through new media technologies in the late 1980s and early 1990s, Jennings's work offers an opportunity to think of black female embodiment and black lesbian sexuality as part of those early experiments in interactive, electronic sounds and images; insofar as she incorporates them into the representational logic of her projects, she generates insights into what was becoming of the identities animated by "black lesbian" during the late 1980s and early 1990s through, against, and maybe even in spite of their encounters with computational media. To the extent *black lesbian* does not appear in her work, despite, perhaps, our desire to find it there, Jennings challenges us to generate other logics and language for what does appear there, prompting us to create concepts for whatever we can perceive in her work.

Creating concepts through computational-based creative expression herself, Jennings enters into the logics of computation and helps us to see differently in and through it. In the summer of 2007 she curated an exhibition displayed at the Rotunda Gallery of the National Academy of Sciences that included select recent pieces of her own work in addition to the work of other "engineer-artists." That exhibition, entitled *Speculative Data and the Creative Imaginary: Shared Visions between Art and Technology*, provided a platform through which conversations between artists and engineers were staged in ways that continued older conversations and opened new ones. In the exhibition catalogue, Jennings asserts, "The creative digital media works in the 'Speculative Data and the Creative Imaginary: shared visions between art and technology' represent a cross section of transdisciplinary research practices that are forging new paths for developing new technologies, discovering new patterns in information, and finding new ways of seeing, knowing, and doing computer and information sciences and engineering."[5]

Jennings's work introduces questions about and explorations within technology, information, and numbers, including algorithms and other calculations, into the twenty-five years of "out African American lesbian media-making" collected in the present volume. This is especially exciting for those of us interested in embracing the history named by and enacted through the publication of this volume, even as we complicate received notions of that body of work by creating new concepts through it. Similarly, because computational media, like all media, operates according to a set of formal logics and constraints that digital media artists work within and against, Jennings's artistic exploration of that media along with her theoretical engagements with and policy recommendations for it provide opportunities for those of us in film and media studies to open new questions about what we currently call "new media."

The range of institutions that have benefited from and supported her work, including higher education, corporations such as IBM, and governmental organizations like the National Science Foundation, is a testament to the variety of ways that Jennings's artistic, scholarly, and scientific activities reverberate throughout American society and culture. It also underscores that there are a range of uses to which computation-based creative expression might be put, as well as the increasing imbrication of creativity, art, and science with commerce and capitalism. Creator of "some of the more progressive works in the canon of new interactive art by artists of color," Jennings offers additional insight into her creative process and unique artistic career in the compelling interview that follows.[6]

Notes

1 Pamela Jennings, "The Book of Ruins and Desire. Sculpture," 1996, accessed September 24, 2013, http://www.pamelajennings.org/index.html (website no longer exists).

2 My reading of *the book of ruins and desire* is based on the information available about it in the interview in this volume, on Jennings's website, and in Erika Muhammad's essay "Black Hi Tech Documents," in *Struggles for Representation: African American Documentary Film and Video*, edited by Phyllis Rauch Klotman and Janet K. Cutler (Bloomington: Indiana University Press, 1999), 298–314.

3 Muhammad, "Black Hi Tech Documents," 303.

4 Allucquère Rosanne Stone, *The War of Desire and Technology at the Close of the Mechanical Age* (Cambridge, MA: MIT Press, 1995), 36.

5 Pamela Jennings, "Speculative Data and the Creative Imaginary," accessed September 24, 2013, http://www.pamelajennings.org/speculative.html (website no longer exists).

6 Muhammad, "Black Hi Tech Documents," 303.

Ruins and Desire

Interview with Pamela L. Jennings, July 27, 2012

Early Career

In the 1990s I lived in New York City. I moved to New York City shortly after graduating from Oberlin College, in Ohio. I lived there for almost a decade, and during that time I was very actively engaged in continuing my pursuit of a career in photography. Photography was my first form of visual art going back to junior high school.

I enrolled in the New York University International Center for Photography master's program because I really wanted to understand what it was to be a photographer. At that time I was very interested in street photography. As a matter of fact, I wanted to be a Magnum photographer, at the Magnum Photo Agency, I just loved the style. . . . They were my idols: Henri Cartier-Bresson and the whole community of photographers from that era of the twentieth century. But what was interesting about that NYU/ICP program was that it was not designed to shape you into becoming a photographer. It was designed more to shape you into becoming an artist, into becoming someone who was thinking critically and theoretically about the work that you do, whether it was photography or other forms of visual, performing arts or creativity. Most people in the program, even though they started off as photographers, ended up as painters, performing artists, or poets, and working in different forms of creative expression. As a result of being in the NYU/ICP program, I started doing more video artwork and electronic sound work. I was gradually moving toward computational forms of media expression at that time called new media art.

There were a handful of nonprofit organizations geared toward supporting media artists in New York City. There were some very important support structures in place too. A small community of people moved between and across those organizations, and collaborations were made.

The independent media industry in New York City was perhaps in a resurgence. It felt young, open, and hopeful. Calling it young is perhaps strange to say because the media industry, beginning with photography, has been around for nearly a century and a half. I think in terms of tools and accessibility for the independent media producer, the industry in the 1990s was experiencing a renaissance. MTV started in the 1980s. Early music videos explored and celebrated the oddly experimental in the moving image and sound. It opened the door to synthesized coolness, which I think brought people not necessarily into wanting to do MTV music videos but wanting to explore this new creative medium for self-expression.

Banff

In 1990 I had my first residency at the Banff Centre in the Banff National Park in Alberta, Canada. Banff at that time was an amazing resource for supporting visual arts and media production and creative leadership development. I went there both as an artist and a work-study program participant. I worked with other video artists as an editor. And I completed the edit of my first video art piece, titled *the silence that allows*, my thesis project for the NYU/ICP master's program. Armed with a suitcase filled with three-quarter-inch videotapes and reel-to-reel audiotapes, I explored every nook and cranny of the Banff Centre state-of-the-art video and midi production labs.

I discovered that Banff was ahead of the game in terms of thinking about electronic music and electronic sound. I spent a lot of time in these amazing studios, kind of discovering and working in electronic sound and music. That was an ah-ha moment. I wanted to learn more about multimedia design. It became almost the perfect medium for me because I was interested in the visual—the photographic, the video, or the filmic aspects of the moving image—and sound. But there were also parts of me interested in performance and performative aspects of creative expression, and in many ways multimedia was a tool that allowed me to start to put all those mediums together.

A lot of incredible artists were at Banff in 1990, like Dick Higgins, founder of the Fluxus movement; writer Tilly Olsen; Attila Richard Lukacs,

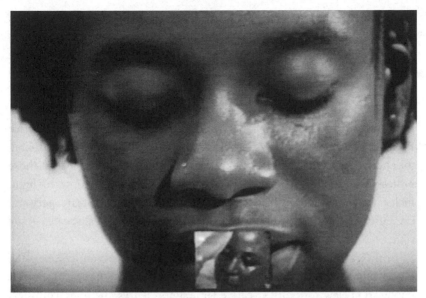

5.1 Pamela L. Jennings, with collaborator Melanie Hope, *the silence that allows . . .*, 1990. Scene from part 3, "the approach." Video composition in four movements.

a bad boy painter who depicted the gay skinhead scene in his larger-than-life paintings; electronic artists Trimpin, Laura Kikauka, and Gordan Monahan. Sharing such an intimate, creative time with that cohort opened my eyes to the international arts community and new forms of technology-based creative expression.

From ACT UP to *In the Life*

In the early 1990s I was honored to have been awarded three New York State Council for the Arts grants to support multimedia projects. This was a time when my photography work started to evolve into video, sound, and new media art. It was a really exciting time. There was a lot of support for media artists, for experimentation, and for documentary forms of media arts. During that time there was an incredible movement happening of international gay and lesbian film festivals. I had the opportunity to show *the silence that allows* in quite a few of those festivals on the international circuit, including its debut at the New Festival in New York City. There were also many opportunities to show interactive multimedia projects at these festivals in salons of computer terminals that were usually set up in the atriums of the film theaters. My first multimedia project, *Solitaire: dream journal*, was viewed by thousands of spectators.

This was also a time when critical social, cultural, and political actions around AIDS became frequent and abundant. I attended quite a few ACT UP rallies and protests, including one of the major protest events near New York City Hall. At that time I liked to experiment with the rough pixelated black-and-white imagery produced by the Fisher-Price PixelVision camera. PixelVision was the antithesis of the video industry's movement toward technologies to make images sharper, hyper-colorful images. The Fisher-Price PixelVision camera was very popular among filmmakers who were looking for alternative forms of image making. I shot quite a lot of footage at those protests with my PixelVision camera. Those images are really interesting to look at even today because the rough, beautiful black-and-white imagery and crystal-clear audio recording matched the emotional political theater of the time.

In the early 1990s I worked in the nonprofit arts community. I was the grants officer at Creative Time, an organization that continues to support public art in New York City. Creative Time supported a sometimes whimsical and always culturally astute spirit of creative experimentation. I was exposed to a context-rich roster of artists, from Jenny Holzer, Bob Flanagan, and Dumb Type from Japan to La Fura dels Baus from Spain.

I also worked as one of the first senior producers for an LGBTQ PBS television show, *In the Life*, that was produced by John Scagliotti. Taking over the abandoned set of the *Jane Pratt* talk show, *In the Life* brought together a very eclectic team of television producers, filmmakers, and technicians, with Kate Clinton as the host. Together we produced the first national grassroots television show for and about the LGBTQ community. Of course we had a nonbudget, so we relied very heavily on volunteers, both behind the camera as well as in front of the camera. Some of the people I interviewed for show segments included Marlon Riggs, B. Ruby Rich, Urvashi Vaid, and the Five Lesbian Brothers. What made the show work was the fact that we were in New York City and that there was an incredible community of creative gay and lesbian, bisexual and transgender, and queer folks who were willing to donate their time, energy, and talents.

Influences and Collaborations

Black lesbian video and filmmaking in New York City flourished in the early 1990s. Several of us were honing our visions and voices at the same time. Cheryl Dunye and Shari Frilot were doing some of their early experimental videos. Jacqueline Woodson's autobiographical work set the stage for her prolific career as a young adult author. As a matter of fact, my video *the silence that allows* premiered in the 1992 New Festival in a program of black lesbian filmmakers including Dunye, Frilot, Woodson, and Welbon. I remember the line to get into the screening wrapped around the corner.

There was a community of artists and producers in New York City running independent media advocacy and support organizations that created the backbone and foundation for the new media movement. One person who comes to mind is Shu Lea Cheang, who was just a wonderful, fantastic, really giving media maker. She had a couple of large-scale productions and collaborative projects that brought the community together to discuss pertinent topics. One such project was a collaborative installation that I and many other women participated in called *Those Fluttering Objects of Desire*. The collective installation was exhibited at Exit Art Gallery and in the 1993 Whitney Biennial.

The purpose of *Those Fluttering Objects of Desire* was to bring together a group of women, primarily of color, to talk about issues of desire. Shu Lea is a media artist who very early on pushed the boundaries of single-channel video and worked in media-rich installations and experimental electronic hacking, as well as film. In *Those Fluttering Objects of Desire*, she rigged pay-phones to require the audience to "pay"—as one would in a porn booth—to watch the short video, audio, and multimedia pieces addressing issues of desire, objectification, and racism.

The project I did for *Those Fluttering Objects of Desire* was created using a very experimental imaging device, I don't remember what it was called, that took sequential photos, rather than video, that were output in video and printed on a paper roll. The images were a beautiful sepia tone that were like a finer resolution grainy PixelVision texture. I later printed some of the images in a series of black-and-white silver halide prints.

At that time I was also training at the feminist martial arts school Brooklyn Women's Martial Arts. I was very interested in the concept of tai chi push hands exercises. I had a friend from the martial arts academy, who happened to be Caucasian, do an exercise of push hands with me. The camera lens was framed tightly on our hands. The video was about hands coming together, pushing, pulling, and coming apart. It was about the tension of attraction. The text accompanying the images was a reading by another friend, who had a very thick French accent, of a section of Anaïs Nin's *Delta of Venus*. Layered into the *Delta of Venus* text were critical texts about the Hottentot Venus and my journal writings about desire.

It was great to have an opportunity to work with Shu Lea Cheang. She gave us the freedom to do our work and to figure out how to approach the questions that she put on the table. I was also part of the film crew when she did her film *Fresh Kill* (1994). That was really exciting because at that point she was working at a professional film level with a couple of young up-and-coming actors who continued their careers in mainstream television and film. I had a cameo that anyone would miss if I were not sitting next to them pointing it out. It was all great fun.

Sleep Now (Version 1 and Version 2)

Most of my creative works started as sketches for much larger projects. I was very interested in American Art songs. I wanted to do a series of videos based on some of the art songs I had learned when I studied secondary voice at the Oberlin Conservatory. In particular I was enamored by the compositions of Samuel Barber, Aaron Copland, Ned Rorem, and other contemporary classical composers.

Sleep Now (Version 1 and Version 2) were videos completed around 1995. "Sleep Now" was composed by Samuel Barber as the setting of a poem by James Joyce about disquiet and longing. In Version 1 I sang and recorded the original arrangement of "Sleep Now" in the Anchorage—a beautiful redbrick, vaulted space with incredible reverberation that sits beneath the Brooklyn Bridge. The visuals included images of my vocalizing, friends from my women's community stepping through a most beautiful Karate Kata, and African drumming.

Sleep Now Version 2 was a more intimate poetic expression. I had residency at the Experimental Television Center in upstate New York. There I did the live mixing of the work. The visual components of the video were shot in my Brooklyn apartment and included grainy video synthesized images of my improvisational hands melding movements from martial arts and expressive dance.

The final video was edited in one live cut using the experimental Sandin video synthesizers and sound mixers at the Experimental Television Center. I played the video on one machine and then I also had a recording of a kalimba thumb piano piece I composed, and I sang a variation of Barber's "Sleep Now" that was recorded live as I watched the video visuals. There was also a text scroll across the center of the frame with my journal entries about desire and select text from Jeanette Winterson's *Sexing the Cherry*. Editing was live. There was no going back for a second edit.

5.2 Pamela L. Jennings, *Sleep Now Variations*, 1992. To Samuel Barber, "Sleep Now," in the *Hermit Songs Cycle*, the American Art Song Project. Video poem, with text from Jeanette Winterson, *Sexing the Cherry*.

Solitaire: dream journal

Solitaire: dream journal (1995) was my first major multimedia work, where I cut my teeth in learning how to write software code. The project began during my 1993 fellowship at the MacDowell Colony. The solitaire board is designed as a tetrahedron (a three-face pyramid), whose triangular sides correspond to the themes of melancholy, flight, and balance. A move made on one side of the tetrahedron randomly opens up a chapter of the three corresponding "books": "the book of melancholy," "the book of flight," or "the book of balance." The idea is to see how many pages you can access. The better your strategy with the checkers-like game, the more chapters you will be able to enter and explore. These windows provide a way for the game player to be placed in a multilayer hypertext context. As Erika Muhammad wrote in her essay about the work in the book *Struggles for Representation: African American Documentary Film and Video*, "In the game, your identity is the sum of your distributed presence. Solitaire is a document of self-discovery and recovery that unfolds dense layers of heterogeneous material culled from personal and popular memory. Mathematical and statistical 'facts' aren't presented objectively or subjectively, but rather, are presented in a conceptual manner in which the player becomes involved in a thick discursive text."

5.3 Pamela L. Jennings, *Solitaire: dream journal*, vignette from *the book of melancholy*, 1992. Interactive multimedia, computer code, algorithmic music composition.

the book of ruins and desire

I wanted to learn more about multimedia production, so I went back to school to the School of Visual Arts MFA Computer Arts program in New York City. Throughout that educational journey, I had a chance to study with artist-engineers who were doing some amazing creative works with electronics, coding, microprocessors, and sensors. The result of that degree was the 1996 interactive sculpture *the book of ruins and desire*. This work, along with my earlier multimedia piece *Solitaire: dream journal*, marked the beginning of my transition from single-channel video work to computational media, writing code, and developing electronic circuits.

the book of ruins and desire was an interactive sculpture that sat six feet long and two feet high. I was really interested in the idea of an interactive book. I think the book idea came about for a few reasons. Early in the multimedia scene a lot of people were trying to figure out how to make an electronic book. It was a term that was used a lot, and I was kind of playing on the rather limited definition of the translation of the book format—an application on a computer screen with a button labeled "next" to trigger a page-turning animation. I started my research for the project in the Special Collections section of the New York City Public Library. With white gloves on, I requested books made of metal. The specimens that arrived at my table included artists' books in film canisters, religious texts incrusted with rare jewels, books with metal pages and bindings. And of course the infamous Madonna *Sex* book complete with aluminum covers.

I started to explore new technologies, sensors, and micro-controllers and integrating media into the experience. My first idea was to create a physical object that looked like a bound book. I researched and experimented with technologies I could access and afford. I came to understand what I as an artist-engineer could figure out how to use and what was beyond my skill set at that time. The idea of a book form blossomed into a bridge-like form influenced by the scaffold structures on the Manhattan Bridge that greeted me daily during my subway ride from Brooklyn to Manhattan. The sculpture, made of wood, emulates that early twentieth-century structural bridge architecture.

the book of ruins and desire was my thesis project at the School of Visual Arts Computer Arts Program. I was becoming fatigued with creating interactive works that were only screen-based. And unlike so many of my classmates, I had no interest in honing skills as an animator for a job in the film animation industry. Being in a school of art, I wanted to explore other creative mediums and disciplines. I wanted to see what I could get my hands on. So I went into the wood shop and made the trusses and cabinets, although I didn't really know how to work with wood. They were beautiful, but structurally a little funky in the most creative manner.

I went into the printmaking shop and took a photo etching class. I wanted the photo etching plates to be the interactive pages. The instructor was a little confused when I wanted to etch the photo plates in the positive so that they could be read. Each page was connected to a brass rod with a potentiometer sensor to measure the degree of the page turn.

I worked with an art song cycle called *Poems of Love in the Rain* by Ned Rorem, a late twentieth-century composer. That song cycle has a very interesting structure. Rorem set nine poems, from poets including Windham, Auden, Moss, Dickinson, Roethke, Larson, Cummings, and Pitchford, to music twice in a dramatic arc because he believed that there was no one way to set these beautiful poems. I thought, "Okay, I have this structure that looks like a bridge balanced with four pages on each side. I'll set his songs to video twice, triggered by opening the page fully." When the pages were opened, sound localized to stereophonic speakers embedded in the supporting cabinet of the sculpture was triggered. Depending on the angle of the page, the sound panned from the left to the right speaker. There was a very small five-inch monitor in the middle of the sculpture. Funny, I think that monitor cost me eight hundred dollars. I could probably find one these days for fifty bucks. The video inside was a combination of animation, graphics, and human movement combining dance, martial arts, and performance art. There was always some form of movement in all of my video work at that period. I worked with Amy Pivar, a dancer in New York City with Bill T. Jones, among other choreographers. And I also worked with a performance artist, Ellen Fisher, a longtime collaborator with Meredith Monk, who I met at the MacDowell Colony in 1993. The martial artist Jan Vanderlinden contributed her beautiful and precise kata execution.

This was my first project that was fairly sophisticated in terms of building micro-controller boards and sensors. On the computational programming side, I integrated a fuzzy logic inference engine, probably on the light side, but still it felt really exciting to be able to understand how control methods for mechatronics could be used in art to control the dynamics of the creative experience. I was introduced to the concept of fuzzy logic during a job interview tour of a mechatronics lab at Rensselaer Polytechnic Institute. I didn't get the job but gained insight into how advanced technologies could be used creatively.

the book of ruins and desire was shown twice. During my MFA thesis show it was exciting to see people not only engage in the moving image but also engage in interacting with the physical device that they had to manipulate for a rich media experience. The piece was also shown at the New York State Governors Conference on media arts that was held at the IBM Palisades Executive Conference Center.

Multimedia Leads to IBM

As a hybrid filmmaker, a media art maker, sound, video, multimedia, and electronics hacker, I found that I had skills required to break into some of the early interactive corporate projects. It wasn't my goal at that time to work for corporate America, but the opportunities to learn from the best producers and researchers in the corporate commercial and research industries were golden.

At that time the dot-com bubble was rising. Every major media company was trying to figure out how to bring interactivity to its product line. There were a lot of great opportunities for creatives, who were getting skilled up in multimedia technology, to work on corporate websites and other experimental interactive platforms.

I worked for Time Warner Interactive on some of their interactive TV trial applications. I worked with NBC Interactive on the team that produced the very first NBC website for the Olympics enterprise during the 1996 Summer Olympics in Atlanta. Today the Olympic websites are a completely different breed of complex technologies. However, back then we were handwriting all the HTML pages at 40 Rockefeller Plaza in a 1990s version of "real time" as producers emailed sporting event images to us.

Somehow I was recruited to work at IBM, and to this day I really don't know how it happened. I joined a team of young media arts, new media, computer science–kind of folks to work on a web property called Alphaworks. This was at a time when IBM was trying to change its public-facing image from stodgy to "we are not your father's IBM any more" hip. We were a group of young upstarts allowed to do anything we wanted to do with the Alphaworks web property. And what we did was pretty extreme for the time. I think IBM's goal was to let us push the boundaries on an experimental site that would help the corporation loosen its grip on conservatism just a bit.

I was interested in Alphaworks because the project was a bridge between computer science and engineering research produced in the global network of IBM research labs and the public. Like an academic research lab, there are many technology inventions and discoveries from IBM's research centers that don't become consumer or enterprise products. This was an exciting time, when the Java programming language was born and web technologies were becoming more sophisticated. The notions of wearable interfaces and augmented reality were just starting to be explored. The Alphaworks project created a public gateway to those new ideas and technologies. My goal was to learn, build my network, and gain access to ideas and technologies for creative ends. As anyone who works for IBM knows, the acronym stands for "I've Been Moved," and that they did. My team and I were moved from New York to Silicon Valley to set up shop at the IBM Almaden Research Center in San Jose, California.

While at the Almaden Research Center I took advantage of the opportunity to work in one of its research labs called the User System Ergonomics Lab. This was a lab focused on human-centered computing, bringing together engineers, cognitive scientists, and designers to develop future technologies and applications to enhance all forms of human performance. Human-centered computing is an area of research that I have been involved in since. From that point forward my creative practice continued to flourish, and it became the driver for my continued engagement in research think tanks and university research, teaching, and federal philanthropy at institutions including SRI International, Carnegie Mellon University, and the National Science Foundation.

There is a continuum in the way I engaged creative media arts from the photography darkrooms to digital imaging and computational media. My work, while always deeply rooted in how I experience the world, has broadened from identity politics of the 1990s to the development of technologies and experiences that explore, question, and promote human potential in the twenty-first century.

Note

Read the complete interview with Pamela Jennings online at www.sistersinthelife.com.

the book of ruins and desire
Interactive Mechatronic Sculpture

The *interactive book* is a term heard frequently in reference to early experiments in multimedia production. But how to translate the concept of the book into a medium that has no paper, no pages, remains a challenge. Is not a book an object one holds in one's hands—the cover affected over time by the acids and oils perspiring from the user's skin, pages turned down and yellowed, torn or marked up? Research could show that the notion of the traditional book has been challenged throughout history. But this challenge has been accelerated with the growing accessibility of new computer interactive and information technologies.

The words engraved on the printed page raise curiosities in our imagination. For some readers, their minds are teleported to a place where the words and their imaginations mingle and twist about each other—creating new notions of experience and reality.

The optimum environment for my kinetic sculpture is a darkened room. In the center of the room stands a simple table with the sculpture object on top. Murmuring from its proximity is a barely audible voice whispering "Touch me." This quiet gesture draws users closer to the object and gives them permission to touch the object. When the sculptural object registers the human touch the sound track changes from "Touch me" to gentle breathing. The manipulator of the object, as the director of the experience, will proceed in composing their own collage of imagery and sound by turning the hinged pages.

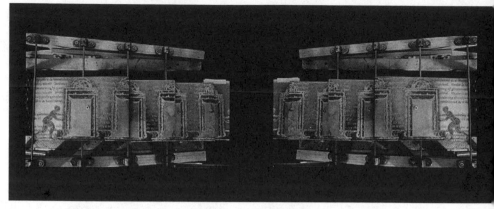

6.1 Pamela L. Jennings, *the book of ruins and desire*, 1996. Interactive sculpture, top view.

The Narrative

Embedded in the wooden cabinet below the scaffold for the book pages is a set of stereo speakers. Placed in between the two sets of metal etched pages is a small video monitor.

When there is no interaction and all of the pages are closed, a video of a black wave is played. As soon as a page is turned the video changes to the spinning rotunda and my hands holding and dropping white pebbles. If the book is left on, touched with all of the pages open, an animation of the Pythagorean theory is played.

Once a page is completely opened a content video is played. There are eight content videos. All but two of them are set to a selection of songs from Ned Rorem's song cycle *Poems of Love in the Rain*. Rorem set each of the poems in the cycle twice to piano accompaniment, claiming that there was no one perfect accompaniment for the poetry. I complemented his claim by setting his music twice to video. The other two videos are set to the song "Sleep Now" by the composer Samuel Barber.

The visuals are lush in this work, but sound is even more important. Turning the pages triggers spoken personal and philosophical texts about desire that amplify stereophonically based on the position and speed of the turned page. An embedded synthesizer plays algorithmically composed music to each interaction taken with the book.

Physical Description

the book of ruins and desire is a simple object run by a complex system of original hardware circuits and 68hc11 microprocessor technology coded

6.2 Pamela L. Jennings, *the book of ruins and desire*, 1996. Interactive sculpture, code and computer systems architecture notebook, with collaborator dancers Ellen Fisher and Amy Pivar.

with a fuzzy logic inference engine. Together they control audio and video processes that are produced with Opcode MAX, a midi programming language. Manipulating the sculpture's pages triggers a visual response on the sculpture's monitor and an audio response from a black box synthesizer and speakers embedded inside the object. The physical book is made from several materials, including metal etched plates and wood. All of the operating technology, except the 1996 Macintosh Quadra 950 computer, is embedded inside the sculpture's cabinet.

Software Description

the book of ruins and desire is operated through several layers of code. The 68hc11 microprocessor board is programmed with C. The fuzzy logic inference engine was developed using a freeware package from Motorola called Fudge. Individual potentiometers are permanently fixed to rods that support the pages. Their readings are interpreted through the inference engine, and three sets of numbers are produced. The sets of numbers describe the page being moved, its angle, and direction of movement. This data is read into Opcode MAX and converted into code that drives video and sound files and midi data. Midi data is created using components of the Real Time Composing Library developed by Karlheinz Essl. This library of MAX objects was developed to allow composers to use algorithmic and serial methods of music making.

A Cosmic Demonstration of Shari Frilot's Curatorial Practice

[Shari] is too black, too proud, and too strong to let the gay white boys get away with anything like ignoring experimental films starring Vaginal Davis. . . . LA, being such an industry monster town, would never feature a film festival of Outfest's caliber made up of nothing but experimental films, like MIX New York. Too many LA-based gay filmmakers are only interested in having mainstream or commercial careers and use film festivals as a stepping-stone to reach that dull goal. Being a subversive rebel, Shari decided to fool Outfest into letting her create a special program two years ago with experimental content. Even old-guard board members like Bruce Cohen gave her the thumbs up when she sold out a retrospective of Vaginal Davis films.
—**Vaginal Davis**

Shari Frilot is a filmmaker and curator whose creative practice has been driven by sustained explorations of sexuality, technology, desire, cosmic and subatomic structures, mixed-raced identity, and chaos. She has often expressed her modus operandi in the following terms: "It's impossible to see a cloud when you're in the middle of it. You have to move outside of the cloud to really get a sense of it." By continually shifting between the outside and inside of a given framework—whether institutional or personal—Frilot has developed keen modes of challenging conventional structures for understanding and engaging the moving image. Her contribution to film culture at large has not only been to open spaces for the creative expressions of people of color and queer people but also to make more capacious the frameworks for audiences to experience the moving image, experimental work, and science through the development of innovative exhibition and curatorial strategies for new media, experimental film, and video that bridge disciplines, fields, and media.

This essay considers Frilot's work as a curator, filmmaker, and creative visionary over the course of thirty years. A self-professed "alien child," Frilot was born outside a marine military base in Oceanside, California, to her Creole father, a former Olympic boxer, and Puerto Rican Taino mother. She was raised in Montbello, a neighborhood of Denver, Colorado, steps away from an arsenal, graduated valedictorian of her high school, and was the first in her family to go to college. She attended Harvard University on an engineering scholarship that lasted until she changed her major to government. Upon graduation, she worked for a program called *Higher Ground* at an NBC-affiliate television station in Boston. She produced a segment of the program that was the first show to talk about black people and HIV/AIDS. After four years as the director of programming of the MIX: New York Experimental Gay and Lesbian Film Festival (Frilot renamed the festival MIX and cofounded MIX Brasil and MIX Mexico), she moved to Los Angeles to program Outfest: Los Angeles Gay and Lesbian Film Festival, where she founded the Platinum section for experimental film and performance. In 1999 she joined the Sundance Film Festival programming team. She is currently a senior film programmer at the Sundance Film Festival, with a focus on American narrative and Latin American films, and is the chief curator and founder of New Frontier at Sundance, a physical exhibition space and curated group of films presented at the yearly festival that explores innovative modes of cinematic storytelling at the intersection of art and technology.

Frilot's early curatorial practice is shaped by her experiences and friendships within a broad, interconnected network of queer artists of color.[1] Her first experience organizing a film festival was in collaboration with Dellon Wilson, a renowned producer of social and cultural events for Black lesbians in New York. They codirected a program of Black lesbian films and videos. In 1991, the year before, Wilson and the filmmaker Dawn Suggs had founded the inaugural program, Through Our Eyes, which they structured as a screening in a club setting, followed by a discussion and reception. Suggs describes the festivals as "one of several that sprung up nationally around this time in an effort to develop self-reliant networks for screening Black Lesbian work within Black Lesbian communities. . . . The *Through Our Eyes Festival* sought to challenge the domination and appropriation of Black Lesbian films and stories mediated by a system of White patronage."[2] But events like Through Our Eyes were rare, and Frilot and her peers became increasingly frustrated with the scarcity of places to exhibit their work and did not find solace in the growing circuit of gay and lesbian film festivals, which consistently programmed their films in the smallest theaters and, regardless of the theme or content of the films, predictably in the "Black and gay" program. Frilot's interests in filmmaking challenged and exceeded notions of both Blackness and gayness.

Frilot's artistic practice began in 1986 with collage, using popular culture images taken from magazines and made with materials as diverse as dollar bills, maps, and clay. She describes her motivation for collage work as reconfiguring the meaning of images found in popular culture to say something different. Her first video, *Cosmic Demonstration of Sexuality* (1992), was intended as a part of a collage. She produced the work in response to a call for work by Jack Waters and Peter Cramer for an exhibition at ABC No Rio on Manhattan's Lower East Side. The original collage comprised two world maps mirroring each other horizontally, the top half darkened in charcoal and covered with the first five planets of the solar system. Earth was cut out, and in its place was projected a circular loop of a sixteen-minute video, *Cosmic Demonstration of Sexuality*. The short video was not intended as an independent piece on its own. Rather the video was to perform connections between sexuality and cosmic structure within the collage.

Cosmic Demonstration was made over the course of eight weeks and cost approximately $1,200. The video is composed primarily of talking-head interviews with Black women about menstruation, sex, the moon, children, and death. Frilot instructed her subjects to relate to her "as though I was an alien, and know nothing about the culture here on earth, nothing about you as an organism, or about earth life." She asked a consistent set of questions to each woman, taking care to not ask questions that would inspire discussion about the specificity of their backgrounds or characters. "They were supposed to be specimens, it was like a test tube." The interviews were intercut with various images—an image of Manhattan in prehistoric times, Earth from the perspective of the universe, a wolf decomposing. The visuals do not directly correlate to the voice-overs but instead are intended to expand their implications.

Frilot's next short film similarly navigates science interpretation from a personal and emotional place. *What Is a Line?* (1994) experiments with narrative structure and the notion of linearity. The video is of a woman riding on a commuter train and having an internal monologue to process feelings of anger, pain, and grief resulting from a breakup. Frilot was curious about

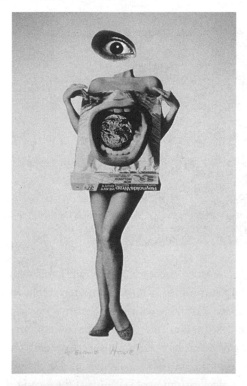

7.1 Shari Frilot, collage.
Courtesy of the artist.

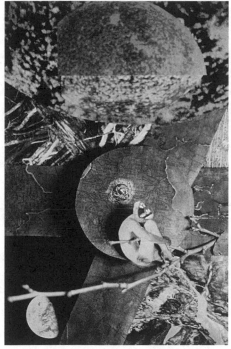

7.2 Shari Frilot, collage.
Courtesy of the artist.

7.3 Shari Frilot, still from *Cosmic Demonstration of Sexuality*, 1992.

observations that straight lines do not exist in nature, and parallels this with her curiosity of how one emotional state progresses into another, never following a rational, straight path. The video was made with $800 over two weeks.

Despite the exploration of scientific themes and sexuality that do not foreground or single out "Black and gay" identity, Frilot's films were repetitively programmed according to essentialist notions of race, gender, and sexuality. She recalls the screening of *Cosmic Demonstration of Sexuality* at the 1992 Los Angeles Lesbian and Gay Film Festival (later renamed Outfest when Frilot became the director of programming in 2001): "The festival was held at the Director's Guild in Hollywood which has two large theaters and one 30-seat video [screening room]. The majority of the works made by people of color were screened in the micro-theater to audiences [that] were overwhelmingly white. Some of my fellow filmmakers of color received poor treatment by the festival staff. . . . I found that the conditions I encountered in Los Angeles were systematic and were likely to be perpetuated since none of the directors of these festivals were from communities of color."[3]

Frilot's concern was how films by makers of color were exhibited. The sixth New York Lesbian and Gay Film Festival invited the filmmakers Thomas Allen Harris and Cheryl Dunye to guest-curate a program, which was called *FIRE!* and was organized around artists from the African diaspora and included films by Frilot, Raúl Ferrera-Balanquet, and others. Dunye and Jocelyn Taylor organized Lookout: The DCTV Lesbian and Gay Video Festival, for which Frilot designed the poster.

In 1993 Frilot and Harris were asked to take a leadership role in the New York Lesbian and Gay Experimental Film Festival (NYLGEFF), founded by

7.4 Shari Frilot, poster for Lookout: The DCTV Lesbian and Gay Video Festival.

Sarah Schulman and Jim Hubbard in 1987. Schulman and Hubbard, along with a newly established board, decided the festival needed new leadership. "In order for the festival to fully represent the entire community," Schulman asserted, "it has to be re-imagined and re-constituted."[4] Frilot and Harris were approached with the opportunity because they were "young, Black filmmakers with substantial roots in the people of color communities and in the art world."[5] While Harris ultimately declined this leadership role in order to focus on the production of his film VINTAGE: *Families of Value* (1995), Frilot saw the chance to remake the NYLGEFF into a space that dynamically engaged her and her peers' work. "In the early nineties, there was an explosion of work by makers of color which engaged the issues of race, class, sexuality, and aesthetics in ways that [were] revolutionizing experimental film. . . . I saw it as a chance to create a festival which encouraged this artistic movement by treating the artists involved better than we were being treated by mainstream gay festivals who often programmed our work in less than optimum (and sometimes racist) ways, and better than the so-called 'ethnic' film festival who program precious few of our works at all."[6]

Frilot asked the Brazilian filmmaker Karim Ainouz to join her as the co-director, and she changed the name of the festival to MIX: The New York Lesbian and Gay Experimental Film Festival. The renaming reflected their desire to mix up the traditional paradigms of festival organizing and exhibition programming strategies, as well as audiences. Frilot described her motivations for accepting the position and "reimagining" and "remixing" the NYLGEFF: "We renamed the festival MIX because I wanted to create a festival on the gay circuit that talked a little more about race and class, as well as queer sexualities. This was in the early 90's, when New Queer Cinema was all the rage, but nobody of color was looking at New Queer Cinema and seeing themselves or thinking that it had anything to do with them. That's where the idea for MIX came from."[7] Frilot was committed to creating more physical spaces of exhibition for films by queer people of color, and her curatorial approach to MIX sought to fundamentally reframe these films as epistemological challenges to how both experimental film and queer film were being constituted.

Whereas Schulman and Hubbard sought to resist the overt cultural invisibility and oppression many of the gay and lesbian artists in their community faced, Frilot confronted the challenge of engaging the rapid commodification and homogenization of gay and lesbian identity. She said, "It's as if the mainstream media have come to play a more important role in determining what a 'gay' film is than the queer festivals."[8] At a time when many gay and lesbian organizations and representations were trying to show gays and lesbians as normative, assimilating people who did not present a threat to society, Ainouz and Frilot sought to transgress traditional notions of sexuality by putting forward explicit images of sex. She explained, "I thought one way would just go to the root of sexuality itself and use the power of the explicitly erotic to really blow the whole thing away, to implode it . . . and create a rich and fertile ground to not only consider cinema and culture but to consider the value of sexuality itself. I was looking for something that was beyond the gay dollar benchmark in the gay revolution that was excluding so many people. . . . I turned to the power of the pussy and to the disarming power of sexuality to undercut all of the momentum of this commercialized movement and reinvigorate it with another kind of power."[9]

Frilot gestured to the cover art of the 1993 and 1994 Festivals as visual representations of her vision. The 1993 cover features a collage imaging the side of a naked male body folded over, wearing nylon fishnet stockings and high heels, the body's head replaced with the mouth of a lion, and a vagina covered with a triangle in its body's fulcrum. The catalogue cover for the 1994 festival depicts an ambiguously raced and gendered head with hair splitting open to let out sperm swimming up to fertilize the planet Jupiter.

Gay and lesbian organizations and publications responded to this explicit show of sexuality by refusing to sponsor MIX, even after Frilot requested support. She wrote in response, "While the Festival is an important force in the liberation of lesbians, gay men, bisexual and transgendered people, MIX does not receive the support of gay institutions which build their businesses and profits on the premise of ensuring the 'community' a voice." Frilot described how the *Advocate* and *Out Magazine* refused to sponsor MIX three times, giving as a reason that the Festival is "too 'risque' and too 'sexually explicit.' " While MIX had historically been supported by the *Village Voice*, the lack of support from these LGBT publications, which supported other gay and lesbian festivals, was telling of the emphatic struggle around solidifying a normative identity around queer sexuality. Frilot called out these "so-called gay institutions who forsake the community of queer people who do not aspire, or absolutely refuse, to merge with mainstream culture." She ends with a provocation: "Perhaps it is time for those who are really dedicated to sexual freedom and freedom of expression across racial, economic, and political lines to build a new movement as we rethink who our allies really are."[10]

At the forefront of Frilot's work with MIX was the idea to "let the festival be re-mixed by audiences and makers who have been traditionally overlooked by the lesbian and gay media circuit."[11] Frilot recounted, "By the mid-1990s, the features were becoming glossier and more mainstream and there was just an unabashed ambition to make a mainstream gay movie, so I wanted to interrupt that. . . . [MIX] was very much in opposition to New Queer Cinema, the gay dollar, and gay commercialism all of which was largely white and male. I didn't feel a part of that at all. . . . But I also wanted to transcend the traditional oppositional approach, which would be just including people: 'What about the women? What about the blacks?' "[12] The goal was not to simply include people of color in the paradigm of gay and lesbian identity but to reconceptualize sexuality entirely so that race, identity, nationality, and class are entangled within its formation.

Meanwhile nationalistic notions of Blackness and queer identity were being called out and challenged by other artists and scholars. Many of these

7.5 1993 MIX Festival catalogue cover.

7.6 1994 MIX Festival catalogue cover.

7.7 Essex Hemphill and Cornelius Moore in *Black Nations/Queer Nations?*, directed by Shari Frilot, 1996.

debates are captured in Frilot's feature documentary, *Black Nations/Queer Nations?* (1996), based on the conference of the same name held at City University of New York in 1995. The conference brought together scholars, activists, and artists to trace how categories of "Black" and "queer" are used as political strategies to redraw the boundaries of nation-states.[13]

Frilot strategically organized screenings thematically rather than around single aspects of race, gender, or sexuality in order to break the LGBT festival standard she and her peers had bristled against. Frilot and Ainouz were committed to "putting together programs where the works actually spoke to one another in some kind of dialectic" rather than strictly along "monochromatic criteria around race and gender" like an all-boy or all-girl program or a race-based program. Frilot continued the guest curator model (originally initiated by Jerry Tartaglia during the festival's early years) by having the majority of the festival programmed by members of community organizations.[14] She described their process for curating and programming the festival: "In a certain sense we were experimenting with the very terms of race, class, and sexuality and trying to expand them in an experimentation of how we put together the programs." MIX's reputation became hinged upon the breadth of thematically arranged, integrated programs of films and videos made by makers of color, international, female, transgender, and male filmmakers, lesbian, gay, bisexual, and straight filmmakers that contest fixed notions of identity and belonging to explore a multiplicity of differences.

Not only did Frilot's programming strategies disrupt the concepts of experimental, gay and lesbian identity, and film "to expand the confines of lesbian and gay media," but MIX's physical spaces were also radically reorganized to hold multiple kinds of audiences and ways of looking. Audiences, participants, and curators were called in by community-organization collaborations (for example, with the South Asian Lesbian and Gay Association) and by the "nontraditional publicity strategy of direct community outreach" to youth and people of color communities through nightlife. An alliance between the filmmaker and club promoter Lisa Collins and Café Con Leche was formative in the festival's efforts to expand its audiences. During this time MIX's mailing lists nearly doubled to "include more people of color, as well as lesbian and gay youth, from around the metropolitan area."[15] The festival also procured a number of "cultural sponsors" that served people of color, diasporic, and international communities.[16]

MIX moved from the Anthology Film Archives, an East Village base for traditional avant-garde film since the early 1970s, to a Chelsea-based performance space and gallery called The Kitchen. "The festival needed to physically break out of that traditional venue. There was a heaviness to the space. . . . It is an archive, it represents the past, it represents preserving a legacy of what was. The very idea of having a festival that was trying to look forward being held at an archive didn't make sense."[17] In 1994 Frilot drew from her background in television to expand MIX's audiences by collaborating with the Downtown Community Television Center's Lookout Festival, which had been showing activist film and video by gay and lesbian artists since 1990. The next year MIX worked with Free Speech TV.[18] With these partnerships MIX became the "largest venue for queer media" as well as the "largest avant-garde film festival in the world . . . mak[ing] queer experimental film and video accessible to more than five million people nationally."[19]

Ainouz and Frilot were also committed to bringing international audiences and work to MIX. From 1993 to 1997 MIX became increasingly international in scope through its diasporic guest curators and connections through a transnational film community of artists of diverse sexualities working with film and video. Working in conjunction with the festival's guest curators, Andre Fischer and Susy Capo, Ainouz and Frilot presented MIX Brasil, a "festival das Manifestacoes da Sexualidade" ("expressions of sexuality"), "the first lesbian and gay film festival in the history of Brazil."[20] MIX Brasil (directed by Fischer and Capo) and MIX Mexico (in 1997 in conjunction with Arturo Catalan and Edna Campos) were not replicas of their sister festival in New York but were organized by people who were familiar with, connected to, and had grown out of "queer" respective Brazilian or Mexican communities. The way MIX New York approached sexuality and experimental film was not neatly exported but rather was used as an inspiration for developing a festival that was relevant for specific communities across Brazil and Mexico.[21] "We are sister organizations who operate independently from each other but support one another by providing programming and advice. Together, we are building a network of festivals which offers unprecedented exposure for Queer work."[22]

Frilot expanded who was feeling called in to participate and attend MIX and also the way people watched and engaged with films and each other. Her approach to the concept "experimental" was not for the content or form of the film or video itself but for the exhibition of the work. Frilot resisted the way traditional theater spaces and film screenings kept audiences, filmmakers, and films segregated in unproductive ways. "I wanted to create a festival that was also a social space where people could go to the movies but then after the movies come and talk about things and digest it, but with a critical mass so that the effect of these experimental films—that are not the easiest things to watch, that operate on audiences in ways that are not that obvious, that are often times visceral, subliminal and subconscious—can be worked out. I wanted a social space to catch the audience afterwards and have the work continue to work in that social context."[23] Different models for exhibiting and engaging with films were developed throughout MIX's programs. For example, the Go!Go!SPOT was a "pre/after show playground featuring café, bar, music, and interactive installations in a leisure lounge setting" that was located in the gallery space of The Kitchen, one floor up from the theater space where the films were screened.[24] Another example is the Video Gong Show, an event where artists could submit their films and videos (under five minutes, anonymously if desired) to be screened in a public setting (a bar), where audiences would cheer to indicate their likes and dislikes to a panel of "celebrity judge drag queens."[25]

The four strategies Frilot employed in the organization of MIX were (1) experimenting with models for exhibiting and engaging with film and video, (2) calling in specific artists and audiences not otherwise interpolated by the festival, (3) disrupting the physical space of the festival,[26] and (4) working with community members in the programming process in the production of Victoria MIX. A "major festival within a festival" taking place during the festival's tenth-year anniversary, Victoria MIX was presented as "the first queer film festival ever to take place in Harlem."[27] Victoria MIX offered "a four-day retrospective showcasing the burgeoning world of queer film and video within the African diaspora."[28] The films included and the descriptions of Victoria MIX go beyond narrowly defined racial identity-based programming.[29] The "Harlem Stories" short films program's description asserted, "Harlem's history is dense, and full of the contributions of people who looked to themselves and their community to define the direction and scope of their expression. The work in this program gives everything from a brief glimpse of a single event, to an elegant visual analysis of how history is not only developed, but also received, acknowledged, preserved, and passed on. Gay and lesbian presence has always been very evident here, and has been a vital part of the thriving culture of Harlem for almost a century."[30]

The questions of belonging, community, and cultural expression raised within these films are read through a lens of what is visible or eclipsed in the telling of history. The organizing principle of a retrospective that cohered work under a neatly identifiable category (ostensibly "Blackness" and "queerness") is also challenged in the descriptions for Victoria MIX: "But don't get comfortable yet. The sheer number of works promises to challenge the very notion of retrospective. The blackness of the 'black' folk who have made these pieces and who are presented within them tends to be a fairly slippery, perhaps even incoherent phenomenon. Male/Female, Latin/Anglo, Dark/Not-So-Dark, Queer/Not-So-Queer, the identities represented within Victoria MIX are necessarily strung together loosely, a fact that is exacerbated by the resistance to traditional narrative found within many of the works."[31] By playing with notions of race, sexuality, and gender, Victoria MIX's programming unsettled fixed categories of race and sexuality on which multicultural paradigms of tokenism and inclusion were based.

In a critical reflection essay published in the festival catalogue, Robert Reid-Pharr recalls the work and place of MIX as it developed over the course of Frilot's leadership:

> Yes, its programming has been remarkably inclusive. Yes, it has offered a venue to artists who have been largely shunned by the mainstream, including the gay and lesbian mainstream. Yes, the curators have experimented with how films can be screened. . . . Yes, many prominent people of color have been nurtured by MIX at early points in their careers. . . . Yes, MIX has premiered more queer works by people of color than any other festival in the world, gay, straight, black, white or otherwise. Yes, MIX New York has helped to initiate gay and lesbian film festivals in Brazil

and now Mexico. Yes, MIX has brought experimental film and video to diverse communities throughout the U.S., including Harlem, Los Angeles, San Diego, and Lewiston, Maine to name a few.

Reid-Pharr found the active participation of different people was the heart of MIX. "This putting oneself into the films and into the festival," while difficult and messy, is the work that "has helped sustain movements, communities and individuals."[32]

In 1997 Frilot passed the leadership of the festival to Raj Roy (currently the chief curator of film at the Museum of Modern Art) and the experimental filmmaker Annie "S8" Stanley (who currently runs an artist retreat workspace called Smokey Belles in the Catskills). Roy was one of Thomas Allen Harris's students at UC San Diego who moved to New York with his classmate and friend Patty Chang to be a performance artist. The two were introduced to Frilot at an exhibition of the photography of Harris's brother, Lyle Ashton Harris. Roy became an intern at MIX and was charged with the task of developing a performance element to the festival. Stanley had been a participating filmmaker at MIX since 1993 and codirected the festival with Frilot in 1995. While Roy and Stanley developed a notably more professional image for MIX, they continued Frilot's investment in problematizing the commodification of gay identity by employing subversive strategies to both attract corporate sponsors looking to market to gay and lesbian demographics and counter the waxing twin trends of commodifying and assimilating gay and lesbian identity and film culture into the mainstream.[33]

Outfest (1998–2001)

These tensions around gay and lesbian identity, commodification of marginal cultures, and the mainstream continued to concern Frilot after moving to Los Angeles in 1996. She remembers leaving New York broke and feeling broken by the demanding, all-encompassing, and underpaid work of organizing MIX. John Cooper, then the director of programming at Outfest, offered her a position as a programmer at Outfest. In an article questioning the essence of queer film by Eugene Hernandez (one of the founders of indieWIRE and the deputy director of the Film Society of Lincoln Center), Frilot wrote, "We are the ones who have played a part in defining what [queer film] is. It can be whatever we want to make it as programmers—our role is inherently a political one." And yet Frilot also recognized that festivals, as social spaces, exceed the purpose of simply screening films. "Part of our major goal is to create a space where gay and lesbian people can come together. It almost doesn't matter what we put on the screen."[34]

In a festival roundup of Outfest 1998 for the *LA Weekly*, the cultural critic Ernest Hardy described the impact Frilot had in her first year working for Outfest:

> Frilot's not only co-programmed, with Shannon Kelley, the best Outfest in recent memory, she's helped elevate it to world-class status: This year's showcase is the film festival, queer or straight, that L.A. has been starved for. . . . In years past, a slow pan of some British boy's ass was the festival's dose of innovation and exoticism, while American flicks, at least as demonstrated by hot-ticket, main-theater fare, became increasingly banal, infantile. . . . Outfest '98 still has its share of crossover dreams . . . and determinedly indie flicks . . . but it's the high number of Asian films . . . films from Israel and Africa, Brazil and Germany, the high-profile slots given to experimental works, the easy balance between lesbian and gay titles, that bear Frilot's stamp.[35]

The following year Cooper hired Frilot as a programmer for the Sundance Film Festival and passed on his position as Outfest's director of programming to Frilot in 2001. Frilot's most enduring legacy at Outfest was carving a section specifically for experimental films called Platinum Oasis, which is referenced in the epigraph by Vaginal Davis.

In 2001 Platinum Oasis manifested in an all-night, one-time performance and installation exhibition, with the performance artists Ron Athey and Vaginal Davis as the king and queen curators and hosts of the event held at the Coral Sands Motel on Western Avenue and Hollywood Boulevard in Los Angeles. Frilot describes her motivations for conceptualizing and organizing the event and how they informed her larger curatorial philosophy: "I wanted to go back to what queer was—how fabulous and wrong and edgy and how dangerous it was. . . . [Platinum Oasis] lasted from the afternoon, and went overnight into the next morning—setting up a landscape for devious curiosity with no bounds. We wanted to create this environment, even if it was just for a little moment, where there was . . . a cornucopia of exploration and adventure alongside sexuality and art."[36]

Each of the different rooms in this "crack-fisting" motel presented some kind of performance: an artist-created "set" or an installation that would call in visitors to participate physically. Davis colorfully describes the event to potential visitors:

> It will be a round-the-clock event featuring artists working in sound, surveillance, vaudeville, life-threatening environments and technical torture devices. It will be 18 hours of durational art—40 rooms of art in every medium imaginable. To give you an idea: the motel's pool will become the G.I.M.P. Geriatric Poolside Lounge hosted by La Diva Davis and El Cholo, the Chicana dagger drag queen (a stone butch dyke with a mustache who does femme drag). There we will introduce the combative talents of Lydia Lunch and the burlesque review Velvet Hammer. You might nonchalantly find yourself in Bruce La Bruce's live and projected photo sessions or get your nails done at the Divinity Fudge Funky Nail Salon. . . . To wind things down, new-fangled country artists The Acres will offer a Sunday morning gospel brunch complete with baptism service.[37]

Toward the end of her short tenure at Outfest, flanked by a group of emerging L.A.-based producers, actors, musicians, and artists, Frilot embarked on making her fourth short film. In *Strange and Charmed* (2003), Frilot explicitly parallels the structure of desire with the quantum structures. The film is told from the perspective of a quark, a subatomic particle that moves in erratic ways across space and time, and is structured around emotional shifts experienced by two women and one young girl who live in the same New York apartment building. Unlikely sex consoles heartbreak, a young crush blossoms into a kiss, and loneliness breeds fantasies of an anonymous ménage à trois. Frilot describes her impetus for centering desire as a way to explore quantum mechanics: "You can be in one place emotionally and then something jostles you and a shift happens and before you know it you're in an entirely different place. Desire is a creative process; it's not logical. I wanted to think about that dynamic through the erratic movement of subatomic particles like quarks. Where desire leads you is completely unexpected." The three women in the film were cast to have a similar look because they are meant to be the same character—the physical embodiment of a quantum particle that moves infinitely across time (their ages) and space (the apartment building). The cinematography mirrors this by assuming the point of view of a quantum particle—zooming in and through cosmic to microscopic scales. Frilot works to develop a narrative structure that can cinematically express expansive possibilities of self and identity through quantum physics. The film

7.8 Still from *Strange and Charmed*, directed by Shari Frilot, 2003.

bears a much slicker production value than Frilot's previous films, although it was never color-corrected and is unavailable for general circulation because music rights were not cleared.

Manifest in three short films (*Cosmic Demonstration of Sexuality*, *What Is a Line?*, and *Strange and Charmed*) and one feature documentary (*Black Nations / Queer Nations?*), Frilot's filmmaking practice has formatively compelled her curatorial work, which by 2001 earned her a spot alongside John Cooper, Geoffrey Gilmore, and Trevor Groth on the programming team at the Sundance Film Festival.[38]

At Sundance, Frilot developed strategies in the programming room to bring in more films by people of color and experimental work and to expand the terms on which those films were considered. For example, after being frustrated with the singular way in which the term *diversity* was used as code for *race*, she began using the word to describe films by or about white people but in terms of the film's formal narrative structure or aesthetic choices. In this way Frilot challenged the term and the framework in which her fellow programmers were discussing films by directors of color during the rigorous selection process. "I focused on demonstrating the value of diversity—as something beyond race, even, but about formalism and difference. I wanted to expand the legibility of what films of color are, the quality they played at.

7.9 Director Shari Frilot and producer Effie Brown on the set of *Strange and Charmed*, 2003. Courtesy of Shari Frilot.

I wanted to make the festival more capacious in terms of the kinds of films it can play, to perhaps surprise programmers by putting these films in front of audiences and seeing the positive response they didn't think that kind of film could get. This was my goal also at MIX, to make the whole landscape more capacious, to make film more capacious."[39]

The highly subjective process of film selection at festivals necessitates a concerted effort to make legible and advocate for the value of films. Of the thousands of films that are submitted for consideration, the hundred or so that are selected for the lineup are deliberately chosen by a committee—not always by consensus, but by persuasion of the film's significance to the larger field and contribution to the lineup.

During her tenure at Sundance, Frilot has successfully advocated for and shepherded through the festival a great many films by people of color, female directors, and experimental filmmakers.[40]

Programming a film by a person of color doesn't just mean the film is invited to the festival. It means that the filmmakers, cast, and crew—many of whom are otherwise marginalized within the broader context of the film industry—enter the space of the festival. Over time these filmmakers bring networks and affiliations of other directors, writers, producers, and actors that literally take up space in the theaters. Given the segregated history of American film culture—both independent and Hollywood—this physical presence is critical to the experience of the film festival and the film itself. As networks of artists of color overlap and accumulate over the years, the constitution of the festival's audiences can be noticeably different and impact a film's overall reception, which in turn influences decisions by critics who write about the film and distributors who might buy the film and the amount they are willing to pay for it. So the work of advocating for marginalized filmmakers can be seen to manifest in not only the increasing numbers of films that are being submitted each year for consideration to the festival but also the growing success of these filmmakers in terms of acclaim, future film or television production, and broader visibility within popular culture.

New Frontier (2007–Today)

In 2007 Frilot's role at Sundance further expanded; besides leading the programming of films in the American narrative and experimental categories of the festival, she envisioned and realized a physical exhibition space at the festival for digital artworks, media installations, and multimedia performance. New Frontier became Frilot's opportunity to "integrate everything I'd been working on up to this point—science, art, a formal engagement with media—into a program that is able to change as fast as the media is changing." Frilot designed New Frontier within a deliberately social setting that fosters collaboration and exchange and has been curated to bring together artists, filmmakers, and designers of new media technologies who are innovating models for cinematic storytelling. In the context of Sundance and its role in the rapid commodification of independent film, New Frontier's retreat-like atmosphere offers respite from the rapid flurry of sales meetings and deals that take over the festival experience for many audiences. Frilot locates her motivation for founding New Frontier in a need to reappropriate screen culture, new media technologies, and cinema for the nourishment of alternative modes of engaging cinema: "When we walk around, screens follow our bodies. Screens are in our pockets and bags. As we move through buildings and terrains, surveillance systems track us. We watch cabs drive by with TV screens. Subways are plastered with screens. You could say that we live inside of a media installation. But you can't really call it that because it is not for art's sake; it is mainly for commerce's sake. I want to reclaim this environment for art."[41]

Frilot's impetus with New Frontier is to resist the occupation of the cultural domain by commercial forces, transforming the conditions within which we engage the cinematic. In her curatorial statement for New Frontier in 2010, she described how the pervasiveness of moving-image technology in everyday life has created an "electroskeleton," an electronically engineered dimension that encrusts our bodies and "structures our modern lifestyle, affecting our ethics and decision-making."[42] Actively refiguring the mode of engagement between audiences and film, Frilot describes her approach to New Frontier as an expansion of audience expectations around what Sundance has traditionally offered: American independent film. Unlike the "white cube" exhibition format traditionally found in the museum and art worlds or the "black box" exhibition format of the conventional theater, it is deliberately not clear what, in which order, or how one is supposed to look at New Frontier. Frilot enthusiastically says, "All those rules are gone at New Frontier. There's no knowing anything there."[43] The location and design of the New Frontier exhibition prompt a productive disorientation that is distinct from other venues at Sundance, which instead depend on film industry professionals (journalists, distributors, producers, and agents, among others) to efficiently organize themselves in order to successfully evaluate the financial and cultural worth of as many films as possible within the limited time frame of the festival.

Frilot characterizes the curatorial methodology that underpins New Frontier as "physical cinema," a framing of the cinematic that calls upon the body to dynamically participate in the process of making meaning from the work. Her early experimentation with exhibition strategies to captivate audiences around film and art become central to her approach to New Frontier. These curatorial experiments aim to "strategically trigger sensual registers" and appeal to audiences through the body rather than isolating the visual. The sensorial elements of the exhibition design foster a space where audiences can be vulnerable. Frilot describes how by "physically seducing [audiences] with soft couches, low lighting, and sexy music," she hopes viewers will "not feel intimidated if they stumble around with their words." As Frilot explains, "for example, it's okay to stumble around with your words in a bar—in fact, it's encouraged. People have really illuminated discussions in bars because of that."[44] The evocation of a bar's atmosphere speaks to the attention Frilot places on how physical spaces and social contexts shape the conditions and terms in which people are able to engage with one another and the implications for this on how audiences might relate to artistic works.

The development and evolution of Frilot's curatorial strategies are aligned with the poet-warrior Audre Lorde's notion of the erotic. Lorde's theorization of the erotic as an invaluable mode of knowing that "rises from our deepest and nonrational knowledge" generates critical paths for curatorial practices that navigate questions of aesthetics, difference, spectatorship, and value.[45] As Frilot's most recent curatorial endeavor, New Frontier offers a kind of cinematic intelligibility that locates the body's position and implicates its physicality as a response to rapidly changing screen cultures and digital landscapes. Frilot's insistence throughout her years of festival work on physical cinema as a curatorial methodology foregrounds the centrality of a kind of "embodied intelligence" that makes sense of work through our bodies.[46] This eclipses a more conventional approach to cinema that relies primarily on textual readings, aesthetic valuations, individual preferences, or commercial assessments. Frilot's long-standing commitments to experimenting with exhibition and curatorial strategies to captivate audiences on an erotic, bodily level open the possibility of refiguring racial, sexual, and gendered subjectivities beyond fixed categories of identity.

Frilot's strategies for conceptualizing and organizing New Frontier around a notion of physical cinema move audiences to recognize, locate, and activate their bodies within a generative dynamic to cinematic production, distribution, and exhibition—facilitating the conditions within which artists, scholars, filmmakers, media scientists, and organizers might forge other ways of loving cinema. The embodied, participatory relationships incited by Frilot's curatorial approaches reframe linear relationships between the spectator and the screen and generate new dynamics that require people's collective presence to experience cinema.[47] Frilot explains that with physical cinema, "your body is moving within the context of the work, completing the story with the information that the body has. The body's movement is consummating the work, and calls the body to react in different ways." This is distinct from the physicality of being moved in one's gut while watching a powerful film. By calling on our bodies to be part of the cinematic experience, meaning is actively generated through our interactions with the screen. Frilot's emphasis on physical cinema in order for the audience to move, in order to be moved, compels audiences to be engaged by the spectacle of technological innovation and the immersion of moving image and also by the provocations at the heart of stories that foreground social, racial, environmental, sexual, and economic justice and well-being.[48]

Reflecting on the trajectory of her creative and curatorial practice, Frilot describes her work as "world-building," a concept she has engaged with her longtime friend and coconspirator cultural theorist José Esteban Muñoz. In *Disidentifications: Queers of Color and the Performance of Politics*, Muñoz argues that "ideological state apparatuses and other aspects of the hegemonic order" (for example, whiteness, heteronormativity, and misogyny) are performative. He critically traces how disidentification neither wholeheartedly identifies nor opposes a fixed identity but rather takes the "majoritarian culture as raw material to make a new world" by "disassembl[ing] that sphere of publicity and us[ing] its parts to build an alternative reality." These disidentificatory spaces are "something new emerging in the actuality of the present . . . within the future and the present."[49] Frilot's approach to New Frontier has been to "create a world within their world" by reconceiving the stakes of an industry-based film festival. "Ironically, my practice of world-making has manifested into ushering in a new phase in virtual reality, marking a very poetic moment in my career," Frilot explains. "My approach was never to become good at playing by their rules, but rather, to break the rules and reassemble a paradigm through which to reevaluate work, to create a path of vision to another world."[50]

Notes

1 This network and their collaborations, support, and concerns are illustrated in a conversation between Raúl Ferrera-Balanquet, Leah Gilliam, Thomas Allen Harris, Brent Hill, Charles Lofton, Alfonso Moret, Dawn Suggs, Jocelyn Taylor, and Yvonne Welbon published as "Narrating Our History: A Dialogue among Queer Media Artists from the African Diaspora" in *XII Black International Cinema*, the catalogue of an exhibition that documents a decade of Black International Cinema from 1986 to 1995, presented by the Fountainhead Tanz Theatre in Berlin.

2 Ferrera-Balanquet et al., "Narrating Our History," 137.

3 Ferrera-Balanquet et al., "Narrating Our History," 137.

4 Ferrera-Balanquet et al., "Narrating Our History," 133.

5 On October 19, 1992, Jack Waters also wrote a response to Hubbard, Tartaglia, and Schuman, asserting the importance of being clear and transparent with the community of artists the festival serves so as to prevent gossip and rumors about the festival from spreading. Jack Waters, "My Two Cents for the Festival," reprinted in *10th Anniversary MIXZine*, 1996, 139–41.

6 Shari Frilot, "Welcome," in *MIX 1996: 10th New York Lesbian + Gay Experimental Film/Video Festival Catalog*, November 14–24, 1996, 1.

7 Shari Frilot, quoted in Ernest Hardy, "Mixing It Up: Outfest '98's Shari Frilot," *LA Weekly*, July 8, 1998.

8 Glen Helfand, "Staying in Focus," *The Advocate*, June 24, 1997, 86.

9 Shari Frilot, interview by author, Los Angeles, September 12, 2008.

10 Shari Frilot, "Welcome," in *MIX: 9th New York Lesbian & Gay Experimental Film/Video Festival Catalog*, November 2–12, 1995, 1.

11 Shari Frilot, "Welcome," in *The 7th New York Lesbian & Gay Experimental Film/Video Festival and The Kitchen Present MIX Catalog*, September 9–19, 1993, 1.

12 Shari Frilot, interview by author.

13 Participants in the conference included the scholars Barbara Smith and Jacqui Alexander, the sci-fi author Samuel Delany, the poet Essex Hemphill, the activist Urvashi Vaid, and the artists Cheryl Dunye, Jocelyn Taylor, Thomas Allen Harris, Dawn Suggs, Karl Bruce Knapper, Lyle Ashton Harris, Kobena Mercer, Coco Fusco, Robert Reid-Pharr, Isaac Julian, and Raul Ferrera-Balanquet, among many others.

14 Film screening programs included challenges to perceptions of racial and sexual identity in "Who's Saying What about Whom" (1993, by Karl Knapper and Alfonzo Moret); the spiritual power of dance across racial, ethnic, sexual, and national lines in "Work the Dance Floor" (1993, Suzy Capo Sobral); an exploration of aesthetic, cultural, and geographic landscapes in "Raat Ki Rani: Tales of the South Asian Diaspora" (1993, Gayatri Gopinath, David Dasharath Kalal, and Gita Reddy); filmic representations of female punk identity in "Punkilingus" (1993, Annie Stanley and Jill Reiter); tracing personal and political experiences through touch within an African diasporic queer culture in "Moto and the Human Touch" (1993, Vejan Lee Smith and Thomas Allen Harris); and contestations of gendered and raced stereotypes by video makers of Chinese descent in "Eat Your Gender Roles" (1993, Ming-Yuen S. Ma).

15 Frilot, "Welcome," in *The 7th New York Lesbian & Gay Experimental Film/Video Festival and The Kitchen Present MIX Catalog*, 1.

16 Canadian Consulate General, New York; Gay Men of African Descent; African Ancestral Lesbians United for Societal Change; Society for French American Cultural Services and Educational Aid.

17 Shari Frilot, interview by author.

18 Free Speech TV was "a new programming service offering activist, community-based, and alternative media to local cable and community access channels" with New York area affiliates broadcasting MIX programs during weeks that overlapped with the festival, including Queens Public Access TV, Staten Island Cable, Bolton (CT) United Artists, New Haven (CT) Citizens Television Cable, Wayne (NJ) William Paterson College, and Pomona (NJ) Stockton. *MIX: 9th New York Lesbian & Gay Experimental Film/Video Festival Catalog*, 3.

19 Frilot, "Welcome," in *MIX: 9th New York Lesbian & Gay Experimental Film/Video Festival Catalog*, 1. MIX Brasil toured São Paulo, Rio de Janeiro, Curitiba, Belo Horizonte, and Fortaleza (*Black International Cinema*, 145).

20 At the Museum of Sound and Image in São Paulo, at Casa Laura Alvim in Rio de Janeiro, and at Usina Cultural Banco Nacional in Belo Horizonte.

21 By 1994 MIX Brasil had become an independent organization of its own, "totally produced and organized" in Brazil under the codirectorship of Andre Fischer and Suzy Capo, presenting queer Brazilian artwork as well as more than one hundred films and videos from around the world. It was supported by MTV Brazil, the Museum of Sound and Image, and the São Paulo State Council of Culture. From October 11 until December 18 the festival toured São Paulo, Campinas, Belo Horizonte, Rio de Janeiro, Brasilia, Fortaleza, Curitiba, and Salvador. (Dates for each city are listed on the back cover of the MIX New York 1994 catalogue.) MIX Brasil established a gay computer bulletin board; a magazine; Club MIX, an association of queer and queer-friendly people; and Mundo MIX, a brand of apparel, sex toys, and "other fun mariconerias." Shari Frilot, "Welcome," in *MIX: 8th New York Lesbian + Gay Experimental Film/Video Festival Catalog*, 1.

22 *Black International Cinema* (1995–96), 145.

23 Shari Frilot, interview by author.

24 Advertisement for Go!Go!SPOT next to introduction in the *7th New York Lesbian & Gay Experimental Film/Video Festival and The Kitchen Present MIX Catalog*, 1.

25 The description of the Video Gong Show reads, "[After] ten years of you (the queer experimental film and video making and viewing public) submitting to our (the Valiant fest organizers) curatorial choices (wise as we feel they may be!). . . . Tonight the choice is yours!"

26 By the tenth festival the locations included the Magic Johnson Theatre in Harlem, the NYU Cantor Film Center, and the Knitting Factory.

27 Victoria MIX was cosponsored by Third World Newsreel.

28 Shari Frilot, "Preface: 10 Year Anniversary, You Go Girl!," in *The MIX 96: 10th New York Lesbian + Gay Experimental Film/Video Festival Catalog*, November 14–24, 1996, 1.

29 Short film programs included "City Lore," "Family Drama," "Harlem Stories," "The House That Identity Built," "Let's Talk about Sex," "Oh Yes It's Ladies Night!," with films and videos by Isaac Julien, Michelle Parkerson, Jocelyn Taylor, Ayoka Chenzira, David Rousseve, Cheryl Dunye, Yvonne Welbon, Charles Lofton, Leah Gilliam, Raj Roy, Vaginal Davis, Felix Rodriguez, Jack Waters, and Kagendo Murungi. Also included was a replay of the 1992 FIRE! short film program, guest-curated by Thomas Allen Harris and Cheryl Dunye, with the works of Raúl Ferrera-Balanquet, Shari Frilot, Dawn Suggs, Vejan Smith, Rupert Gabriel, and Carlo Carmona. The feature films ran the gamut from fantastical political narratives to personal family documentaries, including Marlon Riggs and Christine Badgley's *Black Is, Black Ain't* (1995); Frilot's documentary on the 1995 New York conference, *Black Nations/Queer Nations?* (1995); Sankofa's *Passion of Remembrance* (1985); Thomas Allen Harris's *VINTAGE: Families of Value* (1995); and the special closing-night event, Stephen Winter's *Chocolate Babies* (1996), about "a harsh fantasy underworld where raging HIV+ African American and Asian queer outcasts become terrorists who attack conservative politicians."

30 The program was programmed by the festival committee, and took place on November 22, 1996. For the full description of the program and the films, see *MIX 1996*, 42.

31 *MIX 1996*, 15.

32 Robert Reid-Pharr, essay in *MIX 1996*, 4–5.

33 For a more nuanced discussion of the impact of the commercialization of gay and lesbian culture on gay and lesbian film festivals, see Ragan Rhyne, "Pink Dollars: Gay and Lesbian Film Festivals and the Economy of Visibility," PhD diss., New York University, 2007.

34 Eugene Hernandez, "Dispatch from Berlin: Queer World of Film," *Indiewire*, February 15, 2001.

35 Hardy, "Mixing It Up."

36 Shari Frilot, interview by author, New York City, June 16, 2009.

37 Shari Frilot, interview by author, New York City.

38 See the project's website for background information on the history of Sundance and a lengthy interview between Frilot and Rastegar about her work at Sundance.

39 Shari Frilot, interview by author, New York City.

40 These filmmakers include John Akomfrah, Natalia Almada, Jennifer Arnold, Miguel Arteta, Zal Batmanglij, Diane Bell, Alrick Brown, Mike Cahill, Shelon Candis, Patricia Cardoso, Shane Carruth, Shu Lea Chang, Destin Crettin, Cherien Dabis, Lee Daniels, Zeinabu irene Davis, Youssef Delara, Ramona Diaz, Dennis Dortch, Andrew Dosunmu, Zeina Durra, Ava DuVernay, Karim El Hakim, Rodney Evans, Kevin Jerome Everson, Javier Fuentes-Leon, Debra Granik, Rashaad Ernesto Green, Aurora Guerrero, Tanya Hamilton, Catherine Hardwicke, Sterlin Harjo, Thomas Allen Harris, Lee Hirsch, Maryam Keshavarz, Gina Kim, Braden King, Karyn Kusama, Shola Lynch, Brit Marling, Chris Mourkarbel, Terence Nance, Stanley Nelson, Michael Olmos, Lourdes Portillo, Jennifer Phang, Samuel Pollard, Dee Rees, Marialy Rivas, Alex Rivera, Jackie Salloum, Omar Shargawi, Sultan Sharif, Jill Soloway, Musa Syeed, Hank Willis Thomas, Kevin Willmott, Jessica Yu, among still others.

41 Shari Frilot, interview by author, New York City.

42 "New Frontier Sneak Peek: The Liberated Pixel" (PDF), Sundance Film Festival press release, October 16, 2010.

43 Shari Frilot, interview by author, New York City.

44 Shari Frilot, interview by author, New York City.

45 Audre Lorde, "Uses of the Erotic: The Erotic as Power," in *Sister Outsider: Essays and Speeches* (Trumansburg, NY: Crossing Press, 1984), 53.

46 Vivian Sobchack, "The Scene of the Screen: Envisioning Photographic, Cinematic, and Electronic Presence," in *Carnal Thoughts: Embodiment and Moving Image Culture* (Berkeley: University of California Press, 2004), 135–62.

47 Roya Rastegar, "Curating 'Physical Cinema' at Sundance's New Frontier," *Scholar and Feminist* 10.3 (2012), http://sfonline.barnard.edu/feminist-media-theory /curating-physical-cinema-at-sundances-new-frontier/.

48 Including work by Paul Chan, Matthew Moore, Miwa Matreyek, Lynn Hershmann Leeson, Mark Boulous, Lynette Wallworth, Shirin Neshat, Sam Green, Omar Fast, Martha Colburn, Hassan Elahi, Petko Dourmana, the Bruce High Quality Foundation, Nao Bustamante, and Travis Wilerson, to name a few.

49 José Esteban Muñoz, *Disidentifications: Queers of Color and the Performance of Politics* (Minneapolis: University of Minnesota Press, 1999), 196, 198.

50 Shari Frilot, interview by author, Los Angeles, September 9, 2015.

Identity and Performance in Yvonne Welbon's *Remembering Wei-Yi Fang, Remembering Myself: An Autobiography*

BAKER: One day I realized that I was living in a country where I was afraid to be black, it was only a country for white people, not black, so I left. I had been suffocating in the U.S. I can't live where I can't breathe freedom, I must be free. Haven't I that right? I was created free. No chains did I wear when I came here. A lot of us left, not because we wanted to leave, but because we couldn't stand it any more. Branded, banded, cut off. Canada Lee, Dr. Dubois. Paul Robeson, Marcus Garvey, all of us, forced to leave. . . .

GATES [TO BALDWIN]: And what were your first impressions of life in "exile"?

BALDWIN: I was no longer a captive nigger. I was the exotic attraction of the beast no longer in the cage. People paid attention. Of course you must realize I am remembering the impression years later.

GATES: Did life abroad give you any particular insight into American society?

BALDWIN: I realized that the truth of American history was not and had never been in the White House, the truth is what had happened to black people, since slavery.

—Henry Louis Gates, "An Interview with Josephine Baker and James Baldwin" (1973)

In novel ways, and from a surprising location, Yvonne Welbon's *Remembering Wei-Yi Fang, Remembering Myself: An Autobiography* (1995) explores some of the same dilemmas that earlier African American expatriate artists promulgated, using their time abroad as a window onto America, while relishing the nurturing possibilities of partial escape from American racism. Some of the most complex and insightful observations about America and

American racism have been crafted by African American expatriate artists such as James Baldwin and Josephine Baker. These artists' depictions of their encounters abroad complicate our understandings of American identity and American racism. As Baldwin stated in a film focused on his years in Turkey, "American racism has been crafted from a distance, from another place, another country."[1] Many artists found liberating possibilities in simply leaving the chokehold of American racism behind and reintegrating themselves personally and creatively outside of its confines.

Remembering Wei-Yi Fang offers a meditation on American Blackness that reconsiders and resists the idea of a universal African American narrative from the perspective of expatriation and return, positing a narrative that does not follow a framework of middle passage, generations of slavery, emancipation, great migration, and civil rights movement so frequently reiterated and imagined as "the" African American experience. The film's critique of American racism demonstrates the contemporary salience of slavery to the formation of American racism while emphasizing alternative narratives, including those of the filmmaker's own ancestors, who were free Africans in Honduras, descended from kidnapped Africans who escaped from a slave ship.[2] Yvonne Welbon as narrator and subject resists being fixed or frozen by either American racism or Taiwanese fascination and repulsion with Blackness. While American racism haunts Welbon, the response to her body in Taiwan raises other issues. Like Baldwin, in Taiwan she held "the exotic attraction of the beast no longer in the cage." Yet despite the fascination with her phenotype, and with the idea of Blackness, she nonetheless found Taiwan to be a site where she was able to liberate herself from U.S. racism.

By rendering this alternative narrative, emphasizing the specificity of Black experiences rather than a universal "Black experience," Welbon both performs for herself, engaging her own identity, and offers the viewer an opportunity for self-re-creation and reimagining—an experience Welbon accessed (only) by leaving the United States behind. As the narrator and subject, Welbon demonstrates the transformative possibilities of leaving, recollection, and return while resisting a narrative of deliverance and refusing to idealize the possibilities created by expatriation. With this focus on the perspective offered by her years outside the United States, the film also recalls the idea of exile, but with an implied choice. The narrator can always choose to return, although whether she truly left America behind at all is repeatedly considered. Though the film chronicles resistance and empowerment, it also offers an indictment of American racism: Welbon returns again and again to

8.1 Director Yvonne Welbon and cinematographer Makiko Watanabe on the set of *Remembering Wei-Yi Fang, Remembering Myself: An Autobiography*, 1996. Photo courtesy of Yvonne Welbon.

the idea that being a Black subject in the United States means never being delivered from the shadow of American racism. As Joshua Miller says of James Baldwin, Welbon is a "witness not an exile"; her expatriation and return never fully release her from the problems and promise of home.

This essay considers *Remembering Wei-Yi Fang*'s aesthetic and narrative critique of U.S. racism. I will show that the film resists idealizing the Black expatriate experience, although it does occasionally idealize Taiwan and Taiwanese culture. Welbon adds her voice to a tradition of other Black and queer authors with significant experience writing about American racism from abroad, though she never explicitly cites these artists. Although clearly part of a cohort of identity-focused experimental, performative autobiographical films and videos of the 1990s, Welbon's film resists categorization, as does its subject and narration.

Paul Gilroy's term the *Black Atlantic* is a helpful lens through which to understand the film's conceptions about the meanings and possibilities of Black histories that transcend nationality. Gilroy argues that scholars of race and Blackness have considered Blackness in a transnational context that goes beyond nationality and the boundaries of state and even continent. He shows that ideas about the self and the other are rooted in an intellectual history beyond the Western canon and in conversation across the Atlantic as a result of the trade in slaves, migration, and other movements of people and ideas.

This perspective addresses the marginalization of slaves and the violence to the self that occurs through racism.

Remembering Wei-Yi Fang is located in both the Black Atlantic—in the particularities of Black selfhood emerging from these relocations—and in the Pacific, as Welbon recollects her experiences in Taiwan. Travel is central to the disruptions and realizations explored in this film—travel, imagined and real, forced and voluntary, mediatized and invisible, by bus, ship, motorcycle, and airplane. Travel offers pleasures and possibilities for new narratives enabling Welbon to resist racism, even when returning to the belly of the beast—the United States—home of the formative racism that she escaped by living abroad.

Welbon in Time and Space

Remembering Wei-Yi Fang is a thirty-minute personal, experimental auto-biographical film made with collaged 16mm, Super-8, and video footage. There are several main threads interwoven throughout the film. The primary threads include recollections of Welbon's time in Taiwan, structured by a discussion with her Chinese-speaking Taiwanese alter ego, Wei-Yi Fang, and recollections of her childhood and socialization to racism in Chicago, where she grew up, accomplished with voice-overs, family snapshots, class pictures, and created imagery that works through poetic metaphor. In a fleeting but significant moment of the film, Welbon identifies as a lesbian. We learn that she went to Vassar, an elite, predominantly white liberal arts college. She studied Chinese there and wanted to become fluent; this is the reason she traveled to Taiwan and remained there for several years. In Taiwan, Welbon initially taught English and studied Chinese, but then she became an entrepreneur, starting an English-language magazine called *Bang!* After six years in Taiwan, her life as Wei-Yi Fang ended suddenly when she was in a serious motorcycle accident. After being hospitalized in Taiwan, she returned to the United States to recover.

Welbon's family is another thread in the film, whose strands include a recurring set of images of her great-great-grandmother in Honduras, created with an actor who never speaks in sync sound, and an interview with Welbon's actual grandmother, in which we see and hear her grandmother and hear but do not see Welbon. Some scenes from her grandmother's early years in the United States, where she immigrated from Honduras, are re-created with actors, and these scenes of her grandmother as a young woman working abroad and eventually settling in the United States parallel some of what we learn about Welbon's six years living in Taiwan in her twenties. Welbon frames her move to Taiwan as the result of her interest in learning Chinese, not as directly economically driven as was her grandmother's migration from Honduras.

Welbon, the author, director, and subject of this experimental autobiographical film, uses a metaphor of death and rebirth to frame the experience of escape and return to conditions of American apartheid and its daily psychological violence. She tells her own story, linking it to the story of her mother, grandmother, and great-great-grandmother. Thus the film is partially a memoir of the filmmaker's family history and partially an exploration of her own two-ness—her doubling—as she recalls her Taiwanese self, Wei-Yi Fang, from the perspective of her American self. Welbon/Wei-Yi Fang speaks both Chinese and English in the film and creates a bilingual discussion between her selves.

The Death of Wei-Yi Fang

"In the motorcycle accident, Wei-Yi Fang was killed" are the first words on the sound track. The violence of this sentence, coupled with Welbon's matter-of-fact delivery, invite the viewer to witness the death of Wei-Yi Fang before knowing her identity. This voice-over accompanies a grainy image of a Taiwan street. The score in this sequence, through an eerie repeated series of notes, brings both Asia and the Americas together. The question of the possibilities and limits of death are manifested as both Welbon and Wei-Yi Fang claim their own identity and seem very much alive. This opening introduces the viewer to a persistent motif of the past in the present: Wei-Yi Fang is spoken of in present and past tense, moving her from the immediacy and urgency of the present to the past and back.

As those first words are spoken, a figure in a raincoat on a motorcycle appears on the Taiwan street. After a slight pause and fade to white, an intertitle posits a qualification: "Maybe." This sequence introduces death as a metaphor for the creation and re-creation of identity. Does the "maybe" belie the statement that Wei-Yi Fang was killed? As it becomes clear that Wei-Yi Fang is an alter ego for Welbon, Welbon's question—"Did Wei-Yi Fang have to die" for Welbon to "go on"?—becomes more urgent. The slight pause that surrounds the intertitle allows the viewer to contemplate the possibilities in a moment of stillness.

Wei-Yi Fang is an alternate personality and identity created by Welbon's action of coming to Taiwan and, perhaps more important, leaving the United

States. The film's conceit is this formulation of Wei-Yi Fang and Welbon as their own characters in conversation with one another, with questions from Wei-Yi Fang to Welbon driving some of the organizational structure of the film. It becomes clear that although Wei-Yi Fang speaks Chinese and Welbon speaks English, they are the same person, with one voice, two languages, two accents. The dialogue between them structures much of the film, allowing some of the questions that a viewer might have to be voiced and responded to. Because in the end Wei-Yi Fang and Welbon are the same person, they possess one another's memories, creating an opportunity to reflect on their shared history from two positions.

In the film's opening sequence, Welbon claims, "I still have Wei-Yi Fang's memories." Thus Wei-Yi Fang's perspective is still available to her, despite the film's creation in a present that leaves Taiwan in the past. Although Welbon does not claim it directly, it is clear that Wei-Yi Fang, while enjoying the "American-racism–free zone" of Taiwan, still was haunted by Welbon's memories (her own memories) of the racism she experienced growing up and coming of age in the United States. As Welbon says, rejecting the possibility of forgetting, "Even if I tried, I could never really be rid of them."

Welbon's voice-over informs the viewer that people told her the motorcycle accident was "the only way [she] would stop" living abroad as Wei-Yi Fang. "You brought that accident on yourself, Yvonne," she was told. Welbon seems to agree with this idea, saying, "It was [the] only way I would stop, so I could go on." Again the filmmaker emphasizes the necessity of death to bring life—the idea that only death brings this possibility for reinvention. And yet the film also maintains that death limits and controls. Once again an intertitle appears: "But Did Wei-Yi Fang Have to Die?" And the next intertitle responds, "Maybe." The ambivalence of this response tells the viewer that there are no easy answers here. The film circles back repeatedly to the crash and the death or persistence of Wei-Yi Fang as metaphor for the narrator's identity beginning and ending.

Wei-Yi Fang is very much alive in the film, and her aliveness carries with it the possibility of multiple, coexisting selves without having to extinguish one to be connected to the other. The dialogue between the two is friendly but urgent. Wei-Yi Fang's questions offer a way in to the viewer, who can approach Welbon's story by asking the questions left by the other narratives. It is a pedagogical tool for Wei-Yi Fang to ask, "What about my story?" Welbon responds, "Well, I think we have to start with the past." Wei-Yi Fang responds in Chinese, "Hao la la," which is translated as "All right." Wei-Yi Fang's continued and urgent presence after her metaphorical death illustrates the way that layers of the past linger in the present. This lingering and layering is a repeated theme of this film, urgently reminding us that the experiences of our ancestors' lives, as well as our own previous encounters, create the selves we inhabit in ways we cannot always control.

After the narrator considers whether she "brought that accident on" herself, another slow, grainy, processed, right-to-left pan moves the viewer closer to a photograph of the face of a young child. The narration here is contemplative: "Because I lost myself trying to be Wei-Yi Fang, I forgot who I was—because in Taiwan as Wei-Yi Fang, I had respect. Maybe if you were African American and you found respect in a foreign country, you would forget who you were too." These words are spoken without defensiveness; they charge the viewer with identification, with understanding. Of course, some of the viewers are African American. So the hypothetical "if you were African American" can be a challenge to viewers in different ways; for African American viewers, it is potentially an acknowledgment of shared experience. Without accusing anyone of "forgetting who they are," it reminds viewers that this forgetting is a fraught and dangerous proposition that threatens the very core of the self. After reminding viewers that they might, in a foreign context, forget who they are, the narrator introduces the past and present that structures much of the film by saying, "I did, for six years. I forgot what it feels like to be Black in America." Here, instead of speaking to Wei-Yi Fang or speaking to the viewer in a reflective way, her tone and question confront the viewer—in the first person.

This early scene frames the perspective of the film as being partially about the narrator's time outside of the United States, in Taiwan, which she terms an "American-racism–free zone." This location and perspective become a focal point of the film. Her relocation enabled a reconsideration of her experience of herself (seemingly) outside of the psychic, economic, and physical experience of American racial apartheid. This relocation and reconsideration offered possibilities of both forgetting and remembering, of coming to terms with Black identity even as being outside the yoke of U.S. racism enabled her growth and coming of age.

Throughout this opening sequence, as Welbon both kills and resurrects Wei-Yi Fang, and as she situates the theme of the film and the stories behind it, the sound track signals Asia, or Asianness, on the pentatonic scale. The composer uses a repeated series of notes in a minor key with a synthesized flute sound; the minor key emphasizes tropes that Western music has long used to signify the East. The image track and the sound track are not synched; rather they are edited in a more experimental collage, where sound bridges the edits between fragments of memories in Super-8 and 16mm. When Welbon reflects on the accident and her friends' notion of her own, perhaps subconscious culpability in it, a low sound of thunder is added to the audio mix. Drums in the sound track establish a harmony in relation to eerie, slow, low notes. This insistent music mixes in with the street sound of the black-and-white image of Taiwan to create a sense of both connection and remove. A triple drumbeat underscores the violence of the loss of Wei-Yi Fang and the finality of the accident as it is alluded to at the outset.

The repeated flute notes and the black-and-white street scenes in the introductory sequence are followed after Wei-Yi Fang and Welbon are introduced by a dramatic shift in both mise-en-scène and sound track to an image saturated in the color of an ocean. The image is reframed. The mobile frame shifts up to a woman in period clothes from the turn of the twentieth century, an ankle-length skirt and several petticoats, as described by Welbon's grandmother in the voice-over. Her long hair is gathered into an upswept bun. Accompanying the change in mise-en-scène is a shift in the sound track from Taiwan to the Americas, signifying that the film is connecting Welbon's experience as a Black woman in the Pacific to her ancestors in the Americas and to the roots of her ancestors' experiences in the Black Atlantic. The music here loses its "Eastern sound"—the flutes fade, and a new instrumental sound, which includes the sound of wood on wood, comes in along with the sound of waves and birds. The sound seems to spread out over a vast space, so it has an echo; this vastness, combined with the image of a map, gives us a sense of the global sources of the story. We hear cross-rhythms in the score as the mobile frame scans from Honduras to the port of New Orleans, then up to the Midwest. The frame moves west from California to Taiwan, and then the image transitions from the map to rooftops in Taiwan.

Over these wavy rooftops the first section of the title sequence appears, "Remembering Wei-Yi Fang: Remembering Myself," and the words "An Autobiography" appear over an image of kites in the sky. Welbon herself appears, walking toward the camera and then held in a freeze frame, looking the viewer right in the eye. As we see this image, the words "by Yvonne Welbon" appears. The author is young, female, and black, and we see her pride, her youth, her smile. This title sequence is rich, triumphant. It is one of the only live-action images of Welbon in the film, who is otherwise represented in still photographs from her childhood and her time in Taiwan.

In addition to introducing us to Wei-Yi Fang and Welbon, this opening sequence introduces us to the visual language of the film, in which sound and image are linked in a collage. Taiwan is always a memory, mostly in Super-8, with the telltale blurred edges and Kodachrome color intensity or deep shadows and blurred edges in the black-and-white images. Super-8's blurred edges and intense contrasts create a texture that implies memory in the language of this film, and in the structure of the film Taiwan is always in the past. We are never in the present with Wei-Yi Fang; we always remember her. The re-created worlds are also constituted by different tonalities: Welbon's grandmother's early days in the United States in Yankton, South Dakota, are recalled in a sepia-tone black-and-white and later in bright, washed-out color sequences, with actors playing the parts and no synchronous sound. Her great-great grandmother in Honduras is always shown in saturated color, with long skirts and the sound of the ocean.

Mapping Migration Narratives

"My first memories of American racism belong to my grandmother," says Welbon in the voice-over. To situate her own family story—the story of her great-great-grandmother, grandmother, and mother—Welbon narrates the history of Black Hondurans who escaped before landing in the United States and never became slaves. They, of course, still survived the trauma of the abduction and middle passage, but their experience diverged in history from "the Black experience"—a history so frequently assumed in the United States.

Welbon situates this different historical legacy from that other narrative in several ways: in the personal differences she experienced growing up, a longing for a home that was not the American South but Honduras, with her family's own food, tastes, and smells. She mentions her lack of rootedness in the American South—"We never went down south to see relatives"—and how it gave her a different sense of home. She also repeatedly emphasizes the parts of her family story that differentiate it from the "typical" Black American story as one way to un-enslave her own identity.

She explains that her great-great-grandmother was an entrepreneur, a story that Welbon found inspirational to her own work. Her grandmother too showed independence of mind in her decision to come to the United States and later to leave an exploitative employment situation. The filmmaker implies through her emphasis on inhabiting the memories of others (including those of her alter ego and of her ancestors) the idea that carrying memories and keeping other people alive within the self is not really a choice but an inescapable burden or privilege. The film participates powerfully in a Black feminist literary tradition that urgently argues that an individual person survives and persists through future generations.

Welbon's grandmother, Ellen Smith, says, "[I] used to sit down on the beach and wish to go to England," but she never imagined coming to America. She describes landing in the port of New Orleans and traveling for three days by Greyhound bus to work as a domestic laborer and caretaker for a large white family in Yankton, South Dakota. The tiny, overwhelmingly white locale seemed part of a world as far outside what was possible to imagine for Welbon's grandmother as Taiwan would be for Welbon. Welbon's interview with her grandmother explores the predicament of her grandmother's seeking out the first Black person she found in Yankton after three months of caring for a family of eight children, cleaning and mending, and how she subsequently found a Black community there. As she tells Welbon her story, we see reenactments of her encounters in sepia-tone black-and-white and also in color. Most of these reenactments feature actors, but the sound track is Ellen's narrative in her own voice. One segment highlights the exploitation Ellen faced and how the end of her isolation from the Black community enabled her to repudiate this exploitation. Other Black domestic laborers ask her, "When is your day off?," which is the first time she learns that she is supposed to have a day off. Swing jazz plays over photographs of Ellen playing cards and attending social events in what we can imagine is the Black community in New Orleans.

Citing the way Black Atlantic history and consciousness layer over one another in the present and recent past, the film has Wei-Yi Fang ask, "What was it like for Grandma to come to America?" Welbon answers, "It was like the middle passage—you know, the whole slavery thing." Viewers then see a diagram of bound kidnapped people en route from Africa to the Americas. Welbon places the term *slaves* in quotation marks. She resists a process in which by the very encounter with slave traders, by their very abduction, these people became slaves. In doing so she calls our attention to the idea that to be formed by racism, even in the brutal state of chattel slavery, is not to be denied subjecthood—that these were people and their abduction was a situation. By using voice-over and an explanation of this familiar diagram, Welbon reminds us we are watching a documentary, even as her text and voice-over differ from a typical description of this history.

Through re-creation and interview, Welbon explores the subjective and material conditions of her grandmother's employment in the United States.

8.2 Ellen Smith in *Remembering Wei-Yi Fang, Remembering Myself: An Autobiography*, directed by Yvonne Welbon, 1996.

We see her grandmother's isolation in Yankton. Welbon shows her grandmother both naïve to American racism and seemingly initially naïve to her own exploitation. She learns about the racial slur *Negro* and hears of its roots in the U.S. South. In a confrontation between Ellen's boss and the boss's mother, the boss's mother refers to Ellen as a "nigger" and to the history of slavery. Ellen doesn't know anything about "slave times" because "where she come from they don't have that." This account demonstrates that whites were aware of the performative nature of white supremacist thinking and that if Black people lived outside of the knowledge of how it was "supposed" to go, then racism did not "work" the same way. "She don't know about no slavery," says the grandmother's boss to her own mother, who was chastising her for paying Ellen a birthday bonus. Through this account Welbon explores the process of transnational reinterpretation of self and the process of her grandmother reconfiguring herself in the United States. Somehow this white woman from Yankton, South Dakota, had an idea that racism is more palatable, or at least comprehensible, to subjects circumscribed (as Welbon later was) by growing up with the trauma of slavery, as opposed to encountering it as an adult.

Thus her grandmother, coming to the United States as an adult from Honduras with a history that did not include ancestors forced to work as slaves, learns about this history through an encounter with the memories

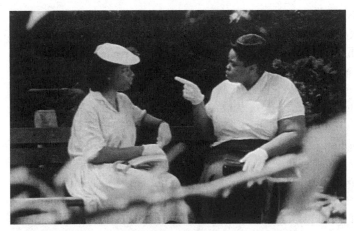

8.3 Ellen (Anita Welbon) and a friend (Jean Garrison) in a re-creation scene in *Remembering Wei-Yi Fang, Remembering Myself: An Autobiography*, directed by Yvonne Welbon, 1996.

and knowledge of slavery. By dramatizing the story of her grandmother's unfamiliarity with American racism in this way, Welbon finds a way to represent her own alienation from American racism through the lens of her own expatriation and her grandmother's rebellion.

Yvonne Welbon, Performing Herself

"I think it was in high school the first time I had to check a box," recounts Welbon in a voice-over, as the viewer sees a hand (presumably Welbon's) grasping a pencil and hovering over a census-type form with a list of racial categories that seems to leave no space for multiple or layered identities. The hesitation persists as the narrative explains, "With one action, I could erase generations of my history." Yet experience trumps the limited racial categories presented on the form. In this film Welbon explores the challenges of embracing hybrid identity in a category-obsessed culture. She returns twice to the violence of checking a box on a census form or some other official document that asks for only one identity category. As Welbon's family story shows, categories such as "Black non-Hispanic" are too reductive. In this sequence we see a hand, presumably Welbon's, resist checking a box, hesitate, erase, and reconsider. Despite this interpretive narrowing and the limited cultural imaginary of the Black American experience, Welbon knew her experience and her family history marked her as "different than the other Black kids." She felt the impossibility of a Black and Hispanic identity, the impossibility of checking more than one box not just for herself and her family but for anyone.

Welbon has less to say, by contrast, about sexuality and gay identity in this film. Yet as a whole, her filmography is very invested in representing Black lesbians, in documentaries such as *Living with Pride: Ruth Ellis @ 100* (1999), as well as a love story, *Sisters in the Life: First Love* (1993), and *The New Black* (2013), a film she produced that was directed by Yoruba Richen. She has also made important work exploring, celebrating, and historicizing the work of Black women filmmakers, such as *The Cinematic Jazz of Julie Dash* (1992) and *Sisters in Cinema* (2003). Thus, as part of the larger context of Welbon's other films, *Remembering Wei-Yi Fang* is primarily concerned with race, the challenge of hybridity, and straddling multiple identities. The psychological terrain of the filmmakers' family is explored in the haunting film about Welbon's "kidnapped" sisters, *Missing Relations* (1994), while *Remembering Wei-Yi Fang* focuses on the filmmaker's family's migration and labor.

While lesbian identity is not the focus of this film, excluding sexuality from identity would deny the film's commitment to the exploration of the hybridity of identity. The implication here, again, is that the action of checking a box is far more than perfunctory: it limits, it can erase generations, it can violate promises and erase struggle and achievement. The image portrays a moment of hesitation, the pencil hovering, checking "gay/lesbian," turning to "African American" and returning. Does checking a box offer a possibility of coming out as well? That it is only in Welbon's later films that she directly addresses gay identities seems to suggest as much. Implicit in this scene are the challenges of embodying these identities and Black ambivalence toward recognizing gays and lesbians within the possibilities of Blackness. These silences and challenges are explored elsewhere, such as in Marlon Riggs's *Tongues Untied* (1989). Here the silence of this moment speaks loudly, though for some viewers—at least, for my students—it also creates desire for more. They want to hear more about Welbon's lesbian identity and how all the aspects of her identity fit together. The film frustrates them in this way, as checking the box is Welbon's only mention of belonging to the category of gay/lesbian in this film.

As the film features Welbon as a character and both Welbon's and her alter ego's performance of self, it appears to embody the type of "performative documentary" Bill Nichols refers to in his taxonomy of documentaries, though it also breaks out of this category. Nichols classifies documentaries into "performative" and "poetic" modes.[3] His taxonomy seems to have responded to a documentary movement already well afoot in the 1990s; indeed it seems the category was a response to films like Welbon's and those of many of her peers. Stella Bruzzi critiques this taxonomy without denying that poetic, performative documentary is a possibility and admitting that many contemporary documentaries are these hybrid creations in multiple modes.[4] Welbon's documentary certainly is. The personal, experimental autobiographical documentary was especially vital, as it explored hybrid entities such as Black and queer or queer and Jewish. Thus notions of the performative documentary are helpful here not to define this film, which creates and utilizes its own language and metaphors, but to understand Welbon's film in the company of its peers, *Tongues Untied, Fast Trip Long Drop, The Devil Never Sleeps*, and *VINTAGE*, among others. All of these works consider queerness with or through and in relation to racial, ethnic, and national identities. In the wake of decades of theory from J. L. Austin, Judith Butler, and others on performativity and performative acts, the term *performative documentary* can be confusing. In understanding Welbon's documentary, both meanings of *performative* are relevant: *Remembering Wei-Yi Fang, Remembering Myself* is both a performative documentary and an examination of the performative nature of racial categorization and resistance.

In his groundbreaking consideration of quare studies (a rethinking of queer studies that moves beyond "racelessness or assumptions of whiteness"), Patrick Johnson considers the possibilities for performing the self that are not just for the other but are also for the self, and not just for the self but are transformative to the self. "The performance of self is not only a performance or construct of identity toward an 'out there' or even merely an attachment or 'taking up' of a predetermined, discursively contingent identity. It is also a performance of self for the self in a moment of self-reflexivity that has the potential to transform one's view of the self in relation to the world."[5] As Johnson elucidates, theories of performance tend to be more historically situated than theories of performativity. Both performativity and performance are productive frames in which to consider this film, in which the very knowledge and recollection of slavery taints, degrades, and haunts Americans both individually and collectively.

Remembering Wei Yi-Fang employs performance of self as well as re-creation: the performances by the filmmaker and her own family are significant both in and of themselves and because the whole category of family has high stakes here. In Welbon's story, representing her family has powerful implications because of the marginalization and pathologization of Black families and especially of matrilineal family structures. Her mention but lack of explicit discussion of her identity as a lesbian also signifies what family is mentioned and who (may be) left out.

Numerous personal experimental works in the 1990s examined representations of the filmmakers' own family as part of the challenge of considering hybrid identities. In *The Devil Never Sleeps*, Lourdes Portillo travels to Mexico to examine the legacies and image her other family members had of her uncle after his death. Documents such as photographs become very important in the detective work of understanding her uncle's life. The occasion of his death allows their perspectives to be spoken aloud. Questions about his sexuality surface and are implied in a rich textual and image collage of telenovelas, recollection, and conjecture. Like *Remembering Wei-Yi Fang, The Devil Never Sleeps* is about travel, about multiple generations of family, about how identities circulate within a wider world of media representations. In VINTAGE Thomas Allen Harris explores the questions of what it means to have a Black queer sibling and talks to his own siblings and to other individuals whose siblings are gay or lesbian.

In both of these cases, the questions of who has the camera and who is telling the story bring a set of power relations to bear on family structures that may not have offered power and agency to the filmmakers before in the same way. The use of reenactments is an important part of Welbon's strategy in this film. Welbon has an actor performing her deceased great-great-grandmother, while her grandmother portrays herself, with reenactments of her younger self portrayed by the filmmaker's sister. All of these films in this same period explore queerness and its push-pull on family boundaries, secrets, and borders from a perspective of national, ethnic, or racialized identity. Overtly Welbon's film seems to be more "about" Blackness than about queerness, except for the moment Welbon literally "checks the box." The moment of coming out is conspicuously disembodied by the shot, which encloses only her hand and the form. Yet this revelation reframes her reconsideration of family, of matrilineal heritage, and of expatriation and return. The film is queer despite its lack of explicitness about gayness in the voice-over, which otherwise is very specific in its approach to viewers. The category of gay/lesbian is an identity in this film, while being Black is a situation.

From the Outside In: Seeing Herself through Taiwanese Eyes

While the hybridity of being gay and Black is mostly unspoken, the film returns to the question of Blackness outside the "Black experience" narrative that is assumed of her in the United States. In Taiwan, Welbon is paradoxically more defined by being American (by dint of language skills, economic possibility, citizenship) than she is in America. Yet Americanness is inextricably linked with whiteness for some of the Taiwanese she encounters as well. Welbon states that when she moved to Taiwan to teach English and perfect her Chinese, she was not consciously trying to leave behind American racism. Indeed she experienced exoticization, which she recounts with a few "incident reports" (incident number 76, incident number 141). These high numbers reflect her numbness to the repetition, the frequency of people literally finding her phenotype "remarkable" and who remarked upon it— and sometimes touching her as well. People touched her skin, surprised that the color didn't come off, and told her that her hair felt like a "carpet." They compared her to "that woman" in *Gone with the Wind* and to Rudy on *The Cosby Show*. While the voice-over says she found the attention for the most part benign and points out that she was in Taiwan at a time when few images of Blackness circulated there, it also acknowledges that the attention could be excruciating.

As images of temples shot on Super-8 or 16mm pass before our eyes, we hear Welbon describe encounters with people she meets on the street, who ask her, "Where are you from?" When she responds that she is American, she experiences what many nonwhite Americans experience abroad, an emphasis on phenotype and ethnicity over nationality. The strangers clarify, "What I want to know is, where are your parents from?" When she tells them that her mother is from Honduras, they are satisfied: "I knew you weren't American." This inextricability of whiteness from Americanness overrides their ability to imagine her as an American, even as the images of Blackness that they are familiar with are primarily American images, and even as Welbon's experience in Taiwan is overwhelmingly structured by American education, language skills, and culture. There is more room in Taiwan for Welbon's story to be specific in one way, for her ancestors to be from Honduras, while in the United States no one even asks. As Welbon's mother told her, "In America, you're Black." Yet in other ways, their ability to see her at all is overwhelmingly obsessed with her Blackness.

Despite this Taiwanese inability to "fix" Welbon as an American, their understanding of her and their framing of her life story helped her to reimagine herself and offers the viewer an alternate vision to the image of deviant Black families in post–*Moynihan Report* America. When they ask her about her mother and father, she says her mother is from Honduras. She accounts for

8.4 Welbon with her students in Taiwan in *Remembering Wei-Yi Fang, Remembering Myself: An Autobiography,* directed by Yvonne Welbon, 1996. Photo courtesy of Yvonne Welbon.

her father's absence from her response by saying, " 'My parents are divorced (I say). My mother raised four children alone.' 'She must be great woman,' they say. 'It is not easy,' they say.' " The repetition of "they say" underscores the importance of their speech to her ears, performativity à la Austin's speech acts. She meets them partway, already framing her experience not as one of deviance but as one of triumph and survival. But this appreciation from strangers offers new possibilities. "I like how my mother is defined in Chinese," Welbon says. This claiming of her mother and pride in this potential redefinition speak to the pathologization of maternal Black families in the United States. Welbon goes on to say, "I like how I am defined in Chinese."

Welbon cannot resist idealizing her Taiwanese experience because of the way it enabled her to get outside the box of U.S. racism. Yet she acknowledges that when she visited tourist sites, many people wanted to take their picture with her, to touch her and remark about her appearance. She recounts that the repetition of this treatment felt like ridicule. She calls the strangers' questioning "only curiosity" but acknowledges that sometimes it feels "like a nightmare." The attention was confusing, a counterpoint to the invisibility and hypervisibility of Black women in the United States. Her idealization of Taiwan breaks down, although it is never fully rejected in the film.

To situate the comparison between Taiwanese fascination with and exoticization of Blackness and American racism, Welbon draws connections between the postcolonial situation of Taiwan and the decolonizing African American mind. When she lived there, Taiwan was not recognized by the United Nations. This invisibility, posits Welbon in the voice-over, was remarkable, yet what was evident was the persistence of Taiwanese identity. Even without international recognition, the self-knowledge and confidence in Taiwan's national identity is evident in everyday life. Though the rest of the world did not recognize Taiwan, the Taiwanese resisted mental colonization. The voice-over says the world "refused to recognize her—as if Taiwan didn't exist any more," yet despite her "newly bestowed invisibility" the Taiwanese went on. The pure capitalism of Taiwan, even in the face of China, also represented the "Taiwan Dream." For Welbon, the Taiwan dream seems too much like the capitalist "American dream," except it lacks what she calls the "American nightmare" of the history of slavery carried forward as racism.

Welbon avoids the question of whether she is implicated as a foreigner with English skills in relation to the privileged status of the English language at that historical moment. She is an English teacher, and the value of this is in the relationship of the English language to world commerce. According to Welbon, for the Taiwanese the 1980s is a moment of economic opportunity where rags-to-riches stories seem plausible in Taiwan, enabling the children Welbon meets to want to grow up to be the "Lao Ban," the boss. The economic possibilities offered by Taiwan allowed her to live the Taiwan dream as well, starting a magazine for the English-speaking communities in Taiwan. The idea of entrepreneurship as a route to empowerment and economic self-sufficiency is rooted both in the Taiwan dream and in Welbon's great-great-grandmother's achievement.

The film uses contrastive exposition to compare the colonial situation of Taiwan and its invisibility to the other nations in this period to Black experiences of being ignored and misunderstood. The film also calls our attention to Welbon's perspective on the most important difference: the Taiwanese know who they are. Rhetorically, Wei Yi-Fang/Welbon asks in Chinese, "Do African Americans know who they are?" English-speaking viewers read this in a subtitle. No answer is offered, but the film implies that this search for identity is what led Welbon to begin to ask these questions in the first place. This focus on ancestors as part of daily life is moving to Welbon, especially in light of the fact that some questions about her own ancestors can never be resolved. A slow-motion sequence of shots of Taiwanese families lighting incense sticks to remember their ancestors on tomb-sweeping day invites contemplation as Welbon compares the confusions and forced erasures in African American lineage and Black experiences in the Americas with the long knowable history of ancestry in Taiwan.

Haunted by Memories of American Racism

Remembering Wei-Yi Fang is a densely textured film, with many overlapping narratives in its twenty-nine minutes. Although a sequence about Welbon's haunting memories of American racism, which Wei-Yi Fang cannot let go of even as she lives the Taiwan dream, is relatively brief, it is one of the most remarked upon and significant portions of the film. We hear whispered questions on the sound track that seem to be voiced from the perspective of a child: "Why won't she sit next to me?" "Why does he think I am dumb?" As these whispered questions pepper the sound track with a relentless internal monologue of anxiety in response to the undermining themes of white supremacist thinking, the image track shows the shadows of individuals converging and moving apart. Then a dog's shadow appears—seeming to attach to or aggress against a person's shadow—but is restrained. Welbon speaks, saying that although she was taught to have self-respect, coming of age in America left her with "very low self-esteem." She describes the two images she heard, growing up, while the viewer sees photographs of Welbon with her siblings and classmates. Messages she received were contradictory—be ambitious and you will be respected—but the racist undertone, implicit in the way she was treated by some people, suggested that a good education would be wasted on her. In response to these memories, Welbon offers this intertitle: "Respect is something you first must give to yourself." This segment of the film is the most pedagogical, although the entire film takes a teaching tone in its expositional style. For the most part the film addresses the viewer as a thoughtful and invested student. Here the viewer is the audience, but, as Johnson argues, Welbon is also conjuring herself, bringing this truth to existence by speaking it.[6]

Conclusion

When Ellen, Welbon's grandmother, tells the story of mistakenly killing and cooking her own grandmother's prized Rhode Island hen, the grandmother, whom the viewer has seen as Welbon imagines and conjures her, silent and regal in her long skirts, did not punish the girl because she told the truth. The admonition "Always tell the truth" appears as an intertitle. The story unfolds in this film's characteristic mix of interview, then re-created footage, followed by an intertitle that addresses the audience directly with a response to the sequence that preceded it. This lesson—"Always tell the truth"—is one of the more explicit in the film, which initially tends to eschew this kind of direct teaching but becomes more explicit as it draws to a close. Yet the film follows its own advice, even when the truth is painful or hard to understand, or even contradictory. There may not be only one truth, but one should still always tell it.

At the end of the film, Welbon makes her own truth explicit and makes certain the viewer understands the lessons of the film. *Remembering Wei-Yi Fang* highlights the importance of performance to the possibilities of identity within the hegemonic experience of racism and in the encounter of travel, migration, and return. Wei-Yi Fang never really lived outside of Yvonne Welbon, yet she was a real person, brought to life by the performative fact of her creation. Welbon/Wei-Yi Fang lived, she went on vacations, she made friends, she studied Chinese in elementary school in Taiwan, she had friends, she earned money, and she started a magazine.

At the end of the film, Welbon explicitly states that she is her own person and has transcended the limits of racism in a prose poem that returns to shadows as images. She invokes Wei Yi-Fang and her ancestors and claims them proudly, saying that they are all part of her and cannot be erased. The film in many ways has already done this work, so this part repeats, makes clear, underlines, so its ending risks overinterpretation. Yet this clarity has made it a beautiful film to teach college students skeptical about the salience of race in the United States and the world. Living in an American-racism–free zone was a formative incubation period for Welbon as a prolific filmmaker, scholar, and producer. But despite the pleasures Taiwan offered, if she could not find freedom at home, she asks, did she really have freedom? This question locates Welbon's film in the company of the work of other returned expatriates and claims a place for her narrative as a unique presence in the tradition of leaving America and returning with insightful theories of American racism and new energy for the struggle for resistance.

Notes

1 Magdalena J. Zaborowska, *James Baldwin's Turkish Decade: Erotics of Exile* (Durham, NC: Duke University Press, 2009), 18, citing a film by Sedat Pakay, *James Baldwin: From Another Place* (1973).

2 Welbon's research at the time located free Africans in Honduras as descended from kidnapped Africans who escaped from a slave ship. Subsequently she found another

history of blacks in Honduras as being descendants of English-speaking contract workers from the Cayman Islands who settled on the island of Roatan in 1838. Most of her ancestors are descendants of this second group. See Harvey K. Meyer, *Historical Dictionary of Honduras* (Metuchen, NJ: Scarecrow Press, 1976), 304.

3 Bill Nichols, *Introduction to Documentary* (Bloomington: Indiana University Press, 2001), 34–36.

4 Stella Bruzzi, *New Documentary: A Critical Introduction* (London: Routledge, 2000).

5 E. Patrick Johnson, "'Quare' Studies, or (Almost) Everything I Know about Queer Studies I Learned from My Grandmother," *Text and Performance Quarterly* 21.1 (2001): 1–15.

6 Johnson, "'Quare' Studies," 10–11.

PART II • 1996–2016

The first ten years of out black lesbian media-making were marked by experimental, documentary, and narrative shorts that primarily reached audiences through film festivals and classroom, gallery, grassroots, and community screenings. During the second period, 1996–2016, black lesbian media makers began to reach larger audiences. The increase was achieved through a shift in the type of media being made and the movement from dial-up modem to broadband or higher speed Internet reaching the majority of American households.

As the emerging directors became more skilled and increasingly interested in having sustainable careers as media makers, they began to move away from experimentation and toward more traditional modes of storytelling that were more aligned with independent and Hollywood feature filmmaking. As noted in the introduction to this volume, through a combination of theatrical and ancillary distribution, feature films generally tend to reach a larger audience than short films, and documentaries and the marketing and publicity generated by the theatrical release of a feature film often bring the director into the public spotlight, creating name recognition and situating both the film and the filmmaker within popular culture.

In the 1990s black women media makers were thriving. They directed more shorts, documentaries, animation, and new media than in previous decades. They also directed more than twice as many feature films as they had in the first ninety years of cinema combined. Black lesbian filmmaker Cheryl Dunye's shift from experimental video short maker to narrative feature filmmaker began with a journey traveled by many first-time feature filmmakers: by directing a more traditional narrative short. *Greetings from Africa* (1994) demonstrated her narrative writing and directing skills. In 1995 the film was screened at a number of festivals, including the prestigious Sundance and Berlin International film festivals. There Dunye took meetings with key players in the independent film industry, like Christine Vachon and Tom Kalin. She thought these independent producers might help her to make her first feature. But nothing came of all the meetings. The entire networking process resulted in Dunye's becoming what she called "morally depressed."[1]

It was the time of Quentin Tarentino, *Slacker* (1991), and *Clerks* (1994), and the independent film world was becoming increasingly focused on what Dunye called "commercially minded white boys with guns."[2] She felt she was being left behind. Considering the kind of work that was being created by independent filmmakers experiencing success and her struggle to raise funding for her first feature, she questioned her decision to make a film focused on black lesbians. Alex Juhasz, her life partner at the time, told her to "stop her crying and kvetching" and offered to produce the film.[3]

Aside from teaching narrative film history and feminist film theory to her college students, Juhasz admitted that she knew next to nothing about feature film production.[4] Her background as a media maker was in activist video production. What she brought to the table was her ability to organize people with very little money. At that time *The Watermelon Woman* (1996) had absolutely no money. Juhasz called on her community of activists, graduate students, filmmakers, and friends and asked them to pitch in. The "ragtag" crew immediately got an office donated. "I don't even know where we had the chutzpah to say that we were going to make this movie," says Juhasz. But make it they did.

Dunye's 1996 feature film directorial debut, *The Watermelon Woman*, is the first lesbian-themed feature film directed by an out African American lesbian. It offers a faux cinema verité story of a black lesbian video maker's search to learn about an obscure black actress known as "the watermelon woman." The film weaves together incidents and details of Cheryl Dunye's own life with those of a fictitious "Cheryl." Because Dunye and her team have to fake so much of what "Cheryl" needs, the movie stresses the importance of preserving black lesbian history and the history of black women media makers. Karin Wimbley's essay in this section, "Stereotypy, Mammy, and Recovery in Cheryl Dunye's *The Watermelon Woman*," explores this aspect of the film in detail.

The Watermelon Woman premiered at the Berlin International Film Festival (the Berlinale) and won the coveted Teddy Award for films with LGBT topics. It was successful in terms of securing a theatrical release, achieving success on the film festival circuit, reaching underserved audiences, and receiving critical and media attention. Twenty years later it remains one of the few black lesbian-helmed films to receive national theatrical distribution. *The Watermelon Woman* marks the beginning of feature film production by out black lesbians. The films that followed—*Nandi* (1998) by Peggy Hayes, *Del Otro Lado / The Other Side* (1999) by C. A. Griffith, *Gotta Get My Hair Did* (2000) and *Hell's Most Wanted* (2001) by Coquie Hughes—did not feature black lesbian protagonists. It wasn't until Dunye's second feature, *Stranger Inside* (2001), which premiered at the Sundance Film Festival and was broadcast on HBO, that audiences were able to experience another feature film that centered on the life of a black lesbian. Theresa Brown added a black lesbian twist to the classic *Cyrano de Bergerac* with *The Right Girl* (2001). Hughes explored intimate partner violence in *If I Wuz Yo Gyrl* (2002). Shari Carpenter focused on lesbian and bisexual relationship dynamics in *Kali's Vibe* (2002). Dunye wrote a black lesbian couple into her third feature, *My Baby's Daddy* (2003), which was produced by Miramax. In 2004 Hughes directed her fourth feature, *Daughters of the Concrete*, and Faith Trimel directed *Black Aura of an Angel*.

In 2005 Angela Robinson released her spy spoof, *D.E.B.S.* (2004). Robinson first realized the project as the short film *D.E.B.S.* (2003) through a training program with POWER UP (Professional Organization of Women in Entertainment Reaching Up), the only 501(c)(3) nonprofit film production company and educational organization for women and the GLBTQ community.[5] In 2005 she also became the second black woman and first black lesbian to direct a studio feature, the Disney film *Herbie Fully Loaded* starring Lindsay Lohan. This moment marked the beginning of the black lesbian media maker hyphenate as Angela Robinson moved to television and began working on *The L Word* as a writer, director, and eventually producer. Patricia White's essay in this section, "'Invite Me In!': Angela Robinson at the Hollywood Threshold," offers an in-depth exploration of her career trajectory.

Tina Mabry is part of this new movement of independent filmmakers moving to television production. She also began by developing her projects through training programs. Her short film *Brooklyn's Bridge to Jordan* (2005), which aired on Showtime, was developed through a Film Independent training program. She was hired by POWER UP to cowrite *Itty Bitty Titty Committee* (2007). She returned to Film Independent and developed her award-winning feature film, *Mississippi Damned* (2009), through their director's training program. *Mississippi Damned* won thirteen awards from participation in fifteen film festivals, including Best Feature Film and Best Screenplay at the Chicago International Film Festival. The film premiered on Showtime in February 2011.[6]

II.1 Promotional image for *Queen Sugar*, 2016. OWN network.

Marlon Rachquel Moore's "From Rage to Resignation: Reading Tina Mabry's *Mississippi Damned* as a Post–Civil Rights Response to Nina Simone's 'Mississippi Goddam' " offers a close reading of Mabry's feature.

In 2010 the script for Mabry's planned second feature, *Country Line*, was accepted into the Film Independent's Screenwriters program. In April 2011 the script participated in Tribeca All Access, where it won the Creative Promise Award. *Country Line* also participated in Film Independent's Fast Track, a film-financing market, which was held during the Los Angeles Film Festival 2011. In 2012 Mabry participated in the Fox Writers Intensive, "a highly selective writer's initiative designed to introduce experienced writers with unique voices, backgrounds, life, and professional experiences that reflect the diverse perspectives of FOX's television and feature film audiences."[7] In 2015 Mabry was hired as a producer and writer on OWN's series *Queen Sugar* (2016), created by Ava DuVernay and Oprah Winfrey. In 2017 she won both the Director's Guild of America Award and the NAACP Image Award for Outstanding Directing—Children's Program for her Amazon-distributed *An American Girl Story—Melody 1963: Love Has to Win*.

Dee Rees took a similar route. Like Dunye and Mabry, she also first directed a short narrative film, *Pariah* (2007). She participated in an industry training program, the 2008 Sundance Screenwriting and Directing Lab, to develop her first feature, *Pariah* (2011), based on the short film. It was picked up by Focus Features and became the fourth film by an African American lesbian to receive national theatrical distribution. Jennifer DeClue explores the narra-

II.2 Lela (Kristine Wallace) in *Holiday*, directed by Jennifer DeClue, 2005.

tive journey from short to feature in her essay in this section, "The Circuitous Route of Presenting Black Butch: The Travels of Dee Rees's *Pariah*." Rees went on to direct the 2015 HBO feature film *Bessie*. It won four Primetime Emmy Awards, including Outstanding Television Movie, and Rees was nominated for writing and directing the film. Her second feature, *Mudbound*, premiered at the 2017 Sundance Film Festival. She is currently working with the producer Shonda Rhimes on an adaptation of Isabel Wilkerson's *The Warmth of Other Suns* for FX.[8]

The period covered in part II, "1996–2016," is marked by the continued production of short films, such as Kara Lynch's road movie, *Me-Ba . . . I'm Coming: A Travelogue* (1997), and a number of comedies by Stephanie Wynne, including *Gay Black Female* (1997), *If Only She Knew* (1998), and *Tantalize* (2001). Dramatic shorts include Jennifer DeClue's *Holiday* (2005), Tamika Miller's *Sarong Song* (2006), and *The Postwomen* (2010) by J. D. Walker, among dozens of others.[9]

The period is also marked by black lesbians taking advantage of the increased online opportunities with broadband penetration finally reaching the majority of American homes. Debra Wilson launched JengoTV (2006), a premier online media network focused on news and entertainment for LGBT communities of color. She is introduced in Candace Moore's essay in this section, "Producing Black Lesbian Media." Amber Sharpe produced *Don't Go* (2007), a self-described *Melrose Place* meets *The L Word* meets *227* that is a pilot for an online series. Shine Louise Houston produced the lesbian porn film *The Crash Pad* (2005) and launched an online paywall site for the *Crash Pad Series* based on the feature. She went on to found the porn production company Pink and White Productions and Pinklabel.tv, a hub for producers of ethical porn.[10] She continued to produce and direct porn features, including *Superfreak* (2006), *In*

Search of the Wild Kingdom (2007), and *Champion* (2008). L. H. Stallings offers a close read of *In Search of the Wild Kingdom* (2007) in her essay in this section, "Shine Louise Houston: An Interstice of Her Own Making."

In 2008 Charmain Johnson launched the extremely popular black lesbian web series *The Lovers and Friends Show*. The melodrama ran for five seasons and was picked up for distribution by Wolfe Video. Johnson wrote, directed, and produced the series set in West Palm Beach, Florida, with Kay "KG" Greene. The show birthed a new genre of black lesbian online storytelling from new voices, especially those from other southern states. Some of the best known web series to come out of the South are *Come Take a Walk with Me* (2010), written and directed by Mina Monshá and produced in Greensboro, North Carolina, and *Let's Talk Lesbian* (2013) from Rock Hill, South Carolina, with over a million views. Aryka Randall's *Girl Play* (2013), set in New Orleans, was launched as part of her online multimedia magazine, *TheFabFemme.com* (2010). The most popular series to come out of Atlanta was Michelle Daniel's *Between Women* (2011). Between Women TV Network currently runs as an online streaming service for $7/month. Other Atlanta series include *StudvilleTV* (2013) and *Sunny Reign* (2012).[11] While this list of black lesbian media being produced in the South is not exhaustive, it illustrates how the rise of online media has helped to break down barriers and bring new voices and their creative output to underserved audiences. There are also dozens of other black lesbian web series, documentary series, reality shows, and other forms of multimedia production that can be viewed online being produced around the country, creating an Internet TV alternative to broadcast television.

Coquie Hughes has also taken her work online. She remade her feature *If I Wuz Yo Gyrl* (2002) as a web series; she recast and renamed it *If I Was Your Girl* (2013). The series has over 3.7 million views on YouTube, making her online work some of the most watched black lesbian media in the world. She also continues to direct feature films, including the urban mockumentary *My Mama Said Yo Mama's a Dyke* (2010) and *The Lies We Tell* (2011). As Hughes states in her interview in this volume, "We're living in a day of technology that anyone can make a film. You can even make a movie with your cell phone and have a distribution outlet like YouTube to put it out there, so we don't need Hollywood validating us. It's an opportunity for everyone to tell their story, and I think that people should just tell their stories." Jennifer Brody offers an introduction to my interview with Hughes in her essay in this section, "Coquie Hughes: Urban Lesbian Filmmaker. Introduction to Yvonne Welbon's Interview with Coquie Hughes."

II.3 Natalie (Namaste) and Miller (Dred Carpenter) in season four of *Between Women*, directed by Michelle Daniel, 2016.

While black lesbian media makers have directed more narrative and experimental films than documentaries, a few emerged during this period that focus on LGBT topics. They include *All God's Children* (1996), a short directed by Sylvia Rhue (and Dee Mosbacher and Francis Reid) that illustrates the human toll exacted upon society by the unspoken stigmatization and alienation of lesbians and gays; *Living with Pride: Ruth Ellis @ 100* (1999), my award-winning documentary about the oldest known out African American, which aired on the Sundance Channel; Debra Wilson's *Jumping the Broom: The New Covenant* (2005), a short that aired on Showtime, focused on four African American lesbian and gay couples discussing gay marriage and the social, political, and cultural impact it has on their communities and long-term relationships; *U People* (2009) by Olive Demetrius and Hanifah Walidah; *Mountains That Take Wing: Angela Davis and Yuri Kochiyama—A Conversation of Life Struggles and Liberation* (2010), directed by C. A. Griffith (and H. L. T. Quan); *The Same Difference* (2014), a documentary about lesbians who discriminate against other lesbians based on gender roles, by Nneka Onuorah; and *The Revival: Women, Wine & the Word* (2015) by Sekiya Dorsett, which focuses on a traveling salon-style performance art show featuring the work of four young, gifted, black, and queer women: singer-songwriter Be Steadwell, poets T'ai Freedom Ford and Jonquille Rice, and poet-founder Jade Foster.

The most prominent feature documentary directed by an out African American lesbian to date is Yoruba Richen's *The New Black* (2013), a film I produced

II.4 Ruth Ellis in *Living with Pride: Ruth Ellis @ 100*, directed by Yvonne Welbon, 1999.

that captures the complex intersection of faith, racial justice, and LGBT rights. With its 2014 premiere at the Film Forum in New York City it became the first and only feature documentary by an African American lesbian to be theatrically released in the United States. The film was broadcast on the PBS series *Independent Lens* (2014) and screened in over seventy festivals and at almost two hundred colleges, universities, community groups, conferences, and corporations around the world. It is the winner of numerous awards, including the AFI Docs Audience Award for Best Feature, the Frameline LGBT Film Festival Audience Award for Best Documentary, and the Urbanworld Film Festival Jury Award for Best Documentary Feature. The film has also successfully been used as an organizing tool in the fight for marriage equality and in the fight for greater LGBT inclusion on campuses of historically black colleges and universities and in churches throughout the United States.

Part II, "1996–2016," begins with Candace Moore's "Producing Black Lesbian Media," which introduces a number of the producers who helped

II.5 Karess Taylor-Hughes in *The New Black*, directed by Yoruba Richen, 2013. Photo by Jen Lemen. Courtesy of Yvonne Welbon.

to make some of these new creative expressions possible. It continues by highlighting the work of a number of the media makers who have helped define the period: Cheryl Dunye, Coquie Hughes, Angela Robinson, Shine Louise Houston, Tina Mabry, and Dee Rees. It closes with an essay by Alexis Pauline Gumbs that provides an overview of queer women of color media training programs that offer alternative opportunities for women interested in becoming media makers.

In 2016 *The Watermelon Woman* was remastered to a digital delivery format (DCP) and rereleased with the generous support of the Outfest Legacy Project, the Toronto International Film Festival (where the film also showed in 1996), and its original distributor, First Run Features. This version of the film, now supported and valued in a manner diametrically opposed to its origins, also premiered at the 2016 Berlinale and is being screened again in many of the same venues (and new ones) where it traveled twenty years earlier. *The Watermelon Woman* stressed the importance of preserving black lesbian history and the history of black women media makers. In the twenty years since its release it has itself become the spark that launched the creation of the black lesbian media history for which the protagonist in the film yearns.

Notes

A filmography, selected interviews, and more information about out black lesbian media makers are available online at www.sistersinthelife.com.

1 Cheryl Dunye, personal interview, January 30, 1997.

2 Cheryl Dunye, personal interview.

3 Juhasz recalls making a deal with Dunye. She had been offered a job at Pitzer College and wanted Dunye to move with her from Philadelphia to California. Dunye said she couldn't leave Philadelphia until she had made her film. Juhasz offered to help her if she promised to move to California. Alex Juhasz, personal interview, April 10, 1998.

4 Alex Juhasz, personal interview.

5 "About POWER UP," accessed August 24, 2017, http://www.powerupfilms.org/index.php?option=com_content&view=article&id=11&Itemid=2.

6 "Tina Mabry: Senior Vice President, Executive Director," Morgan's Mark, accessed August 24, 2017, http://www.morgansmark.com/tina-mabry/.

7 "Tina Mabry."

8 Cynthia Littleton, "Dee Rees, Shonda Rhimes Developing Historical Drama 'Warmth of Other Suns' for FX," *Variety*, May 5, 2015, http://variety.com/2015/tv/news/shonda-rhimes-dee-rees-warmth-of-other-suns-fx-1201487579/.

9 A complete list of films can be found online at www.sistersinthelife.com.

10 "You Need Help: The Quest for Awesome Queer Feminist Porn," *Autostraddle*, February 22, 2013, https://www.autostraddle.com/you-need-help-the-quest-for-awesome-porn-155575/.

11 Links to a number of black lesbian YouTube web series can be found in "Black Lesbian/Queer YouTube Series," *Dark Thoughts of the Rainbow Warrior*, accessed August 22, 2018, http://darkcloudtherainbowwarrior.tumblr.com/post/45968238868/black-lesbianqueer-youtube-series. A list of gay and lesbian web series can also be found on *Televisual* (http://tvisual.org), a blog edited by Aymar Jean Christian that investigates the present and future of television, focusing on web video.

Producing Black Lesbian Media

We have to develop those structures that will present and circulate our culture. . . . It's a struggle but that's why we exist, so that another generation of Lesbians of color will not have to invent themselves, or their history, all over again.
—**Audre Lorde, 1984**

In interviews the comedian Wanda Sykes describes being a successful black, openly gay woman in Hollywood as akin to being a unicorn.[1] Clearly Sykes is majestic. Yet her joke hinges on a bitter truth: the mainstream media industry grants few women, not to mention lesbians of color, access to power. Despite shifts in the cultural imaginary around civil rights, Hollywood continues to maintain an embarrassing lack of diversity in its labor force, especially at decision-making levels. To battle this long-standing reputation, studios have developed diversity-hiring programs. These programs, however, only partially ameliorate disparities and, at worst, act as little more than fronts. For example, women held only 17 percent of the executive producing credits for the 250 most successful films in 2012 and 18.6 percent of TV's top production positions during the 2011–12 season.[2] These percentages are a far cry from census figures that find women slightly outnumber men in America. Producing media by and featuring queer women of color proves particularly daunting in an environment that tolerates such an impermeable celluloid ceiling, and this lack of representation behind the scenes translates on screen. Black women accounted for just 3 percent of the characters in the top 100 films of 2014.[3]

Over the past three decades, however, a few key players have founded production companies focused on minority representation and nurtured films and web series dedicated to the exploration of black lesbian themes. To help detail this history, in this essay I offer portraits of four black female producers and three producer-collaborators instrumental in building the careers of black lesbian media makers. Their successes bringing underrepresented identities to the screen or encouraging lesbians of color to empower themselves within production environments convey the constant negotiations and commitments sustaining minority media production.

Media scholars too often overlook the producer's crucial and collaborative role in the filmmaking process, tending instead to focus on the director as author. Yet the continued spate of black queer media bears a direct correlation to the low numbers of producers more committed to visions of diversity than box office success. As producers within this study argue, these goals do not necessarily have to be at odds. Relying primarily on personal interviews, I explore the strategies of producers working inside and outside of Hollywood, across assorted genres and distribution venues. Detailing the contributions of Morgan Stiff, Effie T. Brown, Catherine Gund, Alex Juhasz, Yvonne Welbon, Debra Wilson, and Stacy Codikow to the project of cultivating black lesbian media, I present their accounts of becoming and being producers, in hopes that such models will act as springboards to help imagine future structures of support for minority filmmakers.[4] To affirm a dedication to studying marginal production cultures is to stress the need to develop understandings of how axes of race and sexuality relate to media makers' professional opportunities and access to training, technologies, social capital, and funding. While examining the hierarchical social relations often in play here, I suggest that queer do-it-yourself artistic collectives, minority-focused mentorship programs, alternative economic models that include a "most favored nations" approach to crew compensation, and not-for-profit studios offer creative methods of supporting media on the margins.

Marginal Production Cultures

In the past decade John Caldwell, Denise Mann, Vicki Mayer, and other scholars have promoted an approach to media studies that focuses less on analyzing media products themselves and more on studying the cultural practices surrounding their production. Production studies, as a subfield, has de-emphasized the director as auteur and understood film and television as created collaboratively by many people, including producers (and producers of different skill sets), working behind the scenes. For the most part, production studies focuses on axes of gender and class as related to media industrial labor and importantly highlights creative labor also taking place "below the line." Caldwell foregrounds the importance of analyses of "very discrete sectors of the production community" and suggests we pay attention to the "self-representation, self-critique, and self-reflection" media producers employ when presenting or describing their work.[5] While Caldwell focuses almost entirely on Hollywood laborers, be they "prestige" or "anonymous," Mayer more broadly defines the media producer, to such an extent that her cultural study considers the invisible labor of underpaid factory workers, often in third world countries, who manufacture television sets. Thus Mayer identifies the dangers of letting mainstream industry practice fully define the media producer, which extend beyond how the term is used in Hollywood to designate a particular kind of white-collar labor. She also importantly highlights the exploitation of low-income workers within a globalized economy.[6] Marginal production studies complements this approach, concentrating its intersectional analysis on considerations of how race and sexuality complicate media production practices. Concerns with distinctions between below-the-line and above-the-line labor, while still relevant, tend to be less central to understanding marginal production cultures, since other, less hierarchical social relations and economic models are often practiced for reasons both political and functional.

By presenting multiple social differences, black queer media, especially media by and about women, becomes triply subject to the so-called burden of representation. In "New Black Queer Cinema" Louise Wallenberg suggests that in figuring blackness and queerness together, black queer films foreground the inclusivity and plurality of this companionship. At the same time, such media challenges the construct of an "essential black queer subject," figuring her instead "in the spaces *between* different communities—at the intersections of power relations determined by race, class, gender and sexuality." For this reason Wallenberg applauds the suggestion by the filmmaker Marlon Riggs that what might seem a "schizophrenic" approach to identity definition fruitfully offers an opportunity to realize, in his words, that "you are many things within a person." Riggs warns against trying "to arrange a hierarchy of things . . . say[ing], 'this is more important than that,'" but instead insists on a celebration of plurality.[7]

While black queer media productions themselves are read for their "representativeness" of a particular subjectivity, so are their producers often called to (and proud to) speak as representatives for an identity group. Kobena Mercer argues, "Insofar as [black gay and lesbian artists] speak from the specificity of such experiences, they overturn the assumption that minority artists speak *for* the entire community from which they come. This is an important distinction in the relations of enunciation because it bears upon the politics of representation that pertain to all subjects in marginalized or minoritized situations."[8] In order to attempt a plural approach to understanding the intricacies and possibilities of black lesbian media production, one that seeks to reduce neither marginal media production practices nor their practitioners, I argue that it is important to turn to the voices of these producers themselves. This study draws on the perspectives of seven female producers, each of whom pursued media-making guided by their strong political commitments. Though different in their approaches, these women similarly created support systems for representing underrepresented populations and articulated their ventures as born out of desire to fill a void.

"Redefining the Mainstream": Morgan Stiff

Morgan Stiff, producer of the feature film *Mississippi Damned* (2009) and cofounder of Morgan's Mark productions, decided to transition from studying dramaturgy to film editing and production because she felt that moving-image media could speak to a wider set of audiences than theater.[9] "I had always been into theater to raise people's social consciousness and for activist reasons," explains Stiff. "I realized I was going to reach more people through television and film. At least the population I was after—they were not going to the theater." After pursuing an MFA in film production at the University of Southern California, Stiff and her partner, Tina Mabry, a screenwriter and director, found themselves in Hollywood having difficulties working on the types of projects they cared about. In response they designed a launching ground for the media they wanted to make rather than waiting for their so-called big break. "With media made by women of color or anyone who's marginalized," says Stiff, "you have to create your own opportunities. I wanted to be an editor, but people wouldn't let me edit black content. Tina was writing and no one was listening to her voice. So we'd sit around and wait and finally we had to create a production company by ourselves." The couple, who have been together since 2003, pooled their funds to finance a boutique studio devoted to the idea that "almost everybody is an other" and that specific, personal stories are more universal than they might seem. They drafted a mission statement with the tagline "Out of the Margins, Redefining the

Mainstream." "We decided if we were going to make this type of investment, let's do it for real," recalls Stiff. "So we developed a five-year plan, we branded the company, we developed a visual identity, we took it seriously. What's a production company that doesn't make anything? We took out loans. We put half of the money in from our own pocket and set out to make a movie."

While planning the first full-scale production of Morgan's Mark, Stiff and Mabry discussed the question of how to ensure that they compensated their cast and crew fairly and treated them properly, despite their company's relatively small budget. They settled on a "most favored nations" business model, which distributed their film budget equally to all of the people working on the project. "We decided to pay everyone the same thing, from the PA [production assistant] to the DP [director of photography], and Tina and I took no fees, because why would we, we'd just be paying ourselves. We created this environment where [our employees] realized that we were honest, they were never paid late, and they were always respected. We had a very strict 'You don't yell on set' policy; it was an even-keeled environment. Why can't this model be the model [for film production]?" By putting into place policies of nondiscrimination based on perceived status or worth, Stiff and Mabry aimed to reproduce their progressive values on an institutional scale.

The first feature film Stiff and Mabry made together was *Mississippi Damned*, an epic, ensemble-cast coming-of-age film that takes place over decades. Based on some of Mabry's experiences growing up in rural Mississippi, the film is, according to Stiff, "personal from top to bottom." Premiering at Slamdance, *Mississippi Damned* screened at many prestigious festivals internationally, including festivals focused specifically on African American or LGBTQ media. The film, which touches on sexual violence, often inspired visceral emotional responses from audiences in the Q&A sessions. "The one thing going to all of these different types of festivals, festivals branded toward certain types of people, showed me was that people were universally affected," Stiff explains. "We had someone at Outfest who was crying and thanking Tina and admitting for the first time in her life that she was molested to this whole audience in the DGA1 [a large theater in the Director's Guild of America building in Los Angeles]. Or in Zurich, where something similar happened, and you're talking about a whole different culture. It showed that this story about a poor black girl growing up in Tupelo, Mississippi, transcends these differences. I was most surprised in Zurich. I felt like we were being looked at because we were the only black people around. Then we show this

9.1 Cast and crew of *Mississippi Damned*, directed by Tina Mabry, 2009.

movie and people are sharing their experiences with us. Like if Tina had just put all of this up there for everyone to see, they could also share in this room."

Though *Mississippi Damned* won awards at many of the festivals, including the Golden Hugo for Best Film at the Chicago International Film Festival, Best American Independent Film at the Philadelphia Film Festival, and the Grand Jury Award at Outfest, the film did not pick up significant distribution beyond the festival circuits. The fact that the film spoke to and across multiple social groups ended up leading to some confusion on the part of networks and film distributors, who often understood the film's prospective audience too narrowly or in conflicting ways. Stiff recognized that "there were gatekeepers who kept us from accessing audiences on a larger level. While *Mississippi Damned* ran on Showtime, if it wasn't Black History Month, it ran really late at night. We had a gay character, Leigh, and the film is made by a production company owned by two lesbians, yet, because Leigh wasn't the main character and because the film explored so many other subjects, there was some debate about whether it was 'gay enough.' LGBT distribution companies weren't necessarily interested in getting our film because they didn't know how to market it." Immaculately shot and full of impressive performances, *Mississippi Damned*'s dramatic focus on the difficulties of working-class African American families in the South and on issues of poverty, addiction, sexual abuse, and incest set it outside of the parameters of LGBTQ distribution companies' notions of the marketable "gay" film. An excessive focus on selling material to niches and notions of a streamlined market for media content prop up ideas of coherent subjectivities organized neatly around identity differentials rather than conceptualizing production and reception at the intersections.

Deeply Involved: Effie T. Brown

Effie T. Brown's career as an executive producer began with *Stranger Inside* (2001), a made-for-HBO feature about two generations of black women in prison directed by Cheryl Dunye, a black lesbian.[10] The next year Brown produced *Real Women Have Curves* (Patricia Cardoso, 2002), an independent title that introduced the actress America Ferrara as a Latina teen coming of age in East Los Angeles and won numerous awards at Sundance and the Independent Spirit awards. Since then, through her company Duly Noted, Brown has produced many other titles that foreground representations of people of color, most recently releasing *Dear White People* (Justin Simien, 2014), an adaptation of Justin Simien's eponymous play about attending-the-Ivy-League-while-black. Brown suggests that even as a child she was always "acutely aware of the images of the other," or at least the lack thereof. Growing up in the 1980s in New Jersey, she recalls watching popular John Hughes movies such as *Breakfast Club* (1985) and *Sixteen Candles* (1984) and wondering "Where is black Jake Ryan?" Recalling having few role models to relate to in the media, Brown pointed to her childhood idol Grace Jones as "the only dark-skinned, black woman who was fierce that I could somehow see." Later, while studying acting at Loyola Marymount College, Brown similarly noticed that, regardless of talent, few lead roles were made available to black women. She switched her major to film production after having what she describes as a "Jesus moment" about her calling: "I have a hard time crying and being vulnerable on stage: I'm a total control freak. I'm a person with a great eye. So what do I do? Produce. It came naturally. I found my thing, pulling people together, telling stories, making it happen." Brown went straight to the head of Loyola's Film Department, Howard Lavitt, and insisted on entry: "I said, 'You don't have many black people, you don't have many women of color in your film department, and I'm going to be huge.' He took a shine to me and laughed and said, 'Okay, I'll take a shot at you.'"

While developing her film production career in Hollywood after college, Brown used her passion for "representing the margins, disenfranchised people, people on the edge, and working on projects about women or people of color" to guide choices she made, while consistently aware she was working

9.2 Promotional image of Effie T. Brown. Duly Noted, Inc.

within a system stacked against her: "I knew that being black and a woman and not having connections in the industry, I had to work twice as hard as my white counterparts, these boys who had connections. What makes [black women] different also makes us stand out amongst all the chaos and the fray. If I were a white man, I would be freaked the fuck out because I would be a dime a dozen. If you're not connected, with the right last name, you're in the same boat, the same hustle. They may not know what my movie is, but it's like, 'Oh, Effie, she's nice, she's that black girl.' Granted it's sometimes tokenism, but I'll take it. All right, let me help you, let me help assuage your white guilt."

Aware that she is both discriminated against and fetishized for her racial difference, Brown relays some of the painful things she put up with to be given a chance, much less taken seriously: "Little black jokes—that's how people [in the industry sometimes] try to relate to me. I've had loads of crazy shit said to me. I knew that I had to do my song and dance and make myself nonthreatening. Make myself funny in addition to having to work my ass off, because nobody gives a shit if you're like funny and charming and you fuck up the money, right?" Ultimately Brown concerned herself with finding projects to work on and people to work with that allowed her to be successful while also standing up for herself and against discrimination.

Looking for a way to network and find mentors who treated her with respect, Brown joined the Film Independent program Project Involve, to which she, in many ways, credits her career. Originally founded to provide young women of color specifically opportunities in the media industries, the diversity program now provides mentorship opportunities, workshops, and short-film funding to filmmakers from underrepresented communities more broadly: "Then, Project Involve was just for women of color, and they would introduce you to the town, so you are able to build these relationships and connections. I met Laurie Parker, who used to be Gus Van Sant's producer, and she taught me how to be a respectable producer. I'm so glad she caught me when she did, because I'm naturally kind of a selfish person. She said, 'Effie, the greatest lie that they tell us is that there's only room for one of us—there's room for all of us. That's why I'm reaching now and pulling you up, and then when you get up, Effie, you have to reach down and pull somebody else up.' I care about mentoring others, and I'm very involved in Film Independent now. I am a sucker for somebody who has a vision and a passion that is different from the norm. Sometimes the only thing we have in common is not doing anything that is common."

Brown fondly recalls her experience as a new producer working on *Stranger Inside*, describing herself as something of an A personality on a lax set: "Producing on a film with black lesbian content was funnily enough my first job. *Stranger Inside* was my first straight-up, real-deal producing gig with HBO. The film is about black women—though they're all in prison. While making the movie, I was so square that it was literally five or six years later that people told me of all the sex and drugs and fun stuff that were happening on that set. I was like, 'No wonder you guys were always so fucking late.' I was so stressed making sure that everything was perfect and pulled together, I had no idea that people were having a blast." Often mistaken for a lesbian, Brown attributes this misrecognition to the queer and feminist projects she often chooses to work on, but also the fact that she is "a good-looking strong black woman that is business and is in charge." "I often feel like I'm passing," she jokes. "If I could really get down with women, I would be married, I would be happy, my life would be full of friends, but unfortunately I'm heterosexual."

After finishing *Stranger Inside* and while making *Real Women Have Curves*, Brown started her own company, Duly Noted, to allow her to mount productions independently. "I'm a full-fledged producer of nuts and bolts, to creative, to delivery at the end to the studio. I do the full circle," she explains. "I'm really passionate about women and people of color being seen. I'm so sick and tired of us doing the same shitty subservient bullshit role. Why can't we be our own complicated types of people? Why are we always Bagger

Vance?[11] My job is to make sure that my content is the way that I want to see the world. Which is, you know, all colored up and different with different types of people."

Now that Brown has been successful in the film industry, she feels she has paid her dues. "I'm a known quantity, and maybe that buys me a little bit of room to be sassy. When people say stuff off the cuff that is just racist, wrong, and offensive, I have a righteous indignation." As a producer at the head of a team of eighty or more people, she describes her ability to "cuss people out" as crucial in her business. "It's like that old southern saying, 'Give someone enough rope and they'll hang themselves.' When people get to talking, they tell you about themselves in a heartbeat. The first two minutes will be something PC and some bullshit that they want you to hear. But if you keep them talking, the next five to ten minutes will be where they really land. It's like they're puppies: they get confused. I have to slow their stroll." Brown is frank about the talk that goes on behind closed doors at the expense of women, gays, and people of color within the mainstream entertainment industry: "People will talk about gay men, they'll talk about Asians, they'll talk about Jews in front of me. So I have to be like, 'Okay, this is where I have to stand up and stop you.' I'm hoping that my white friends will do the same thing if someone starts calling us the 'n word' or something like that. Cease and desist."[12]

The head of an independent production company who provides mentorship to others, like Stiff, Brown consciously crafts ethical working environments and sets a progressive production agenda. She is able to facilitate the type of environment she would like to see behind the scenes as well as offer new opportunities for other women of color who are just starting out in the industry.

Strategies of Cultivation and Distribution: Debra Wilson

One of the first black LGBT streaming media websites, Jengo TV, began in the middle of the first decade of the twenty-first century, founded by Debra A. Wilson.[13] Wilson began her career as a producer and director of the films *Butch Mystique* (2003) and *Jumping the Broom* (2006) and was coproducer of Tina Mabry's *Mississippi Damned*. She created her first thirty-five-minute documentary film, *Butch Mystique*, after attending the first Zuna Institute National Black Lesbian Conference and feeling excluded from a conversation about black female masculinity: "They had a workshop on butch-identified lesbians. Just out of curiosity, I went to sit in and they kicked me out because

I wasn't butch-identified. They felt I should not be there. I get it, but, after that, I was like, 'Well fine, I'll just do a documentary on my own.'" After researching the topic, Wilson asked friends, acquaintances, and strangers who identified as black butches to speak to her on camera about their experiences with their gender and sexuality. She describes using an open-ended process in all conversations, which were filmed in a sit-down style: "There were lots of questions that I asked people, but mainly all of my follow-up was based on the sharing process. So I'd ask a question, and maybe they would say something that intrigued me. I didn't want to be married to my questions." Sensitive to some of the problems with ethnographic approaches and the risks of further othering her interviewees through the framework of her documentary, Wilson treaded carefully, trying to avoid presenting herself as an expert on an identity she did not claim: "That was my biggest thing: let people speak for themselves. I didn't want to put my biases in. I wanted to see their ideas about [being a black butch] and how they think of themselves. Sometimes when you look at documentaries they're so heavy-handed with their stories. They try to put themselves in this voice of always knowing everything."

Butch Mystique played at numerous film festivals, including Fusion, a then new festival organized by Outfest for films by or about LGBT people of color, and the San Francisco International Lesbian and Gay Film Festival, where it won an audience award. Wilson also entered the film in Showtime's black filmmakers' showcase competition, which offered $30,000 and distribution on the premium network. "I submitted it on a whim," she recalls. "I thought they were not even going to take this seriously because it was about black butch lesbians. There wasn't *The L Word* on or anything like that. So I got a call saying that it won. What a shock!" The film was also picked up by the LGBT basic cable network LOGO: "I ended up having separate deals with LOGO and Showtime to screen *Butch Mystique* even though they're under the same umbrella. To me it would have been exciting if BET [Black Entertainment Television] wanted it, but BET would never have shown *Butch Mystique* then. BET may have changed in terms of being open [to more LGBT material] at this point."

Gaining distribution and funding for *Butch Mystique* opened up the possibility of working on other media projects on black gays and lesbians for Wilson, who used her award money from Showtime to make the film *Jumping the Broom*. Wilson summarizes *Jumping the Broom* as a "film about gay marriage as a civil rights issue. The biggest reason I made that movie, really, was because I felt like if I didn't tell this story about the black gay and lesbian

9.3 Promotional image of Debra Wilson. A State of Mind.

community, nobody else would." Wilson also met Stiff and Mabry while touring LGBT film festivals and ended up helping to produce *Mississippi Damned*,
working alongside Stiff as an associate producer on set. Clarifying her role
on the picture, Wilson, like others I interviewed, pointed to the broad range
of meanings associated with the work of production: "There are all kinds of
different producers—producers who make the money to get the project off
the ground; there's a creative producer who comes on board. You can be a
producer, but that doesn't mean you're going to stay for the whole project.
On *Mississippi Damned*, I wasn't the producer who got any of the money, but
I was the producer who helped run the set."

Wilson channeled some of her skills as a producer and director into creating a distribution platform that would provide like-minded individuals a
place to share work with larger publics. Recognizing early the possibilities for
streaming media, Wilson decided to develop online content and a space for
content by others about LGBT people of color: Jengo TV. In the early 2000s
ideas about the form television or film would take on the Internet were still
experimental, tentative, and formally diverse. Wilson saw Jengo TV as not
just another website; using the model of television distribution, she con-
ceived of the potential for an expansive media venue, consistently providing
new content to its audience: "through Jengo TV, I was creating in my mind an

entire network. I was the CEO, producer. The trouble with Jengo TV was just acquiring content, creating a resource and an outlet that wasn't there before. I still don't think anyone has really incorporated so many kinds of content on gays and lesbians of color online. Today they have web series, but there's not a network. It wasn't always the best-produced stuff, but it was a place people could go and watch."

In some ways this dedication to the creation and distribution of a field of black gay and lesbian media *willed* into being such a field (rather than a handful of examples), to use Juhasz's term. Production quality may have taken a backseat, as Wilson admits, because of available funding, but the *practice* of producing material relevant to this community, the establishment of a virtual space for this expression was the website's foremost aim. Wilson began with the goal of premiering new content every two weeks and used social media as well as offline events to spread news of the site: "The only thing that was available to us to get it out there was MySpace at the time. We would try to connect with different [LGBT] Pride festivals and be sponsors." The site also encouraged viewers to submit their own content: "I had one idea about if you go to Pride and take footage, we'll put it up on Jengo TV. Just use your phone! But people weren't thinking that way yet." The site operated mostly on DVD sales and contributions: "People would go and look at media online, and then they would go and buy the DVD. That model totally worked then. So the artists, the directors made a little bit of money." Wilson tried to reach out to more established LGBT media distributors to encourage partnering in the efforts to stream LGBT content, but suggests that, sadly, she was "a little bit ahead of the curve. I approached LGBT distributors like Wolfe, and I said, 'I have this player that I'll help you with, and you could stream your movies through Jengo TV.' Then they're like, 'What are you talking about?' and now they're doing it. I knew that one day people would watch material over the Internet or through different devices."

As of 2015 Jengo TV's streaming videos are no longer available online since the costs of keeping the project going eventually became untenable: "The videos aren't available now, and there's no new production of media for the site. It was hard to keep going, because at the end of the day it's really about money. We were relying on a third-party player to stream everything, but we didn't have a proprietary player. This was 2006, 2007, the economy was really horrible, and we're black, so we weren't going to get the kind of venture capital that everyone else was getting."

Jengo TV serves as an example of an online venue, which, like other channels that seek and disseminate queer of color media such as festivals, television networks, DVDs, and theatrical distributors, works to cultivate a viewing public and an actual community where creatives and consumers meet. However, the sustenance and growth of such a media culture necessitates an infrastructure of support on the front end that helps defray the costs of production, provides access to equipment and education, organizes collaborations, and brings together people with differing expertise. This is where sustainable production companies focused on minority media and internship and award programs come in and help facilitate minority media production within a broader media environment that subtly, and not so subtly, discourages such work.

Empowering Others: Stacy Codikow and POWER UP

Over the past decade the Professional Organization of Women in Entertainment Reaching Up (POWER UP) has emerged as one of the central organizations providing mentorship and funding for fledgling LGBT media makers.[14] Stacy Codikow, executive director and founder of POWER UP, describes it as "the only all-volunteer, nonprofit, gay and lesbian film studio in the world." The studio, based in Los Angeles, emerged out of a networking organization for gay women in Hollywood, established in 2000, which broadened its scope and membership to include gay men. In the face of the Proposition 8 vote in 2008, which struck down gay marriage in California, Codikow claims POWER UP "realized that as a media organization, we have a lot of influence and power. That's when we made a huge effort to include men and become more integrated." Members of the group volunteered their time to create public service announcements as part of the "No on 8" campaign. The organization also brought in celebrities and aid from other activist organizations such as the Feminist Majority to make commercials.

POWER UP produced a number of short films over its first four years. These films evolved from contests aimed at newcomers to the industry, who were paired with established mentors and offered on-the-set training: "Directors, writers, and producers had the opportunity to submit themselves to be financed and for POWER UP to produce their short. Each year we went to Sundance with shorts. [Since then] we've made two features so far [*Itty Bitty Titty Committee* (Jamie Babbit, 2007) and *GIRLTRASH: All Night Long* (Alexandra Kondracke, 2014)], and we're about to start a third." POWER UP continues to draw from new talent: "We run a mentorship program that is

9.4 (*clockwise from top left*) Angela Robinson, Guinevere Turner, Jamie Babbit, Jane Lynch, Lee Friedlander, Colette Burson, Stacy Codikow, and Honey Labrador at POWER UP's annual Sundance Film Festival dinner.

about giving people a chance to participate in the many different areas of filmmaking and get a real, hands-on experience. We have usually about forty mentees on a movie, who come in for the period of shooting and for a few weeks before and a few weeks after. They get to learn to be in different departments and start relationships in the industry."

One of POWER UP's first mentees, the black lesbian writer, director, and producer Angela Robinson, developed a long-standing relationship with the organization that grew from writing and directing one of its first productions, the short film *D.E.B.S.* (2003), which Screen Gems later released as an eponymous feature film (2004), to mentoring fledgling directors herself. Since joining POWER UP as a volunteer, Robinson has worked as a producer and writer for the television shows *True Blood* (HBO, 2008–14), *Hung* (HBO, 2009–11), and *The L Word* (Showtime, 2004–9) and has helmed the successful feature *Herbie: Fully Loaded* (2005) with Lindsay Lohan. After the full-length version of *D.E.B.S.* debuted at Sundance, Nina Jacobson, head of Disney, offered Robinson a three-year deal and hired her to direct *Herbie*. "Angela was the only black woman to direct a Disney picture, let alone the highest grossing Disney picture of that year, but she didn't want to continue to only make Disney movies. Angela wants to create things that she can put her signature on," says

Codikow, clearly proud of Robinson's career trajectory. "When I met Angela Robinson, she was a PA for us, on our first set of shorts. This was 2001. Angela was thirty-two and working in the industry as a color-timer on the graveyard shift. She worked all night long while she wrote scripts and did things to try to promote her career."

Robinson submitted to both of POWER UP's first writing and directing contests. In order to decide on writers for their first three short films, POWER UP took around 250 submissions. "From that we would take the top twenty-five scripts and give them to super-big Hollywood producers, writers, and agents. Each time seven or eight people would read them and decide on the best script. Hands down, Angela got the highest scores all along." Robinson's work almost fell through the cracks, however: "*D.E.B.S.* was almost not made. I had a woman working for me who said, 'Oh, that's just too expensive' and just pulled it from the list. Jamie Babbit, who was on our board of directors, asked, 'What happened to *D.E.B.S.*? It's missing. It should be in here.' I sat down and I read it. I laughed my head off. I called Jamie back, [and] I said, 'You're so right. This movie's wonderful.' We didn't want to originally have people direct and write their film, because in Hollywood, 90 percent don't do it that way. Somebody writes it, someone else directs it. Having read the script and realizing, oh, my God this is fantastic, I sat down and said, 'She's going to have to direct it,' because she was also winning the directing contest. We were looking at them separately. You submitted your directing reel and you submitted your script. Well, she won in both categories. So it was like, 'This is silly—she should get this opportunity.' That's how it started."

POWER UP has also helped advance the careers of other African American lesbian filmmakers, including Tina Mabry, who answered an ad to write the script for POWER UP's first feature film while still in graduate school. "We hooked up Tina Mabry with another girl named Abby Shafran and they wrote *Itty Bitty Titty Committee*. Jamie Babbitt and Andrea Sperling pitched the idea for the film to Mabry and Shafran, and we oversaw their writing as they worked with us for four months. Tina wrote the script and was on the set. She got her first feature film produced by us, which won Best Feature Film at the South by Southwest film festival, which is huge and put a feather in Tina's cap. She's a great writer. Then she went on and did *Mississippi Damned*."

In the nearly fifteen years that POWER UP has been around, the organization has acted as a resource for many filmmakers like Robinson and Mabry, in numerous ways: "We may have participated in maybe another hundred or so shorts and films by people who come to us for help, and we're able to give them guidance or help along the way." POWER UP fundraises and asks for donations of labor and equipment from the larger Hollywood community: "Because we're a nonprofit, we can make a movie for, you know, two hundred thousand dollars, where a movie would normally cost two million dollars, but we're getting a million paid in free gifts and services." Remaining nonprofit, POWER UP continues to act as a mentoring and networking service for aspiring filmmakers even as it has shifted from an activist organization for lesbians in Hollywood to a full-fledged studio. Structures such as POWER UP facilitate the production of works that might otherwise go underfunded or unseen.

Group Authorship

What all of these pioneers and innovators in black lesbian media production have in common is a sense of shared responsibility for the identity representations that make it to the screen. Each producer I spoke to described herself as part of a bigger community, but also as beholden to it and dependent upon it in the most fruitful ways. By teaching people who have never used a camera how to do so, encouraging folks to tell their own stories and that their creative visions matter, and also communicating or inventing their own stories, these women have made a whole body of work possible. These producers recognize that media-making is a social endeavor and that of the films they want to see get made through collaboration, even those in charge need to ask for help. By transforming their focus from the authorial fame or making it to the top of some mysterious hierarchical food chain, to creating organizations that aim to sustain minority media production over time—the independent company, the nonprofit studio, the mentorship program, the online television network—these producers have, importantly, enabled others to produce.

Notes

Epigraph: Joseph F. Beam, "Interview with Audre Lorde," in *Conversations with Audre Lorde*, edited by Joan Wylie (Oxford: University Press of Mississippi, 2004), 130.

1 Stratton Lawrence, "Funny and Proud: Wanda Sykes Grows into Her Role as Comedy's Activist," *Post and Courier* (Charleston, SC), October 10, 2012.

2 Martha M. Lauzen, "The Celluloid Ceiling: Behind-the-Scenes Employment of Women on the Top 250 Films of 2012" (2013), Center for the Study of Women in Television and Film, http://womenintvfilm.sdsu.edu/files/2013_Celluloid_Ceiling _Report.pdf, 2; "Independent Women: Behind-the-Scenes Representation on

Festival Films" (2012), Center for the Study of Women in Television and Film, http://womenintvfilm.sdsu.edu/files/2012_Independent_Women_Exec_Summ.pdf, 3.

3 Casey Cipriani, "Sorry, Ladies: Study on Women in Film and Television Confirms the Worst," *Indiewire*, February 10, 2015.

4 Essays about the contributions of Catherine Gund, Alex Juhasz, and Yvonne Welbon to the project of cultivating black lesbian media can be read online at www.sistersinthelife.com.

5 John Caldwell, *Production Culture: Industrial Reflexivity and Critical Practice in Film and Television* (Durham, NC: Duke University Press, 2008), 7, 5.

6 Vicki Mayer, *Below the Line: Producers and Production Studies in the New Television Economy* (Durham, NC: Duke University Press, 2011), 40.

7 Louise Wallenberg, "New Black Queer Cinema," in *New Queer Cinema: A Critical Reader*, edited by Michele Aaron (Edinburgh: Edinburgh University Press, 2004), 129, 133, 136.

8 Kobena Mercer, "Skin Head Sex Thing: Racial Difference and the Homoerotic Imaginary," in *Bad Object Choices, How Do I Look? Queer Film and Video* (Seattle: Bay Press, 1991), 204–5.

9 Information and quotes in this section are drawn from my interview with Morgan Stiff on May 28, 2013.

10 Information and quotes in this section are drawn from my interview with Effie T. Brown on June 10, 2013.

11 Bagger Vance is the character played by Will Smith in *The Legend of Bagger Vance*. Brown uses the name as shorthand to describe the role Smith plays in the movie defined by some cultural critics as a "Magical Negro." This is a benevolent, somewhat mystical black character who is supportive of the white hero and always seems to have the right words of wisdom to help the white hero succeed.

12 See HBO's *Project Greenlight* season four opener, where Matt Damon and Effie Brown have a conflicted discussion on diversity, to see how this plays out for Brown in her work environments.

13 Information and quotes in this section are drawn from my interview with Debra Wilson on May 19, 2013.

14 Information and quotes in this section are drawn from my interview with Stacy Codikow on May 20, 2013.

Stereotypy, Mammy, and Recovery in Cheryl Dunye's *The Watermelon Woman*

The Mammy has been in our field of vision as a popular icon representing black womanhood for more than a century in literature, film, and television and in consumer and material culture.[1] Described as an asexual, rotund slave of older age whose sole responsibility is to take care of her master's children, Mammy is a beloved character who represents all that is nurturing and maternal. She is dark-skinned and boisterous and thought to have mannish features such as large feet and hands. Mammy wears a large skirt, hiding her sex, and covers her nappy hair with a bandanna or handkerchief. The qualities ascribed to Mammy, "her deeply sonorous and effortlessly soothing voice, her infinite patience, her raucous laugh, her self-deprecating wit, her implicit understanding and acceptance of her inferiority and devotion to whites—all point to the long-lasting and troubled marriage of racial and gender essentialism, mythology, and southern nostalgia."[2] Above all else, she is a servant to whites, knows and accepts her inferiority without malice, and cares for her white charges with utter devotion.

The Mammy stereotype was popular among whites because she legitimized the popular myth of the Old South, which grew out of post–Reconstruction era anxieties about the newly freed slave population in the mid- to late nineteenth century. Her image captured in the American imagination the idea that the South, prior to the Civil War, was one large hamlet where all was well between the races: slaves were happy children and whites their gentle benefactors. Moreover it referenced the Old South myth that figures the pre–Civil War South as a location for plentitude and beauty that was unnecessarily disrupted and destroyed by the North's interference in the South's genteel slavocracy. Mammy supported this ideology, for she was the happy darkie for whom slavery was a blessing. According to M. M. Manring, "the Mammy of the Old South mythology was a collaborator in [slaveholder] society, a reassuring figure who, despite her breeding, comforted her white betters, offered advice, kept black males in line, and put food on the table."[3]

When dealing with issues of black womanhood, the representational practice of stereotypy engages with the Mammy stereotype to produce a fertile site where African American womanhood can be recovered, (re)constructed, and (re)interrogated. As I define it in this essay, stereotypy—whose most familiar icons can be traced to the post-Reconstruction South—is the use of black stereotypes in African American politics, art, literature, and performance by black scholars and artists. Specifically, stereotypy is a signifiyin(g) practice that illumines the racial stereotype in representation in order to deconstruct and revise the stereotype, negating it as a legitimate or authentic articulation of blackness. As a discursive, rhetorical, aesthetic strategy and representational practice, stereotypy contests racialized regimes of representation by confronting how the stereotype functions in representation.

For instance, as a site for recovery, the Mammy figure has been an abundant site for the African American female artists Betye Saar (*The Liberation of Aunt Jemima*), Marcia L. Leslie (*The Trial of One Short-Sighted Black Woman vs. Mammy Louise and Safreeta Mae*), Breena Clarke and Glenda Dickerson (*Re/membering Aunt Jemima: A Menstrual Show*), and Cheryl Dunye (*The Watermelon Woman*) to interrogate what it means to be black women in the United States during the last three decades of the twentieth century.[4] Dunye's *The Watermelon Woman* (1996) employs stereotypy—the Mammy stereotype in conjunction with parody—as a means to recuperate negative images of black women in the American cinematic tradition by utilizing the black womanist recovery project; it is in this way that Dunye is able to reclaim Mammy as a precursor to a black lesbian film tradition. By positioning Mammy as a site for recovery, Dunye constructs a black lesbian matrilineage that begins with the Mammy stereotype in *The Watermelon Woman* and ends with Dunye as a benefactress of this black lesbian film tradition.

A symbiotic relationship exists between self-reflexive parody and stereotypy. Though definitions of parody depend on historical period and cultural production—interpretations ranging from Aristotle and the ancient Greeks to Bakhtin and the Russian formalists and beyond—for the sake of argument, I will focus on the metafictional aspects at play in this genre and the narrative technique that speaks directly to the reflexivity active in the film.[5] One general working definition, taken by the Russian formalists, reads parody as "the commentary of one text on another, or on literature in general, within a single work, exposing the methods and processes of art while it makes use of them."[6] Margaret A. Rose argues that parody of the original or target text illumines the very means of critique the parody is making about the target text, "so that it is at once a fiction and a fiction about fictions."[7]

As a master parodist, Dunye also suggests that the use of the stereotype in a work of art or a text is complicated because the target text of parody, like the black stereotype, is often seductive. There is something about the original text, in its own terms, that attracts the parodist while at the same time wanting to destroy it. In the case of *The Watermelon Woman*, the target text is the Mammy stereotype—and by extension, its role in the American cinema. Dunye's manipulation of stereotypy and parody to (re-)create and posit a lesbian participation in American film history is revolutionary in its creation of the fictional character Fae Richards and the multiple frames of reference that spectators travel through in Cheryl's quest for a lesbian foremother. Dunye is part of a womanist tradition that employs the Mammy stereotype to reconstruct and recuperate black womanhood from the pervasiveness of the racial stereotype.[8]

The Watermelon Woman as a Black Womanist Recovery Project

Released by First Run Features and partially funded by the National Endowment for the Arts, *The Watermelon Woman* occupies a unique space in cinematic history, for it remains only one of a handful of feature-length films directed by a black lesbian to receive national distribution in the United States. The film's central narrative directly comments on the difficulty black lesbian directors have finding spaces for cinematic distribution, a serious indictment of American cinematic production practices. *The Watermelon Woman* is the story of Cheryl—a videographer, video store clerk, and aspiring filmmaker— and her first documentary film project on the actress Fae Richards (Lisa Marie Bronson), also known as the Watermelon Woman. The plot follows Cheryl's investigation into the life of Richards in archives and through interviews and Cheryl's personal life: her friendship with Tamara (Valarie Walker) and her romantic, interracial relationship with Diana (Guinevere Turner).

In the first talking-head address of the film, Cheryl explains that in searching for a topic for her film project, she discovered the black-and-white film *Plantation Memories*. She shows us a scene from the film, which is a parody

10.1 Cheryl Dunye in *The Watermelon Woman*, directed by Cheryl Dunye, 1996.

Dunye has created of the Hollywood plantation film popular in the 1930s and 1940s. For the character Cheryl, the budding filmmaker, the beauty of the Mammy figure in *Plantation Memories* becomes the impetus behind her project. The Mammy character, named Elsie in the fictional film within the diegesis, catches Cheryl's attention as "the most beautiful Mammy she has ever seen." For Cheryl, Mammy Elsie is sexy and "has it going on." Elsie's sexual desirability inspires Cheryl to investigate the life of the actress who plays Elsie, simply named the Watermelon Woman in the film's credits. By employing a mixture of cinematic methodologies and approaches, including stereotypy, parody, metafiction, reflexivity, and documentary strategies, Dunye advocates for the representation and, if necessary, the invention of narratives that reflect black lesbian participation in American cultural production.

The multiple levels of reflexivity and parody within the film provide Dunye with the authorial voice to critique the erasure of black women's presence in twentieth-century cinematic history in the United States. Indeed there are multiple levels both within and outside the diegetic frames that comment on and about one another. For instance, there are two distinct representations of Cheryl Dunye: we have Dunye, the director of *The Watermelon Woman*, and we have Cheryl, the protagonist who works in a video store, who is a videographer and "wants to be a filmmaker." Here Dunye is able to reference herself as an auteur through the character of Cheryl while simultaneously revealing her own approaches and cinematic practices operative in the film. The action of the film transpires in two distinct frames: the diegetic frame shot in 16mm film in which all the actions and other frames of *The Watermelon Woman* take place and the video documentary Cheryl shoots as an amateur filmmaker. The fact that the viewing audience is unaware that *The Watermelon Woman* is a mockumentary is part of Dunye's cinematic genius as a master parodist.

In a parody of the documentary form, the subject of the mockumentary provides spectators with a critique of the sociocultural world around them. The mockumentary employs a hybrid of aesthetic devices directly derived from the documentary, including interviews, hand-held video, and archival documents such as pictures, maps, and cinematic footage. In order for mockumentaries to function as a parody of the real, this "hybridity [of devices] depends upon indexical icons, re-creations that bear close, motivated resemblances to the real and to representations of the real."[9] Reflexivity in the mockumentary has as its referent the documentary itself, so that the form of the mockumentary is already (before the subject of the mockumentary is introduced) reflexive. Furthermore, in the case of *The Watermelon Woman*, the mockumentary frame creates and archives the construction of black lesbian subjectivity. As Ann Cvetkovich explains, "One of the ways that documentary film and video expands the archive is by documenting the archive itself."[10] In Dunye's use of reflexivity, the narrative structure and media technologies at play in the film work in harmony to constitute an authorship that is both black and lesbian and a film that at once celebrates and mocks the womanist recovery project.

Alice Walker's *In Search of Our Mothers' Gardens* (1983) is the ur-text of the womanist recovery projects, and Dunye uses humor to parody the relationships between mothers and daughters. The difficulty in finding African American women role models is more complicated than just asserting their nonexistence. Rather, argues Walker, black women artists have always been present as mothers, sisters, grandmothers, and aunts. Hindered by poverty, sexism, and racism, African American women found alternative ways to express their creativity, most notably in the tending of their gardens and the stories shared and passed down through the generations. Yet instead of searching through her mother's "garden" to find information about Fae Richards, Cheryl is left to sift through her mother's junk-ridden basement in the urban space of Winfield, Pennsylvania. Filled with old papers, costumes, records, the remains of her dead grandparents' collection of things, the basement is in disarray. Frustrated and in a state of confusion, Cheryl is unable to find anything of specific use and humorously remarks that her mother is "a collector of sorts." In contrast to Walker's organic garden, interior chaos defines Edith Irene Dunye's space; the basement is crowded and lifeless, filled with inanimate objects, whereas Walker's idea of women's storytelling and artistic beauty passed down by the generations has an aliveness. The potential for the garden to be socially reproductive is replaced in this basement model, where materials are discarded and forgotten, tucked away from vision. Though Cheryl tries to invoke Walker's narrative of womanist communication between mother and daughter, Dunye instead opts for a humorous exchange between Edith Irene and Cheryl that forecloses such romanticized narratives of matrilineal piety.

Spectators witness video footage of Cheryl's mother fixing her hair and putting on her earrings and the microphone before the interview. She asks, "How do I look, Cheryl?" Slightly impatient, Cheryl replies, "Fine," and starts the interview, reminding her mother to just be herself. Then the caption "Edith Irene Dunye, Cheryl's Mother" pops up on the bottom of the screen. Cheryl is behind the camera for the duration of the scene; we only hear her voice as she prompts her mother with questions about the Watermelon Woman. Edith Irene does not quite know what Cheryl is talking about, so Cheryl becomes more impatient. Scolding, Edith Irene reminds Cheryl, "You don't talk to your mother that way!" Apologizing, Cheryl takes another approach with the interview and asks about her moviegoing in the 1930s and 1940s. Though this scene may seem inconsequential, the behind-the-scene view of the interview (the putting on of the earrings and microphone) makes readily available for the viewers an up-close and personal example of mother-daughter interaction. When asked about the Watermelon Woman, Edith Irene has no idea what her daughter is referring to, which, unlike the mothers and grandmothers in *In Search of Our Mothers' Gardens*, speaks to the lack of language that essentially exists between the two women. Just prior to this interview scene, Cheryl is seen searching through the basement and speaking with her mother outside the frame, to which her mother responds, "You never listen to me!" This disconnect is an ironic play on Walker's womanist philosophies. Rather than seamlessly passing down stories generationally from mother to daughter, Edith Irene and Cheryl seem to have communication problems, foreclosing the social reproductivity that such an inheritance would proffer.

After some time Cheryl offers some redirection and shows Edith Irene the film box for a film called *Jersey Girl*, directed by Martha Page (Alexandra Juhasz), in which the Watermelon Woman has a part. This is another

Dunye faux film within the diegesis, though not shown in the interview but conveyed through Cheryl's voice-over. Edith Irene tells Cheryl she never saw the Watermelon Woman but does recognize her as one of the club performers from that era. Though there is clearly love and affection between them, Edith Irene and Cheryl still struggle to communicate with one another, first because Edith Irene doesn't have the answers Cheryl is looking for, and second, Cheryl is not asking the right questions or listening to her mother's answers. Eventually Edith Irene's account of her own life and friendships provides Cheryl with crucial information; Edith Irene introduces Cheryl to her friend Shirley, who in turn alerts Cheryl to the fact that Fae Richards was a lesbian. Dunye represents their mother-daughter relationship as a fraught, comic exchange characterized by misunderstanding and frustration, yet Cheryl and Edith Irene reinforce Walker's claims about the power of Black women sharing stories cross-generationally.

Despite Dunye's parody of Walker's recovery project, Dunye is still invested in "the (lesbian) family" and in recovering the story of Fae Richards as representative of a part of American cinematic tradition in which black lesbians are absent. At the conclusion of the film, June Walker (Cheryl Clarke), Fae's partner of more than twenty years, urges Cheryl to tell Fae's story. In a direct-address shot, Cheryl sums up her search for Fae by reading the letter June wrote before she went into the hospital. As June tells the story, it "troubled [Fae's] soul" to play mammies and domestic help in her career, but June reminds Cheryl that Fae "paved the road" for people like Cheryl to make films. The letter entreats, "Please Cheryl, make our history before we are all dead and gone," emphasizing Cheryl's role as part of Fae's history as a documentary filmmaker. Here June legitimizes Cheryl's claim to this black genealogy in which Fae is the progenitor, as well as the other black women who have helped Cheryl on this journey. But this journey, as well as this matriarchal line, is a black lesbian genealogy, for as June tells Cheryl, "If you are really in the family, you know we only have each other." Here "the family" has a double valence, as part of the gay community as well as part of a community of black women entertainers, historians, and archivists that have gone before her and "paved the way" for her own work as a black lesbian filmmaker. Like Walker's need for a matrilineal tradition in which to solidify her literary identification, Dunye creates a tradition based on Richards as a mother figure and cinematic ancestor with whom she can identify. At the film's conclusion, Cheryl sheds her hesitancy to call herself a filmmaker now that she has a predecessor with whom she can identify. This shift in subject

10.2 Fae Richards (Lisa Marie Bronson) as Mammy in *Plantation Memories* in *The Watermelon Woman*, directed by Cheryl Dunye, 1996.

position is the direct result of her identification with Richards, the "sexy" Mammy of the faux film within the diegetic *Plantation Memories*.

Queering *Plantation Memories*

In *Plantation Memories*, Dunye mocks the nostalgia for the Old South that proliferated in Hollywood films such as *Jezebel* (William Wyler, 1938) and *Gone with the Wind* (Victor Fleming, George Cukor, and Sam Wood, 1939) in 1930s and 1940s American cinema. During her first talking-head address to the camera, Cheryl explains her documentary project by introducing *Plantation Memories*. She turns the camera away from the seat that she was sitting on and focuses it on the television and VCR unit as it plays the ending scene of the film. In this scene we see the mistress of the plantation standing by a tree on a beautiful plot of land, distressed because her husband is leaving to fight in the Civil War. A thin and beautiful Mammy named Elsie rushes to her mistress and begins to comfort her, reassuring her that her husband "is comin' back . . . I just knows he is. . . . Don't cry, Miss." Elsie pulls a handkerchief from her pocket and gently wipes the tears from her mistress's eyes. At the end of the scene Elsie puts her hands on her mistress's shoulders, and blackout. Cheryl turns the camera away from the television and VCR and comes back to talk once again in direct address.

The Mammy in *Plantation Memories* differs from the traditional Old South stereotype. This Mammy is young and attractive and has a name other than Mammy. The mistress calls her Elsie,[11] and her proximity to her mistress in age and beauty, as well as her proximity to her mistress in the shot, suggests a level of intimacy that is far more sexually evocative than traditional renderings of Mammy. Elsie gently wipes her mistress's eyes, and Elsie's sex is not hidden under a large skirt; rather we see a small waist slightly emphasized by the tie of her apron strings. The intimacy suggested between the two women might even highlight the potential for a sexual relationship with the husband's absence (foreshadowing Richards's sexual relationship with the faux film's white director, Martha Page, as well as Cheryl's relationship with Diana). Dunye departs from the traditional reading of Mammy in another way: in placing the Mammy stereotype at the foundation of her cinematic matrilineage, Dunye reinstates Mammy's sexuality through Elsie, and through Elsie we have the potential "mother" of black lesbian cinema.

Dunye frustrates the reading of this Mammy as asexual and disengaged from her own progeny in service to her master's children, allowing for Cheryl's identification with Richards. She "has it going on," and the sexual attraction Cheryl has for Richards's Mammy becomes complicated as Cheryl's quest for identification with a potential black lesbian predecessor. So, on the one hand, just as Walker's search for Zora Neale Hurston leads her to a literary predecessor to whom she can lay claim, Dunye finds a mother figure and potential lover in Richards. The sexual attraction Cheryl feels toward Richards foreshadows Richards's own lesbian identity, in which Dunye can also identify. In psychoanalytical terms, Mark Winokur argues that this tension between the sexual attraction to Richards's Mammy and the desire for a mother figure with whom to identify is a direct representation of the "negative Oedipal stage in which both identification with and desire for the body of the black lesbian mother" occurs.[12] The historical import of this identification is multidimensional: Mammy is no longer relegated to stereotypes that would see her as asexual; to the contrary, the Mammy of Dunye's making is young, beautiful, and sexually desirable, with the potential for reproductive agency and the opportunity to be maternal to her own progeny. This move away from traditional representations of Mammy opens up the horizon for Cheryl's attraction and subsequent identification with Richards. Additionally Cheryl's identification with Richards affords her a model and cinematic predecessor for her own quest as a budding filmmaker.

Dunye's parodic direct address both celebrates and mocks readings of Mammy that would reduce the stereotype to tragedy. While clearly acknowledging the racism Mammy typifies in the American cultural imagination,

Dunye complicates how representations of Mammy are understood by way of Cheryl's imitation of Richards's Mammy. In another talking-head address for her video, Cheryl dons a handkerchief in the same style as Elsie, sits next to her VCR, and plays again the last scene from *Plantation Memories*, dramatically lip-syncing Elsie's speech, adding grotesque movements and facial expressions to mock the scene. Before the film ends, she takes off the handkerchief and shakes her head in disbelief. Clearly Cheryl recognizes and provokes engagement with the irony behind African American women resigned to playing stereotyped roles in American film; though she ridicules Richards's Mammy, she also distances herself from the action of *Plantation Memories*. Dunye plays with this scene, highlighting the ambivalence that stereotypy brings; by placing herself in close proximity to the action of the faux film, Cheryl is identifying with Richards's Mammy role while her gestures mark a level of misidentification, or at the very least a stance that is critical of this identification. This ambivalence is part and parcel of parody's character as an imitation of the model it seeks to critique. The ambivalence here is tracked by Cheryl's own behavior and marks a subversive move on Dunye's part. This is a prime example of parody's reflexivity as a discursive force in challenging cultural norms. On the other hand, Dunye manipulates the Mammy stereotype as a means to create Richards, recuperating agency from the Mammy stereotype. However, Dunye the parodist takes this ironic, comic scene one step further by commenting on the intellectual absurdity that recuperative readings of Mammy could entail, thus collapsing the very recuperative model she posits.

Later in the film Cheryl shows photographs of famous black women in cinema and entertainment, including Hattie McDaniel and Ella Fitzgerald. Interlaced in these pictures are photos of Richards playing domestic help from various films.[13] What is significant here is the fact that Cheryl/Dunye has chosen to take a moment to record on video a photo archive inserting the Watermelon Woman as a means of also inserting a black lesbian presence within the context of real black women made famous in film and entertainment. This presencing is achieved by including not only pictures of Richards in the series; Cheryl's face is also included as she holds up the photos for the camera. She shows the pictures as if to say she holds the key to this past and these women. By placing herself within this frame she is also placing herself within a film tradition.

In Swarthmore, Pennsylvania, Cheryl conducts a talking-head interview with the cultural theorist and iconoclast Camille Paglia, who plays this scene

10.3 Dunye's direct-address parody in *Plantation Memories* in *The Watermelon Woman*, directed by Cheryl Dunye, 1996.

as a parody of herself. Consistent with her criticism of second and later third wave feminism, Paglia made her reputation by making assertions against feminists and the white middle class.[14] So when she renders her reading of the watermelon as representative of African American culture, the irony continues. Linking it to her own Italian heritage, Paglia makes fun of herself before the camera as she claims that images of little black children eating watermelon is a site and sight of pleasure and joy. Her public persona as an iconoclast fits neatly with the parody that Dunye insists upon in *The Watermelon Woman*. When addressing the Mammy stereotype, Paglia compares the strength and sass of Mammy, "a great favorite of [hers]," to her own Italian mothers and grandmothers. For Paglia, Mammy in her largess represents "abundance and fertility, a goddess-like figure," and she takes to task African American critics for reading representations of Mammy as "desexualizing, degrading, or dehumanizing." Paglia even goes so far as to claim, "My Italian grandmother is the spitting image of Hattie McDaniel in style, in attitude, in ferocity." Dunye manipulates Paglia's cultural cachet and status as a famous intellectual to parody readings of Mammy that emphasize the power of black motherhood in the Mammy myth by reinstating Mammy's sexuality and ability to have a productive relationship with her own progeny. Paglia's interpretation of Mammy's significance in American culture invigorates Dunye's own reading of the Mammy as sexual, yet Paglia's ridiculous comparison of the Mammy to an Italian tradition of womanhood displaces the significance of the racist narrative inherent in the racial stereotype. Dunye's employment of stereotypy both ridicules and disavows readings of the Mammy as sexual and motherly and, by doing so, complicates both narratives of negativity and recuperation.

Journeying the Archives

The scene with Paglia brings to bear another of the framing devices in *The Watermelon Woman*: the scenario. In her book *The Archive and the Repertoire*, Diana Taylor eloquently maps out the relationship between performance epistemologies and cultural memory by means of the scenario, "a paradigm for understanding social structures and behaviors." Taylor sees an interconnectedness between the archive and the repertoire, one that allows for a dynamic system of knowing and the transmission of knowledge about the past. Archival memory represents embodied but stable material knowledge (photographs, documents, texts, maps, etc.), while the repertoire represents the enactment of embodied knowledge (plays, songs, verbal and nonverbal practices and performances) that "requires presence: people participate in the production and reproduction of knowledge by 'being there,' by being part of the transmission."[15] Both the archive and the repertoire require physical mediation in order for the transmission(s) of knowledge to occur. By filming the journey through various archives that Cheryl and Tamara encounter, a system of scenarios are created that enact the black womanist project. It is this creation of scenarios that allows for the development and creation of a cultural memory of and for black lesbians in the American cinema.

In the film, both formal and informal archives are abundant. In looking through her mother's basement, Cheryl realizes that though her mother is "a collector of sorts," her basement archive has no rhyme or reason. Indirectly Cheryl's mother gives her a clue as to how to build an archive; the basement represents a space of collection gone past the point of manageability and reconcilability. As Cheryl begins her journey in search of Richards, she finds examples of the trappings and potential pitfalls of archive building. One clear danger is allowing the archival impulse to lead the researcher astray in the collection of materials without setting up a system of referents and classification. With a hunch and her mother's help, Cheryl digs through her mother's things and finds the contact information for her mother's former friend Shirley Hamilton, a lesbian who explains that Richards was a "Sapphic sister."

In another comic scene, Cheryl and Tamara visit Germantown and the home of a collector of black cinema memorabilia, Lee Edwards (Brian Freeman), a self-proclaimed collector, exhibitor, and lecturer of race films from 1915 to 1950. Clearly more orderly in nature than Cheryl, Tamara records on video their journey through Edwards's house. In his cinema archive, Tamara and Cheryl learn about the vibrant nightlife in Philadelphia in the 1920s and 1930s, well into the Great Depression. They learn that early theaters and clubs, such as the "Dunbar, Standard, and Royal," were black-owned and -operated. In these locales African Americans enjoyed leisure in an open public space. In *Migrating to the Movies*, Jacqueline Stewart explains, "African Americans used the cinema as a literal and symbolic space in which to rebuild their individual and collective identities in a modern, urban environment."[16] This explains why this section of the film is so crucial. Understanding the cultural history of the cinema in African Americans' lives during this time period connects Cheryl's project to a larger narrative of community building. As her mother articulated earlier, she and her friends went to the movies and clubs often during the 1930s and 1940s. Dunye includes this history in telling the story of Fae Richards; specifically, in the scene following the meeting with Edwards, we see footage of the Standard in urban decline along what was once a vibrant avenue. Juxtaposed against the footage of dilapidated buildings and boarded-up storefronts are black-and-white photos depicting black urban modernity in its heyday. Dunye the director interlaces shots of these photos with a voice-over by Edwards. Shot in video, this montage suggests that Cheryl is constructing it as part of her project; however, it is Dunye the director who is masterfully directing the documentary to create and support a narrative of black lesbian participation in film (i.e., through Cheryl).

This archive gives a spatiotemporal component to Cheryl's project by providing the milieu and time period of Richards's career that Cheryl was unaware of prior to visiting the collection. Thus the periodization of Philadelphia's pulsating nightlife and commerce proffers the collection an authenticity and legitimacy, but only so far as the collection says more about the collector than it reveals a narrative of history. This becomes central to understanding the idiosyncratic behavior of the collector. Though he serves as a curator to his collection, it is clear that he has a specific organizing principle for the collection that speaks directly to his own tastes and tendencies. For instance, Tamara senses early on that Edwards is not necessarily woman-friendly, as he himself describes women as "not his specialty." Edwards is drawn to the black female bodies on movie posters of the 1930s and 1940s only as decorative display items in his collection.

The third archive Cheryl and Tamara visit is the Philadelphia Public Library, the most formal and traditional archive they explore. With a jazz soundscape, Cheryl searches through the "black" section of the library. The formality of the library is expressed through the reference desk librarian (David Rakoff), whom Cheryl asks under what section she might find the Watermelon Woman. Impatiently the librarian suggests that they look in the "black" section. Having already searched the stacks, Cheryl insists that he search his database, which he does begrudgingly. Unsurprisingly he finds only Martha Page, Richards's lover and the director of several Watermelon Woman films. Page is in the "woman in film" section, though the Watermelon Woman is not. Her absence in both sections speaks directly to the exclusion of black lesbians in film and black studies. Moreover, if we read the librarian as part of the "space of governmental power and where things commence," then the Watermelon Woman fails to be socially constituted for lack of name recognition. When the librarian calls up her name on the computer database, this interpellation does not successfully occur. Fae Richards does not exist in this archive because she has not been properly named in an Althusserian sense.[17] It is no wonder, then, that Cheryl has difficulty locating the Watermelon Woman by these formal channels of information flow.

The most useful archive Cheryl encounters is the Center for Lesbian Technologies (CLIT). This scene is a major source of comic irony and parody in its representation of white (second wave) feminist archives. On the recommendation of Annie, her coworker at the video store, Cheryl travels to New York City to explore a feminist volunteer-run archive. Here Dunye is parodying as the target text the famous Lesbian Herstory Archive (LHA), founded in New York in 1974.[18] CLIT, like LHA, is a communal archive funded by donations and run by volunteers. The humor of this scene runs rampant throughout. The acronym CLIT, short for clitoris, already positions the scene as satiric parody. The archivist M.J. (Sarah Schulman) is a nervous woman who seems to have had too much coffee to drink. According to M.J. the black lesbian section was funded by a "hysteria grant," and so the collective took all the pictures with black people in them and crossed out any white faces also in the photograph. Though ironic, the point is well taken: black lesbian history can often be oversimplified or even absented in feminist archives. Though the word *technologies* appears in the name of the archive, there is no technology functioning in either of the ordering systems. Part of this may be because the technology from the archive is missing. The collective has put all the material in boxes, hoping that volunteers will one day sort and index them. Despite the "box system," Cheryl finds pictures of Richards and has Annie record them on the video camera. However, M.J. insists that copying and recording information is against archive rules; in order for them to have access, they must have consensus from the collective, which meets once a month. The irony here is that the collective exists on one level to disseminate information but becomes bogged down by the politics of the very collective that runs the organization. Cheryl decides to copy the pictures anyway and leaves the archive with the information she sought. On the backs of the photos are inscriptions, dates, and signatures—valuable information for Cheryl's journey. The irony is that, although the archive is called the Center for Lesbian Information Technologies, the use of any technology to record elements of the archive is prohibited.

Despite the humor of the trip to CLIT, Cheryl is able to locate June Walker,[19] Richards's African American partner of more than twenty years. A professional photograph of Richards, sold in a nightclub in which she performed, was signed "to June Walker." At CLIT items that seem unimportant or insignificant are housed as a way to document gay and lesbian experience. Cvetkovich addresses the information that these informal lesbian archives offer as archives of feeling: "The archive of feeling is both material and immaterial, at once incorporating objects that might not be considered archival, and at the same time, resisting documentation because sex and feelings are too personal or ephemeral to leave records. For this reason and others, the archive of feelings lives not just in museums, libraries, and other institutions but in more personal and intimate spaces, and significantly, also within cultural genres."[20] CLIT, like the LHA, is a space of intimacy and takes donations from individuals who believe their items are important in documenting personal experience(s) as gay and lesbian subjects. Although Cheryl has no official record of who donated the items that deal directly with Richards, as the items are donated anonymously, she finds Walker's telephone number and makes contact with her.

Conclusion

Film spectators learn that Fae Richards is merely another fictional character in *The Watermelon Woman* during the sequence when the documentary is revealed. Interlaced in the narrative of Cheryl's documentary are the credits and production values of *The Watermelon Woman*, instantly marking it as a mockumentary, a fact unknown to the film audience until these closing credits. With the knowledge that Richards is a construction, the film audience is left to ponder what they just witnessed, as if to figure out what was true and what was not. According to Dunye, "Narrative is as true as we want it to be. We believe in narrative as truth."[21] So the question becomes not "What does it mean that Fae is a fictional character?" but rather "How is meaning created in the film?"

Dunye employs parodic reflexivity to state her case for black lesbian womanhood on and off the silver screen. This is not to say that Dunye or Cheryl ever becomes a unified subject called "author"; rather Dunye's employment of parody celebrates and enhances the multiple levels of authorship at play in *The Watermelon Woman*. Parodic reflexivity is a decisive tool that comments on target texts and practices such as stereotypy while offering a critique on the sociocultural landscape that creates, circulates, and reifies such images. There is also a Hegelian overcoming: Cheryl is now a filmmaker, but by her own admission she still has a long way to go, marking the ongoing process that being a filmmaker necessitates.

Notes

1 Though there are examples of characters in pre–Civil War American literature who are slave women who take care of the master's children, the Mammy stereotype we have come to know finds its antecedents in post–Civil War performance and consumer culture. Kenneth Goings, *Mammy and Uncle Mose: Black Collectibles and American Stereotyping* (Bloomington: Indiana University Press, 1994), 64; Kimberly Wallace-Sanders, *Mammy: A Century of Race, Gender, and Southern Memory* (Ann Arbor: University of Michigan Press, 2008), 3. For an extended discussion of literature depicting black nurses and nannies before the Civil War, see Wallace-Sanders, *Mammy: A Century of Race*, 16–31.

2 Wallace-Sanders, *Mammy: A Century of Race*, 2.

3 M. M. Manring, *Slave in a Box: The Strange Career of Aunt Jemima* (Charlottesville: University of Virginia Press, 1998), 23.

4 African American male artists are also part of this tradition of recovering black womanhood through the Mammy figure as an act of recovery. For example, see Murray N. DePillars's pen, Conté crayon, and ink drawing *Aunt Jemima* (1968).

5 However, it is important to note that not every metafiction is a parody. See Margaret A. Rose, *Parody: Ancient, Modern, and Post-Modern* (Cambridge: Cambridge University Press, 1993), 91–101, especially 93–94. I take the definitions from the Russian formalists because they afford readings of texts that focus on structural reflexivity. The double-coded characteristic of parody, the renovation of older forms into newer ones, can be attributed to the Russian formalists for laying bare the functions of each literary device.

6 Michele Hannoosh, "The Reflexive Function of Parody," *Comparative Literature* 41.2 (1989): 113, quoting Margaret A. Rose.

7 Simon Dentith, *Parody: The New Critical Idiom* (New York: Routledge, 2000), 13–14.

8 For my discussion of stereotypy and the womanist tradition of recovering Mammy through the work of the artist Betye Saar, visit the website www.sistersinthelife.com.

9 Steven N. Lipkin, Derek Paget, and Jane Roscoe, "Docudrama and Mock-Documentary: Defining Terms, Proposing Canons," in *Docufictions: Essays on the Intersection of Documentary and Fictional Filmmaking*, edited by Gary D. Rhodes and John Parris Springer (Jefferson, NC: McFarland, 2005), 23. I am using parody here as a type of narrative device that is active in the mockumentary and therefore activating the irony and satire working throughout the film. This narrative frame works in tandem with, say, Diana Taylor's scenario, which functions as the theoretical frame.

10 Ann Cvetkovich, *An Archive of Feelings: Trauma, Sexuality, and Lesbian Public Cultures* (Durham, NC: Duke University Press, 2003), 251.

11 Though the Mammy Elsie is given a name, in the credits for *Plantation Memories*, Fae Richards is listed only as the Watermelon Woman. This is certainly a moment of irony, for Mammy is given a name, but the actress playing Mammy is not.

12 Mark Winokur, "Body and Soul: Identifying with the Black Lesbian Body in Cheryl Dunye's *The Watermelon Woman*," in *Recovering the Black Female Body: Self-Representations by African-American Women*, edited by Michael Bennett and Vanessa D. Dickerson (New Brunswick, NJ: Rutgers University Press, 2001), 244–45.

13 Cheryl Dunye and Zoe Leonard, *The Fae Richards Photo Archive* (San Francisco: Artspace Books, 1996), 36. It is unclear if film spectators are expected to recognize these photos of the Watermelon Woman, nor is it clear that these photos are from fictitious films also created in service of the larger fiction of Fae Richards.

14 Within the scene the crosscut to three white, horrific-looking, anorexic women's studies students who have never heard of the Watermelon Woman Fae Richards illustrates an exaggeration and irony of Paglia's indictment of the white middle class.

15 Diana Taylor, *The Archive and the Repertoire: Performing Cultural Memory in the Americas* (Durham, NC: Duke University Press, 2003), 29, 33, 20.

16 Jacqueline Stewart, *Migrating to the Movies: Cinema and Black Urban Modernity* (Berkeley: University of California Press, 2005), 17.

17 Judith Butler, *Bodies That Matter: On the Discursive Limits of "Sex"* (New York: Routledge, 1993), 121–22.

18 For an in-depth discussion of the LHA archive in *The Watermelon Woman*, see Cvetkovich, *An Archive of Feelings*, 240–44.

19 This name is a possible reference to Alice Walker and June Jordan.

20 Cvetkovich, *An Archive of Feelings*, 244.

21 T. Haslett and N. Abiaka, interview with Cheryl Dunye for the Black Cultural Studies Web Site Collective, April 12, 1997, http://blackculturalstudies.net/dunye/dunye_intvw.html.

Coquie Hughes: Urban Lesbian Filmmaker
Introduction to Yvonne Welbon's Interview with Coquie Hughes

Toni Morrison purportedly began her career as a novelist because she noticed a dearth of books about black women. As a result of this limitation, Morrison desired to write books "for people like [her], which is to say black people, curious people, demanding people—people who can't be faked, people who don't need to be patronized."[1] Similarly the writer, director, and filmmaker Coquie Hughes (born Latasha Iva Hughes in Chicago in 1970) has produced narratives that feature an array of queer black women—"Girls Like Us" as she calls them in her web series—who are curious, demanding, flawed, and not "faked." Hughes has written and/or directed several feature-length films about contemporary black urban queer and lesbian life, making her part of the still small cadre of black woman filmmakers, writers, and producers (of whatever sexual orientation) working today.[2] Her IMDb profile, over a decade in existence, lists her as the writer, director, and/or producer of a number of films, including *The Lies We Tell but the Secrets We Keep* (2011), *My Mama Said Yo Mama's a Dyke* (2010), *If I Was Your Girl* (2012), and *Kuchi Costs Money and CoKane Keeps the Cable On* (2016).

Producer, writer, director, editor, teacher, and *mentor* are the words Hughes uses to describe her own cultural labor. After attending Xavier University in New Orleans and Columbia College in Chicago she became a playwright, activist, mother, and CEO of GirlCrushTv.com. Given her large audiences and movement from theater to screen, one could think of her as the Tyler Perry of black lesbian productions; however, she does not work in slapstick comedy and her actors are not from the star system. She works in a form she describes as urban lesbian filmmaking, and her actors are largely from her community.

While they both share an entrepreneurial spirit and passion for filmmaking, Tyler's rise to fame and control of resources have been "successful" and hers remain ascendant.

Hughes speaks of her background as a ward of the state in the Illinois foster care system, and of its impact on her creative focus. In an extended interview with Yvonne Welbon, she explains, "I would go into my own little creative world of making up stories about having a different life. I remember when I was in seventh grade I had created this incredible story that I was from Germany and that I had these parents that were like spies. It was ridiculous. But what I liked is that people believed me, and it was fascinating to keep this story going for my entire seventh grade school year. And even though people would say that I was a liar, I just thought I was being creative."[3]

Her life in Chicago influenced her aesthetic sensibility, which blends hip hop, popular culture, and social themes about domestic violence, queer love, church, and family relations. Her greatest influence was the unexpected death of her brother. She tells Welbon a compelling and revealing story about the impact of his death:

> At that time I was heavily involved in the church, and you know the church can be very close-minded. A lot of those thinkings were also inside of me as far as being very conservative and very close-minded. But a lot of things really changed about me when he died because I said, "I'm not going to live my life for no one else, cause you just never know." And my brother was twenty-five years old and he just went to sleep, didn't wake back up. So I just said that I'm just going to step out on faith and make my movies.

Hughes works in a post-deregulation era, where some of the most innovative and "daring" programming of "difference" emerges from Internet venues such as Netflix and Amazon. As Herman Gray notes, "Representations are more than free-floating signifiers cut loose from the social and historical moorings that make them intelligible in the first place. . . . Media representations continue to bear the traces of their productions and the historicity of their time and place."[4] To this end, Hughes founded the SeeTruePeace Entertainment Group as a means to oversee her various "subsidiaries." Like Oprah Winfrey with her Harpo Productions, Hughes desires to profit from her work even as she seeks to distribute it widely for pedagogical purposes. Although she has worked in many genres, she describes herself as now interested mostly in realism; certainly her work addresses actual situations that black women confront every day (sex, coming out, domestic violence, divorce, money problems, adolescence, and more).

Her body of work fits well under the rubric of New Queer Cinema or perhaps postindependent American film, which features contemporary stories that need not conform to "positive" images.[5] As such she can be read as an exemplar of the new creative culture industries.[6] "When I did *My Mama Said Yo Mama's a Dyke* I began to develop a style of being uninhibited, being audacious and raw and gritty and just true to life and real," recalls Hughes as she describes the birth of her signature urban lesbian filmmaking style. "I took it even further in *The Lies We Tell* with the conversations, the dialogue, the intimate scenes, the violence. I just went there and I think that is the reason why the urban community could relate. It was so relative to what they knew and it was relative to what I knew and what I saw and I wasn't afraid to expose it."

Most of her work appears in digital format that she, like many media makers of her generation, has chosen for its low cost, convenience, and immediacy. Despite having greater access to such means of technological production, Hughes continues to struggle with funding her work, but not with finding her audience. Her YouTube channel has over 57,000 subscribers and 8,790,203 views (as of August 2017). Her attempt to create a diversified brand that includes "subsidiaries" such as the now defunct GirlCrushTv has been only partially successful.

Following in the path of the director and writer Cheryl Dunye, Hughes initially relied on local friends and community members to help her make her work. She worked with nonprofessional actors and used local homes for her set. Thus her work reads as "realism" and features quotidian life and "everyday" people. The urban lesbian films that she presents are melodramatic sitcoms that tell local stories of interrelated community members. This commitment to a local urban lifestyle marks most of her films. For example, the screenplay *My Mama Said Yo Mamma's a Dyke*, which Hughes characterizes as an urban mockumentary, was written, produced, and directed after she conducted interviews with a number of lesbian mothers in Chicago. The plot hinges on a group of teens who become fed up with their lesbian moms and then decide to enlist them in an uncanny camp that specializes in "de-lesbianism." Although the project originally started off as a documentary in which the director interviewed various African American lesbian and bisexual moms along with their children, funding difficulties found Hughes deciding to make the story fictional instead. She devised scenarios from the interviews with African American youth from urban communities struggling with queer mothers. Unlike the Hollywood hit *The Kids Are All Right* (Lisa Cholodenko, 2010), which features white stars Annette Bening and Julianne Moore as chic L.A. lesbian moms, Hughes's characters have grit. Her film's mise-en-scène eschews the consumerist glamour as well as the "house and garden porn" featured in the Hollywood production and instead gives us a mash-up of production styles that are representative of urban lesbian filmmaking.

In Hughes's feature *Girls Like Us, Part I* (which remains unfinished) the main characters repeat the line "Real lesbians aren't tryin' to share their girl with another girl, let alone a nasty-ass man." The characters in this film skew along rather strict lines of butch and fem, the latter being those attracted to and interacting with men. This stereotype, despite the diversity of characters (most minor and sometimes not well drawn), reinforces types within groups of black lesbians and is a key component of the urban lesbian filmmaking genre. Another aspect of the style that is represented is the attempt to show how class connects and divides the characters (two are lawyers with their own homes; others share a house) and where "straight" and "lesbian" desires intersect.

In an advertisement for her digital filmmaking class, she develops an intriguing marketing tag: "The registration fee is 100% refundable upon successful completion of the class." All the films she has completed in the past decade she now distributes for free. It may be significant that Hughes decided to standardize the title for the web series from the film—from *If I Wuz Yo Gyrl* to *If I Was Your Girl* for the web series. One further critique of Hughes's work is the issue of determining the quality of so-called "amateur" versus professional productions. Hughes herself has commented in online interviews on the shift to "do it yourself" productions, saying that initially her work didn't look the way she wanted it to look but that now she has access to good equipment and so can have better production values.

Despite these struggles, Coquie Hughes can be credited for her industriousness, her vision, her vitality, and her verve. In her feature work, such as the challenging *If I Wuz Yo Gyrl* and *My Mama Said Yo Mama's a Dyke*, she makes space for new narratives to enter the world and addresses major issues in what too many see as "minor" lives: the lives of still overlooked and underfilmed black lesbian subjects. Hughes is managing to harness do-it-yourself industriousness through low-budget technology that gives her viewers direct access to her urban lesbian filmmaking. The question remains: How do we undo the perpetual cycles of minority representation that follow a capitalist logic of boom and bust? Is the current consumer's choice for "quality TV" a space where more black lesbian filmmakers and content can flourish?

Notes

1 Toni Morrison quoted in *Voices from the Gaps*, February 2007, 10, University of Minnesota Digital Conservancy, http://hdl.handle.net/11299/166281.

2 See also Claudia Springer, "Black Women Filmmakers," *Jump Cut: A Journal of Contemporary Media*, no. 29 (February 1984): 34–37.

3 Coquie Hughes, interview by Yvonne Welbon, July 27, 2012. Subsequent unattributed quotations of Coquie Hughes come from this interview. Read the full interview online at www.sistersincinema.com.

4 Herman Gray, "Where Have All the Black Shows Gone?," in *Black Cultural Traffic*, edited by Harry Elam and Kennell Jackson (Ann Arbor: University of Michigan Press, 2005), 333.

5 B. Ruby Rich, *New Queer Cinema: The Director's Cut* (Durham, NC: Duke University Press, 2013). Sadly, no black woman filmmaker is listed in the introduction.

6 Anne Balsamo, *Designing Culture: The Technological Imagination at Work* (Durham, NC: Duke University Press, 2011), 2.

Stepping Out on Faith
Interview with Coquie Hughes, July 27, 2012

Coming of Age

I grew up on the West Side of Chicago, where it was infested with gangs and drugs and violence. But I was always the type of person that wanted to be better than my environment, and I was also the type of person that didn't want people to underestimate me because of where I came from. And so I made up in my mind, even as a young child, that I wanted to be somebody.

I love making movies. I've wanted to be who I am ever since I saw Sidney Lumet's movie *The Wiz* (1978). When I saw the stage production of *The Wiz* when I was in fourth grade, I thought that was one of the most amazing things that I had ever seen in my entire life. I wanted to become the one that was behind it all.

I was raised by my aunt. She ended up getting custody of me and my brother because my mother at the time wasn't able to take care of me. So she was a single parent, who was a foster mother to me and my brother, doing the best that she could despite the problems that she was having.

I would go into my own little creative world of making up stories about having a different life. I remember when I was in seventh grade I had created this incredible story that I was from Germany and that I had these parents that were like spies. It was ridiculous. But what I liked is that people believed me, and it was fascinating to keep this story going for my entire seventh grade school year. And even though people would say that I was a liar, I just thought I was being creative.

I had a teacher who really took an effort in trying to pull that creativity out of me with writing short stories and plays and stuff. Unfortunately my aunt

12.1 Coquie Hughes in *My God Is Not a Bully,* 2013. The Church Within A Church Movement and E3 Radio.

wasn't as encouraging with me wanting to create stories. So when I wanted to go to a performing arts high school and I got accepted, she was like, "No you can't go there."

So I had to go to some neighborhood high school, and they really didn't have the activities that I desired. By this time I had excelled academically in school. I had a lot of conservative mentors in my life who felt that I needed to go into a field that was stable. I was being groomed to go into politics. I got a scholarship to go to college and I had an internship working for this judge. But I really wanted to go to, like, a creative school, like film school, like Columbia [College in Chicago]. I walked away from the opportunity. I think I did, like, two years in liberal arts college at Xavier, and then I transferred to Northern at DeKalb and I was a polysci, prelaw student. I didn't have to pay for college when I first went. But like I said, I really wanted to go to film school and tell stories and learn how to make movies and things of that nature. I walked away from that in hopes that I would get some money to go to Columbia. The scholarship programs were like, "Well, you either go to a school that's in the field that you're supposed to be in or we're not going to give you any money to go to Columbia." So I was like, "I'm going to Columbia."

Learning How to Make Movies

So I prayed and sacrificed and went to Columbia for a semester and couldn't afford it and dropped out. And then I learned that—I know this is kind of grammatically wrong—but I started learning myself how to make movies, and I started working with kids, and they were like my . . . students but I was learning as they were learning so they were my students, but they loved me so much they forgave a lot of my mistakes. And so I learned how to direct and how to make movies by working with inner-city kids that lived in the projects that my real mother lived in. And it was working with those kids that live in Rockwell Gardens Housing Project that really helped me develop my craft. I spent several years learning how to write and how to shoot and how to direct.

I didn't have any money and so I learned a lot of the stuff that I know by just doing it. I was blessed to get a job back in '98 working for the Chicago Park District as a drama instructor, and so I had access to produce community theater, because in the years before, in the early '90s, I worked with kids to learn how to put on plays, and then I would up my game and I started putting the plays on at church, and they started getting recognized by people who were in influential positions, and so I was offered a job opportunity to teach theater.

Teach theater! Now mind you, I had no degree in theater. My productions were engaging enough or compelling enough that these influential people thought that, you know, I could teach. And so I had access to have a facility to put on my shows. So I would raise money through my plays and buy equipment and stuff and I would read the tutorial. So I taught myself Final Cut Pro and taught myself Premiere. I really don't want to sound braggadocious either. I think because I walk into a situation and I command what I'm looking for it makes me seem like I know what I'm doing when really I don't have a clue. So people tend to give me opportunities to do things because they think I know what I'm doing. Hence, it's how I learned how to direct. I'm so commanding in what I'm saying, they just take me at my word and be like, "Okay, she knows what she's talking about," when really I don't know what the fuck I'm doing [laughs]. Well, back then. I don't know what I'm doing. I'm sorry for cussing.

Deciding to Become a Filmmaker

It was when my brother died. His name was Laurie Lashawn Hughes. He was named after his doctor, you know, the birth doctor. He was twenty-five. He was a writer and he was also a copycat. He was always trying to do everything that I did. He was a year and two months younger than me. He wanted to become a writer and he moved out to LA. And wow, he was twenty-five years old, and he just died of natural causes in his sleep. At the time I wasn't really working in film. When he died it was like this moment in my life that I said, "Okay, I'm going to live one time, have my life one time, and so I might as well do it doing what I love to do." And I really wanted to make movies and so I was like, you know, "I'm just gonna do it."

And I mean, like, make real movies, not working with little kids and stuff like that. At that time I was heavily involved in the church, and you know the church can be very close-minded. A lot of those thinkings were also inside of me as far as being very conservative and very close-minded. But a lot of things really changed about me when he died because I said, "I'm not going to live my life for no one else 'cause you just never know." And my brother was twenty-five years old and he just went to sleep, didn't wake back up. So I just said that I'm just going to step out on faith and make my movies.

I had wrote this screenplay called *Sunday after Church*. My brother he had died in August of '97. I think I wrote the screenplay in September '97 and tried to make it in October. Didn't have the money, so one of my friends invited me to go to the boat [casino] with him, and I had won like $500. I used that money to try and make my first film, *Sunday after Church*. I never finished it, but I tried. I did get a trailer out of it.

Coming Out

I'm very rooted in my faith. I like to incorporate films that deal with having faith in God and have perseverance and being able to overcome, you know, struggles.

I was a lesbian for quite some time and I really wanted to come out, but because I was heavily involved in a very close-minded church, I was very afraid of the repercussions. And so I would cloud it with making these Christian films and, you know, try to, you know, hint at it.

Back in 2001, I was involved in a relationship with this woman—actually she was my first—and when she broke up with me she ended up going with this other woman who was very abusive.

I tend to, when I really want to express myself, do it in either a play or do it in a movie without having to necessarily say it with my words. And so I wanted it to be about domestic violence in same-sex relationships and at the time I had just finished a very powerful urban Christian film that the church was really advocating and telling other people about. But I knew what was going on personally in my life with my friend. Even though she broke up with me, she was still my friend and I still cared about her. I hated that she was experiencing what she was experiencing. So I wanted to also come out too.

So I made this work-in-progress version of *If I Was Your Girl* back in 2001 about domestic violence in same-sex couples. It was when I decided to come out as well.

Film Themes

I'm actually very selfish with the type of films that I like to make. I like to make films that I want to see. I mean my thing is there are 7 billion people in the world and I can't make a film for 7 billion people, but I can make a film for me. So I just make films that I want to see and hopefully there are others who want to see it as well.

I like violent movies. I like very raw and gritty movies. I like directors like David Fincher. He did *Fight Club* (1999). You know if white people can do it with money, why can't I make films like that? I love Quentin Tarantino and Robert Rodriguez and so I like those kinds of films. And I make those kinds of films because I find them quite entertaining. Not saying that it's my life, you know, but I have also been told that a lot of my films tend to have, like, this grittiness to it. But it'll have humor in it and I like that I do that.

Some of the films that I've made . . . My first film was *Gotta Git My Hair Did* (2000). The second film was *Hell's Most Wanted* (2001). The third film was *If I Wuz Yo Girl* (2002), the work-in-progress version. . . . The fourth film was *Did I Just Look at Her* (2004). It was a lesbian short film. And I think that was the first film that had got me attention from industry folks. And that was pretty cool, being able to have a film in film festivals and stuff. Even though *If I Wuz Yo Girl*, the work in progress, was in a film festival. Then I made a movie called *Daughters of the Concrete* (2004).

Having Children

I had made up in my mind a long time ago. When I say long time ago, I mean like maybe ten or fifteen years ago. I said, "I don't care what is going on in my life, I'm going to have kids at thirty-five years old. I'm going to have two kids, a boy and a girl, and I'm going to be pregnant and have them." And so in 2005 I stopped making movies. I took a four-year break and I started working on my family 'cause I knew I was going to be thirty-five years old in November. So the beginning part of 2005 I started, you know, getting myself stable so that I could have a baby, and so I did.

In the summer of 2005 I did some research about a sperm bank, went online, ordered the sperm, took the sperm home, and inseminated it and got pregnant on the first try with my first baby, a little girl. I did it in November, which is my birthday, and had her in August of 2006. And then on her birthday, when she turned one, 'cause when I was pregnant with her I said, "Okay, when this baby turn one years old in 2007 of August, I'm going to get pregnant and have another baby, I'm going to have a little boy," so that's what I did. I ordered the sperm, brought it home, inseminated, got pregnant on the first try with him, and he was born in 2008. So I took a four-year break from 2005 to 2009 to have kids.

Filmmaking Sabbatical

I taught inner-city kids how to make movies because I had learned how to make movies, you know, in an unconventional, guerrilla-type way, and the way that I learned it, it warranted an awesome lesson plan that was great for inner-city kids. Organizations and funders, they liked the vision that I had. It was something to spend money on and get kids off the street, and so they were throwing money at me to teach kids how to make movies.

I wanted to become what I was looking for, and so I had always had an affinity for disadvantaged youth and youth who were, you know, underestimated because I was one of those youths. I knew that there may be some individuals who had stories to tell, some young people that had stories to tell, like I did. I didn't have anyone to serve as a mentor because a lot of stuff that I learned I literally learned on my own. But basically I just woke up one day and I said, "I want to become what I'm looking for . . . teach media arts education."

There was a lady at the church. She was really good at getting money for nonprofits. So I just went to her and I said, "Look, I have this idea." I was very good at writing proposals and stuff like that, or just writing period. So I wrote this proposal and she loved it and she was very impressed with it, and she was like, "I can get you some money," and I was like, "Okay, cool. That's why I came to you." And so she was able to get $32,000 for me to teach the community.

Now at the time it wasn't for youth. It was to teach the community how to make a movie in ten weeks. The students would come twice a week and they would come for . . . I think they would come for, I think it was four hours. We bought all the equipment and everything, and it was a successful program. It was initially called the Urban Strive Filmmakers. But then it ended up being some, some impropriety with that woman. Her and I had a falling-out as it relates to the funding and I was like, "Bump this." And so anyway a week after the program had ended and, you know, her and I had a disagreement about the funding to continue an additional ten weeks. I was like, "Know what, I'm just going to just teach kids." Because initially I was teaching adults.

And so I had went to this poetry set that Pow Wow had and there was a lady there who worked with this organization called After School Matters.[1]

Let me just say this: I'm a faith walker and I truly believe that what you are seeking is also seeking you. So anyway, I went to this event and she got up on the microphone to make an announcement: "Anybody that's a artist that likes kids, we have some money to pay you and the kids to do a program." I was like, "What?" That was Jacinta Terry. May she rest in peace. She died a couple years ago. She was the one. That spiraled to working with other community-based organizations like Girls in the Game and the Chicago Park District because my curriculum became so popular because it was specifically designed for disenfranchised youth, at-risk kids, and it was very successful. Maggie Daley would invite me to come and speak at some of her board meetings to some of her funders to highlight some of the successes of the After School Matters. Maggie Daley, by the way, was Mayor Richard M. Daley's wife—she passed too.

Returning to Filmmaking

From November 2010 until right now, July 27, 2012—would you say that's a year and a half or two years?—I've made four feature films. Three of them were lesbian-themed, which is exciting. I make movies like you change underwear. Every time you turn around I'm making another movie.

So anyway, I was talking to this girl, I really liked her, I thought we were going to be together forever and ever and she was going to have two more babies for me too. But then, she didn't like me. And she dumped me. And I was sad and I didn't want to be depressed, you know, especially for my kids' sake. So I said, "I'm going to make a movie. I'm going to make a mockumentary of *My Mama Said Yo Mama's a Dyke* to make myself laugh and be distracted."

When I was working on it there was this young lady named Milan Parker. She had approached me about some book she had wrote and she was like, "Um, when we finish working on this film"—'cause she was an actress in *My Mama Said Yo Mama's a Dyke*—"could you take a look at my book?" So I was like, "Yeah, yeah, yeah, yeah, yeah." Because I also have a short attention span. One project at a time. So I was like, "Yeah, I'll deal with it when I get done." But I was serious. I really was going to pay attention to her when I was done. And sure enough, when I finished *My Mama Said Yo Mama's a Dyke* thing, I said, "Okay. Let me read your book."

She sent me her book, and it was a really interesting story. It needed a lot of work. But, hey, I was at a time in my life where I just wanted to be busy because I didn't want to be sad. Like I say, I'm the type of person that I like to become what I'm looking for. So I always wanted someone to unequivocally, undeniably, unapologetically believe in me and come at me 100 percent and help me with my moviemaking business. So, I said, okay, I'm going to help this kid out with her piece. So I was like, "Okay, I want you to write the screenplay." I wanted to see how serious she was because I really didn't want to waste my time with somebody. Making movies is more than a notion. I had written the first four pages and told her, "Okay, you write the rest." So she had started on it. She didn't know what she needed to do. So, I was like, "Okay, I'm going to write the script." So I wrote the script, and of course her and I collaborated, because even though she wasn't a writer, she was a great storyteller.

Milan knew what kind of story she wanted to tell, and I knew how to execute it. So her and I collaborated and we created this amazing urban film called *The Lies We Tell but the Secrets We Keep*, and it was based on her book and also of course based on ideas that I contributed to the screenplay. It triggered an enormous wave of support, especially here in Chicago. It was such a collaborative effort of the actors and the crew that worked on it, because everybody did it for nothing. They did it free, including myself, because as I said I wanted somebody to unapologetically give me the attention that I was giving to this person. It's all about energy with me.

Challenges and Staying Focused

There was so much personally going on in my life. I was having personal conflicts with Milan. But I was committed to the project and I wanted to see it to the end. So I cowrote it, at times I shot it, I directed it, I edited, everything.

I got evicted. It goes back to my brother. You know, you only live once—especially now that I have children. I'm motivated by people that underestimate me. I don't ever want my children to think that their mother gives up. I don't give up. Hence sometimes it takes a lot of perseverance and a lot of sacrifice.

Now even though we got evicted, you know, the Lord took care of us. My landlord, he was so cool he asked for my autograph when he was evicting me. He said, "I don't know why you're doing this 'cause this doesn't seem to work for you." But, he said, "I admire your perseverance. Let me get your autograph, so when you do make it, I can be like, 'Yeah, I evicted Coquie Hughes.'" He was so sweet when he evicted me he rented the truck. He paid for me to put my stuff in storage. He was a great landlord.

The Birth of a Genre: Urban Lesbian Filmmaking

The Lies We Tell but the Secrets We Keep wasn't a perfect movie, but it was made with perfect passion. It really triggered a ripple of excitement in urban lesbian filmmaking, here in Chicago. And, to me, it has transcended to other states and the world.

When I did *My Mama Said Yo Mama's a Dyke* I began to develop a style of being uninhibited, being audacious and raw and gritty and just true to life and real. It was like I was making films where you actually felt like a fly on the wall. I took it even further in *The Lies We Tell* with the conversations, the dialogue, the intimate scenes, the violence. I just went there and I think that is the reason why the urban community could relate. It was so relative to what they knew and it was relative to what I knew and what I saw and I wasn't afraid to expose it.

The "bootleg man" got hold of it and he was impressed with it. He put it out on the street. And when I say bootleg man, I mean figuratively. He essentially put that movie out there, which gave it the popularity that it has.

I just came up with this idea that whatever movie I make I'm going to make it freely available online. I needed a following because I want to do a web series for *If I Was Your Girl*. And I've seen some examples of how it's done, and it seems to work like with *The Lies We Tell*, Part One. Tyler Perry, he created a fan base with his stage plays before he made his movies. It's a couple of people that have web series where they produce them like every other week and maybe have like 100,000 views during season one. So when it came time for them to do season two, they had this 100,000-plus fan base they were willing to spend money to see what's next.

I think it's pretty awesome the opportunities filmmakers have available to them now via social networking sites. That has shown why this movie has garnered the popularity with the, you know, thousands and thousands of YouTube views on the trailer. People are reaching out to me and to Milan. I had wrote the screenplay for a movie called *Girls Like Us*. They were shooting somewhere and the people saw Milan, who was also starring in that movie, and they, like, just fell head over heels because it was like, "Oh my God! This is the girl from that movie." It's just like hearing the constant stories about the

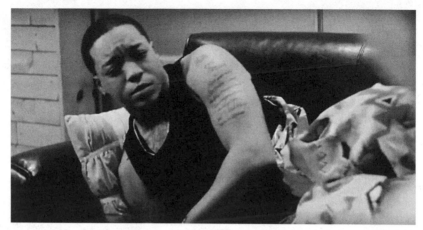

12.2 *Catfishin*, a dark comedy about Brooks (James Moses Jr.), a trans man who is interested in dating only straight women. Directed by Coquie Hughes, 2017.

film that gives credentials to how this movie has gotten out. People who I've never even heard of or seen before are reaching out to me and reaching out to the people that were a part of that because they find it very exciting.

Milan ended up making a part two of *The Lies We Tell*, which she actually wrote and directed herself. I did another film which was based on a work in progress in 2001. I did the updated version of *If I Wuz Yo Gyrl*, and that had been like a ten-year process. I had finally gotten the cast and the producing partner that I had always wanted. We shot that film and we had a sold-out premiere. That was in April. Milan's premiere for her movie in June was sold out. Then the very next day, the movie *Girls Like Us* where I wrote the screenplay was sold out. So it's like Chicago has unofficially been put on the map as making these urban lesbian films.

I think it's sad that I am credited as the only black female filmmaker to have made as many feature films as I have. I think that filmmakers, particularly women, should not be afraid to tell their stories, regardless of the funding or regardless of what the powers that be say what constitutes your film being a legitimate film. I think people should just tell their stories and not be afraid, like me. I mean, we're living in a day of technology that anyone can make a film. You can even make a movie with your cell phone and have a distribution outlet like YouTube to put it out there, so we don't need Hollywood validating us. It's an opportunity for everyone to tell their story, and I think that people should just tell their stories and forget the semantics, just tell your story. People like stories. They forgive production quality. If it's a

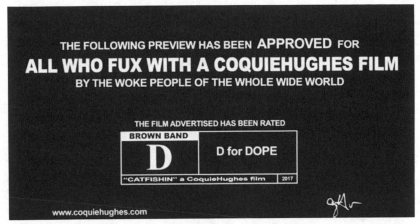

12.3 *Catfishin*, directed by Coquie Hughes, 2017.

story that comes from your heart and it reaches their heart, they're going to be compelled to want to see it again and tell others to see it. You know people have created projects and put them up on YouTube and have become instant millionaires and famous because of that. So we're in a day and age of modern technology. . . . There's no excuse. People should tell their stories.

Notes

Read the complete interview with Coquie Hughes online at www.sistersinthelife.com.

1 Performers or Writers for Women on Women's Issues (POW-WOW) was a weekly open mic poetry and performance safe space for queer women of color and their allies held on the South Side of Chicago at one of the city's oldest gay bars.

"Invite Me In!"

Angela Robinson at Hollywood's Threshold

One of the first of Angela Robinson's (b. 1971) publicly screened works was *Chickula! Teenage Vampire*, a four-minute, black-and-white queer vampire spoof that made the LGBT film festival rounds in 1995. While she's launched an impressive career in mainstream media since then, she hasn't strayed far from these mythical origins. Robinson served as executive producer for the final season of *True Blood* (2008–14), having joined the HBO show as co-executive producer two seasons previously, just before its openly gay creator, Alan Ball (Academy Award–winning writer of *American Beauty,* creator and head writer of *Six Feet Under*), stepped down as show runner. Delivering on premium cable's promise of sexual titillation, *True Blood* queered the deal. The show's vampires and fairies (yes, fairies) are persecuted minorities generally accepted as allegorical stand-ins for queers and PWAs. Robinson herself has been out throughout her career as a film and television writer, director, and producer, and she welcomed *True Blood*'s license "to explore all sorts of crazy shit like race and sexuality. It's a mishmash, and I'm always pushing to put in those themes."[1] She is even able to get away with this on network television; as consulting producer on *How to Get Away with Murder* (2014–present) she finds common ground with the creator Peter Nowalk, also openly gay, and the African American television tastemaker Shonda Rhimes, whose company, ShondaLand, produces the show. "For the last twenty years I've been doing the same thing," Robinson remarks. "I've always tried to find the crosshairs where a pop sensibility and progressive politics around gender, race, and sexuality converge."[2] Presenting Robinson with the Fusion Achievement Award at the tenth Outfest Fusion LGBT People of Color Film

13.1 Angela Robinson. Photo courtesy of Angela Robinson.

Festival (for "all-around biracial awesomeness"), Rutina Wesley and Kristin Bauer van Staten, who played the interracial maker/makee vampire couple on *True Blood*, called her "the patron saint of lesbian nerds everywhere."

By any criteria, Robinson has shaped a remarkable career across independent and mainstream film and television. Born in San Francisco, she studied theater at Brown and then attended film school at NYU. Her class was very diverse, and she found Spike Lee an encouraging presence. Robinson is one of the still-small number of African American women to direct a studio feature: her debut, *D.E.B.S.* (2005), was financed by Screen Gems as an expansion of her 2004 independent short film of the same name, and it in turn got her a gig directing the Lindsay Lohan vehicle *Herbie: Fully Loaded* (2005) and a first-look deal with Disney. In her Fusion Award speech, she recounted what it was like to show up at Disney for work: while the receptionists invariably directed her to the messenger entrance, African American security personnel gave her a VIP parking space. "I was probably the only black director, the only woman director, the only lesbian: I was definitely the only black lesbian!" But Robinson is always quick to credit those who invited her in: the out lesbian producer Nina Jacobson was head of Disney's live-action films at the time.[3]

Robinson's career path to date is a strong example of tapping into the power of the culture industry, as Julie Dash's impassioned protagonist Mignon

Dupree vows to do at the end of the short film *Illusion* (1982), about a black woman inside the Hollywood system during World War II. Separately and together, women's, queer, and black film critiques have long circled around the tension between making films within the mainstream that are accessible to underserved audiences and fostering politically and formally challenging work in the independent realm. As long as access to the industry was so restricted, the question of *how* to fight within the system was more or less moot. Without taking for granted the security of Robinson's position within the industry (after all, even Jacobson was fired), I would suggest that her career offers a new twist to such debates about cultural production by women, queers, and people of color.

The opposition between mainstream and independent may be an economic one, but it may no longer be as potent an aesthetic or political one, and not only because studio classics divisions have created something called Indiewood. Two of Robinson's favorite TV shows growing up were *Facts of Life* and *Josie and the Pussycats*; she read comics and watched horror movies. Generations younger than Robinson are even more immersed in popular culture, and their earliest production experience is likely to be the mash-up, arguably an exercise of what bell hooks calls "the oppositional gaze." Television is our era's reference, and television is where Robinson has landed.

Hollywood filmmaking, in the age of megabudget comic-book blockbusters and anxiety over new delivery platforms, functions like a walled fortress. In 2016 only 7 percent of directors of top-grossing features were women.[4] And Robinson's frustrating experience as writer and producer of the musical comedy-action film GIRLTRASH! *All Night Long* (2014), directed by her partner, Alex Kondracke, brings home how any mode of feature film production can be fraught with uncertainty. A dispute with POWER UP (the LA-based company founded to promote gay women in film that backed the short version of *D.E.B.S.* [2003]) delayed the release of the highly anticipated film, and creative issues around the final version remain unresolved. After *Herbie Fully Loaded* in 2005, Robinson went more than a decade before directing another feature.

Instead, like many independent women directors before her who have had difficulty sustaining careers in film after promising debuts, she turned to television, finding opportunities as a writer and director on premium cable before entering the network realm. Indeed her career to date might be seen as a best-case scenario for lesbian filmmakers in the wake of the New Queer Cinema boom of the 1990s. Even the most successful, Kimberly

Peirce (*Boys Don't Cry* [1999], *Stop-Loss* [2008], *Carrie* [2013]) and Lisa Cholodenko (*High Art* [1998], *Laurel Canyon* [2002], *The Kids Are All Right* [2010], *Olive Kitteridge* [2014]), faced difficulty financing feature film projects. An alternative route to practicing her craft and gaining visibility was afforded to Robinson by *The L Word*. Created by Ilene Chaiken with Kathy Greenberg and Michelle Abbott in 2004, the show enlisted *Go Fish* director Rose Troche to direct the pilot. Troche's partner on *Go Fish*, writer and star Guinevere Turner, wrote several episodes for *The L Word* and played a recurring character. Troche later came on as co-executive producer—a role with considerable power. Co-executive producers participate in the writers' room and are charged with carrying out the design of the show runner and executive producer. Other lesbian feature film directors—Cholodenko, Peirce, and Robinson's friend Jamie Babbitt (*But I'm a Cheerleader* [1999], *Itty Bitty Titty Committee* [2007])—directed an episode here and there. While the Showtime series is consistently and rightly referenced as a definitive platform for the coming out of lesbians in the media, this behind-the-scenes networking dimension of *The L Word*'s production culture is at least as significant for television history as what is on screen. Both have their analogy in the Chart, a device introduced by Alice Pieszecki (Leisha Hailey) in the pilot to map the complexity of lesbian sociality through linking women by their sexual histories.

Robinson came on as co-executive producer on *The L Word* in the show's last two seasons. Of all the New Queer Cinema talents who came to Hollywood with the show, it is she who leveraged the experience most directly into a successful career in premium cable. Having worked in independent and feature films as well, Robinson asserts, "I can say with certainty that I, by far, am most creatively satisfied in the world of cable television."[5] She claims she was initially tapped for *The L Word* because they needed a funny lesbian in the writers' room. Contacted by Troche, Robinson was willing. She wrote the episode "Longing" for the first season of the drama in 2004 before going into production on *Herbie Fully Loaded*.[6] She found the culture of the show very encouraging: "[*The L Word*] was so awesome to work on, because Ilene often allowed me a lot of freedom to do whatever I wanted creatively." She has credits on twenty-seven episodes of the show, including producing, writing (six episodes), and directing (eight). Asked whether she prefers one to the other, she replies, "In general, I prefer directing movies and writing television. In the movies, the director is in charge and the writer usually doesn't have a lot of power. In television, it's the opposite: the writers have all the power and the directors do what they say. It's all a collaboration. I'm speaking in generalities." As for doubling down, she adds, "Directing on a show you're writing on is usually a matter of scheduling: you have to take time out of the writer's room to prep and shoot your episode, so it kind of depends on the show and the demands on you. I love to do it when I can."

When *The L Word* ended, Robinson moved to the HBO show *Hung*, about a down-and-out high school basketball coach who makes money in sex work on the side. *Hung* was co-created by Collette Burson and Dmitry Lipkin, and Robinson wasn't the only woman writer on the show, but she was the only African American. The same was true for *True Blood*, which Robinson joined in 2012 after *Hung* ended. Is the cable niche for New Queer Cinema talent mirrored in opportunities for black independent filmmakers trying to sustain a career and hone their craft between features? Discussing the cultural politics of black representation in the postnetwork era, Herman Gray writes, "Despite their domination by Western corporations, a broader range of service delivery options and the rising importance of television programs as sources of product identity . . . promise greater opportunities for black and minority representations to circulate more in market niches."[7] A higher percentage of black households than of the general population subscribes to HBO, with shows like *Oz* (1997–2003) and *The Wire* (2002–8) drawing record numbers of viewers. In 2015 HBO Access launched writing fellowships to bring diverse talent to the network and green-lit projects by the young African American women directors Dee Rees and Issa Rae. At the same time, producing for premium cable and streaming platforms is becoming more attractive to elites. Robinson laments, "Now everybody knows how great [cable] is, so all the movie people are coming over—Scorsese, Fincher, Soderbergh!" As Gray notes, "Negotiating the logic of the market as a terrain on which forms of community, identification, and association [are] . . . structured is as tricky as it is potentially productive" for black producers.[8] In this climate network television reaped the rewards of African American audiences' loyalty with shows with African American leads, like Rhimes's *Scandal* (2012–present) and *How to Get Away with Murder* (2014–present) on ABC, and predominantly black casts, like Lee Daniels's *Empire* (2014–present) on Fox.

Robinson's projects almost always include black principal characters; however, to date none has been set in a predominantly black world. While she is name-checked on lesbian sites like *After Ellen* and widely acknowledged in LGBT film and television circles, she has been less prominent in conversations on black film and television. "Almost every job I've done in LA,

13.2 Annelise (Viola Davis) and Eve (Famke Janssen) in season two of *How to Get Away with Murder*, 2015.

somebody gay hired me—the gays have really had my back," she says. Joining *How to Get Away with Murder* in its second season as consulting producer—a credit that acknowledges a high-level writer who has had executive producer credits on previous shows—Robinson found by far the most racially diverse writers' room she'd ever encountered. She thought, "I have been in a totally segregated Hollywood my whole career!"[9] Network television may be more mercenary, but "I'm intrigued because I feel like it is about much more than a segment of the market." Under her contract with ABC studios she writes a few days a week for *How to Get Away with Murder* and works on her own projects. The success of diverse voices on television may be beginning to affect feature filmmaking opportunities. Robinson returns to feature filmmaking as writer-director of *Professor Marston and the Wonder Women* (2017), executive produced by *Transparent* creator Jill Soloway.

It would be a mistake, indeed an impossibility to separate out any one aspect of Robinson's identity and experience as it informs her work as media maker. She isn't a lesbian filmmaker *or* a black filmmaker any more than she is exclusively an indie filmmaker *or* an industry media worker, a writer *or* a director. Her work goes beyond *True Blood*'s mishmash of race, gender, and sexuality to explore their intersectionality.

In a *Variety* article titled "Female Directors on the Hunt for Work," citing the pick-up work in television as a trend, Robinson is quoted about the range of media in which she works. "Diversify. Diversify. Diversify," the author sums up, bringing together the two connotations of *diversity*—business strategy and identity politics—that are at stake in any conversation about the politics of representation in mainstream media. Robinson tells the trade paper, "I am a woman, I am black, and I am a lesbian, too, so statistically, I am nonexistent!"[10] Cynically put, she's a three-fer. Enthusiastically embraced, she's a superhero, like the other sisters in cinema countering the erasure of blacks, women, and lesbians in film and television. Importantly, Robinson tips the scales toward a different kind of visibility through her play with icons, a practice characteristic of a key dimension of all her work: genre.

Robinson has stuck with stylized genres since her film school days; in addition to *Chickula*, she made a dyke film noir and a spy spoof called *The Kinsey 3* (1999) and wrote for DC Comics. She successfully draws on commercial filmmaking conventions from Batman and Bond to Valley Girl to tell her stories and engage her audiences. Genres give us a map of what things look like in a particular world, how characters behave, what is imaginable. Plot taken care of, genre films can focus on style. Some genres allow for the most outlandish things, like female power or black heroism; some make the invisible visible. And to keep things fresh, every genre film needs a twist, demanding novelty and eventually parody. Robinson taps into this subversive—and pleasurable—aspect of genre, acknowledging dimensions of sexuality and race that speak to queers and people of color.

Robinson's first feature, D.E.B.S.—an acronym for discipline, energy, beauty, strength—is set in a secret spy academy for girls who've scored high on a special test hidden inside the S.A.T. The very premise riffs on at least two exploitable film genres: spy film and boarding school film. (Both have important lesbian variants.) The first PG-rated lesbian-themed movie, D.E.B.S. is a teen romance, its kink hidden in plain sight in details of the mise-en-scène, including handcuffs and plaid miniskirts. The arch villain (Jordana Brewster) falls in love with the leader of the schoolgirl spy posse (Sara Foster), and the lesbian couple eventually goes off into the sunset. The film barely missed an R rating: the offending scene showed the central couple in bed under the covers.

The film is crammed with in-jokes and references to other films. The head of the D.E.B.S. spy academy, Ms. Petrie, is played by the deliciously bitchy Holland Taylor. Robinson later introduced Taylor's character, Peggy Peabody, on *The L Word*. Both the wealthy art collector and Ms. Petrie pleasurably evoke the predatory lesbian stereotype, in all her elegance and snobbery. Ms. Petrie's disdain for her inferiors is marked by her inability to remember names. Giving her girls an assignment, she references another

13.3 Lucy Diamond (Jordana Brewster) and Amy (Sara Foster) in *D.E.B.S.*, directed by Angela Robinson, 2004. ABC.

movie: "the one with Jodie, and the little dog, and the girl in the hole in the ground." *Silence of the Lambs* (Jonathan Demme, 1991): her assistant supplies the title. The joke lies not only in the light reference to a creepy film (protested by the LGBT community at the time of its release for its transphobic depiction of the serial killer) but also in the character's claim to be on a first-name basis with Jodie, a nod to the star's singular status and lesbian fandom. Her orders given, Ms. Petrie disappears in a column of blinking lights—*Star Trek's* Holodeck meets *Bewitched's* Endora; Taylor's tony diction even emulates Agnes Moorehead's.

Written and directed by Robinson, *D.E.B.S.* is the work that perhaps most fully represents her sensibility to date. But she also brings her touch to material she writes or directs in collaboration with others. One of the most brilliant meta-sequences ever on *The L Word*, in Robinson's episode "Luck Be a Lady," brings the principal characters together in a multiple split-screen effect as they connect over their cell phones. Robinson says, "I told [Ilene Chaiken] that I wanted to write the longest phone tree ever in the history of television that encompassed the stories of all the characters, and she told me to go for it. I think the sequence goes on for ten minutes. It was fun to bring some of my *D.E.B.S.* aesthetics to *The L Word*." The sequence uses form to show the pleasures of soap opera narration: every character knows something different about all the others, and viewers get it all. The split-screen effect evokes another graphic representation of lesbian connectivity on the show: the Chart that links the small world according to who has slept with whom.

Robinson's works are also littered with the tropes of action filmmaking—weapons, special effects, sexy women—and formal devices like split screens and graphic transitions. D.E.B.S. started out as a comic strip, a genre with which Robinson feels at home. Rather than going the route of realism, she reaches for a balance between serious and spoof; to Robinson's credit, even her lower budget work gets it right. *Variety* concludes its D.E.B.S. review: "Surprisingly, lesbian teen fantasy not only hangs together but becomes progressively more enjoyable."[11] Robinson turns stereotypes inside out, celebrates outsiders, and subverts gender, sexual, and racial expectations. In other words, she revels in the tried and true pleasures of popular genres—and of previous decades, with the 1970s of her early childhood high on her list of aesthetic influences. Entrusting her with steering *Herbie Fully Loaded* wasn't such an oddball choice. I am not the only kid whose fantasy life was stoked by Disney live-action fare—think of the double heroines of *The Parent Trap* (David Swift, 1961; Nancy Meyers, 1998). In the original they were played by Hayley Mills, later reincarnated by Lindsay Lohan, in a direct line of descent to Disney's *Herbie* sequel.

As long as her "quality television" résumé may be, Robinson finds influences in the sleazy side of independent film history. The transitions, music cues, and decor of her films pay homage to blaxploitation and cheesy action shows like *Charlie's Angels* (she directed an episode of the reboot). Yet she gets far less attention for the originality of her pastiche of exploitation genres than male directors like Quentin Tarantino and Robert Rodriguez. When she quotes these styles, she's connecting with black screen history and feminist reassessments of girl gang films: *Chickula!* is the bastard progeny of *Blackula!* (William Crain, 1972) and AIP's *Velvet Vampire* (Stephanie Rothman, 1971). On *The L Word* she even had the chance to write for the iconic blaxploitation star Pam Grier as Kit. (Besides *Foxy Brown* [Jack Hill, 1974] and *Coffy* [Jack Hill, 1973], Grier appeared in *Scream Blacula Scream* [Bob Kelljam] in 1973.) Robinson is one of the few media makers who is in a position to tap these traditions and their complex legacy for black women, to echo viewers' pleasure of recognition and shape it with her own creative voice.

In other words, what is special about Angela Robinson is not just that she appropriates commercial genre conventions in her independent work as a shortcut to our understanding and pleasure but also that she includes queer and black subcultural styles and sensibilities in her mainstream work through the same genre codes and references. An exchange of glances (and a display of fangs) among incarcerated women in *True Blood* reads as dyke drama. Although Annelise's (Viola Davis) sexy season-two lesbian affair on *How to Get Away with Murder* was already planned before Robinson joined the show, she was consulted first on the scenes. Robinson solicits our recognition not only through gay content—and not at all through the earnest realism of positive characters—but also through form: double-entendre dialogue, crosscutting, musical counterpoint, the energy of her own synthetic style. Her stuff has bite.

But to conclude that Robinson is an "insider" overlooks the precariousness of her position in the economic and power structures of Hollywood. We can be pretty sure Angela Robinson isn't going to be tapped for the next Batman movie, however attuned her sensibility might be to the genre's potential. I find it productive to think of her instead as a threshold figure. In *True Blood* a vampire lurks in doorways, demanding of mortals, "Invite me in." When the invitation is extended, it is with unpredictable but often riveting results.

This discussion of Robinson's representational strategies and professional tactics as poised on the threshold is well illustrated by the 2007 web series GIRLTRASH! The series consists of nine episodes plus outtakes; she and her crew ran out of money before it was completed. Made with Kondracke while Robinson was working on *The L Word*, the series was hosted on the show's web 2.0 tie-in *OurChart.com*, which emulated the social networking site that the fictional Alice Pieszecki (Leisha Hailey) runs on the show. Like *The L Word*, GIRLTRASH! follows a (somewhat) multiracial cast of largely femme lesbians in LA. The difference in production values between the glossy Showtime soap and the black-and-white web series is obvious. And instead of moping about the Planet, Robinson's heroines kick ass. At heart a buddy/love story between punky dyke bad girls Tyler (Michelle Lombardo) and Daisy (Lisa Rieffel), the show has them draw down the wrath of big bad Monique, played by Rose Rollins. Rollins was also a late-series cast edition on *The L Word*, where her character, Tasha, an African American butch in the armed services, addressed some of the audience's objections to that show's spotty record of diverse representations in race, class, and gender presentation.

Meanwhile, back on GIRLTRASH!, Monique kidnaps Daisy's kid sister and her friend and ties up her hostages. Colby and Misty are played by Mandy Musgrave and Gabrielle Christian, who portrayed the popular and groundbreaking teen lesbian couple Spencer and Ashley (Splashley, in fanspeak) on the N network's cable drama *South of Nowhere* (2005–8), whose pilot was directed by Rose Troche. Acting like a fan herself, Robinson brings the couple together in peril; to viewers' delight, they make out in captivity. Monique, the African American character, is the big bad villain. Disappointingly, the series' hiatus meant a disruption in Monique's story arc before it was possible to tell where this citation of gangsta and blaxploitation stereotypes was heading. While it is still rare for a web series to sustain itself financially, it was virtually impossible in 2007, at the dawn of the genre. Yet, like the first *D.E.B.S.*, *GIRLTRASH!* earned in subcultural capital what it couldn't in dollars, marking the presence of wide swaths of underrepresented people and potential audiences on the Internet. Later web successes like Issa Rae's *The Mis-Adventures of Awkward Black Girl* owe something to its efforts.

Luckily HBO work paid Robinson's bills. While *Hung* was a chance to hone her skills, *True Blood*, with its Louisiana setting, racially mixed cast, and potent mythology, offered especially fertile ground for exploration at the intersection of race, gender, and sexuality in characters like the show's vampire ur-goddess, Lilith, as played by Jessica Clark, a mixed-race lesbian actress and model—she's as much Lilith Fair as the biblical figure reappropriated by 1970s feminists—and the black queen Lafayette Reynolds (Nelsan Ellis). Lafayette's cousin Tara (Wesley), *True Blood*'s principal black woman character and heroine Sookie Stackhouse's lifelong friend, had embarked on a promising character arc when Robinson came on. After a few seasons of bad luck with men and her mom and a lot of viewer discomfort, Tara had "turned"—first lesbian, then vampire. Says Robinson, "I love Tara's character, especially as a vampire. One of my favorite scenes I've written on the show was in my first episode, 505, when Tara and Jessica discuss what it means to be a vampire and compare their experience. . . . I think Tara is a strong, capable, damaged, vibrant character who feels deeply alienated from the world and keeps looking for a way to connect. I liked examining the maker/makee relationship between her and Pam." From talk and no action in the Jessica-Tara conversation about bloodsucking being "better than sex" (unless combined with it, of course), actions speak louder than words in the Pam-Tara pairing. Pam is blond, statuesque, and brusque; Tara is always hungry. The show's "femslash" fandom fills in the blanks in online fictions spinning out the characters' love, lust, and eternal bond.[12]

True Blood's queerness extended beyond what fans call a "canon lesbian relationship" (one that actually exists in the show) like Pam and Tara. In a particularly eventful Robinson-penned episode in season 6, "F**k the Pain Away," blond heroine Sookie Stackhouse (Anna Paquin) is overwhelmed when her ex—vampire Bill, who's caused her trouble since episode 1—shows up in the middle of a romantic evening designed to entrap the new-in-town Ben. With

13.4 Promotional image of Tara (Rutina Wesley) and Pam (Kristin Bauer) in the season five finale of *True Blood*, 2010. HBO.

her exasperation at Bill's arrival—she has things under control—the show makes a feminist point about Sookie being surrounded by misguided losers and bad news. But then the scene adds a queer twist: the two men go off together, maker and spawn, and Sookie is left standing in her underwear. Later most of the main vampire characters have been rounded up and placed in a secret internment camp. Tara steps between the naïve Jessica and a beautiful brunette inmate who's curious about the pretty redhead. Jessica herself is not so innocent; she's just eaten four fairy girls and confides she found it sexually arousing.

Play with in/visibility and bodily and sexual difference has been an appeal of the horror genre since the beginning of screen history, and many artists and scholars have discovered queers and people of color lurking in those generic shadows. *True Blood*'s particular iteration of vampire lust—pro-women's sexuality, tinged with BDSM, racially attentive if not always nuanced—consciously draws out this potential. But maintaining control over connotation is hardly possible; the show has been challenged for its perpetuation of African American stereotypes. Its power relations can be disturbingly racialized, as when Tara confronts Pam: "So I'm basically your slave." "Yes," Pam drawls. Tara didn't make it to the series' end, and the show's white characters remained central. We have seen how conservative, heterosexual, and sexist appropriations of the vampire mythology in the romance can be, in what we can only hope is the twilight of Stephenie Meyer's megaseries' influence.

Although her creative input was considerable as co-executive producer, and she brings a unique perspective as consulting producer to *How to Get Away with Murder*, Robinson's job is to realize the show runner's vision in the writers' room, even on episodes for which she is a credited writer. An "encoder" whose contributions audiences will "decode" in many different ways, Robinson cannot authorize particular interpretations. Artists can deploy particular tropes in order to connect with discerning audiences, but wider cultural meanings always filter these acts of communication. The rules of its genre allowed *True Blood* to talk about race and sex outside the law; the particular mix of sensationalism and empowerment that characterizes ShondaLand affords a similar possibility in *How to Get Away with Murder*. Both have provided excellent opportunities for a maker like Robinson. But American popular culture, history, and society mix sex with race in volatile ways. Opening up taboos as these shows do also raises ghosts that are hard to put to rest.

The language of encoding and decoding is borrowed from Stuart Hall's seminal work in cultural studies, and bell hooks's term for black women spectators' oppositional gaze is derived from Hall's discussion of the "resistant" and "oppositional" readings of mass culture brought by audiences who are at odds with dominant culture. Much criticism to date that is sensitive to issues of race, gender, and sexuality has necessarily focused on decoding. Greater numbers of women, queers, and people of color behind the scenes in the entertainment industry change the equation on the encoding side. While queer encodings have catalyzed remarkable change in television since the 1990s (in the structure of the industry as well as in stories and images), race has tended to be reinscribed in the dominant key. Robinson's articulation of race and sexuality together becomes all the more important.

Robinson's career raises all the usual questions of crossover success and the commodification of identities. She does not so much work in an alternative tradition as turn mainstream genre conventions to other purposes. As an African American lesbian media maker she excels at this strategy of citation instead of opposition. In an era of online mash-ups, user-generated content, and sophisticated fan vids, it is likely that younger artists will follow Angela Robinson in turning the clichés of mass culture to queer-of-color purposes. (It isn't for nothing that *D.E.B.S.* is aimed at tweens.) For cultures of production (encoding) to change, facilitating mentorship and collaboration is crucial.

Professor Marston and the Wonder Women, just released at the time of publication, tells the true story of the man who invented Wonder Woman in 1941, his wife, and their female lover. With this queer take on superhero cinema, on the threshold of film and TV, indie and industry, as both author and fan, black and lesbian, Angela Robinson stands her ground.

Notes

1 J. Halterman, "Angela Robinson on Her Fusion Achievement Award and How She Brings the Lesbians In," *AfterEllen*, March 21, 2013, http://www.afterellen.com/angela-robinson-on-her-fusion-achievement-award-and-how-she-brings-the-lesbians-in/03/2013/.

2 Interview with author, October 18, 2015.

3 Famously fired while at the hospital with her partner, who was delivering their third child, Jacobson formed her own company and went on to produce the *Hunger Games* franchise.

4 Martha Lauzen, "Celluloid Ceiling: Behind-the-Scenes Employment of Women on the Top 250 Films of 2014," Center for the Study of Women in Television and Film, San Diego State University, 2015, http://womenintvfilm.sdsu.edu/files/2014_Celluloid_Ceiling_Report.pdf. In May 2015 the ACLU called for an investigation of rampant gender discrimination. Cara Buckly, "Citing Bias against Women, ACLU Wants Investigation into Hollywood Hiring Practices," *New York Times*, May 12, 2015, http://www.nytimes.com/2015/05/13/movies/aclu-citing-bias-against-women-wants-inquiry-into-hollywoods-hiring-practices.html?_r=0. Statistics for people of color directing feature films were not available, but a report issued by the Directors Guild of America covering the situation on episodic television during the same period found that 13 percent of shows were directed by white women, 15 percent by men of color, and 3 percent by women of color. "DGA TV Diversity Report: Employer Hiring of Women Directors Shows Modest Improvement; Women and Minorities Continue to Be Excluded in First-Time Hiring," DGA, August 25, 2015, http://www.dga.org/News/PressReleases/2015/150825-Episodic-Director-Diversity-Report.aspx.

5 Angela Robinson, email communication with author, September 15, 2013. Unless otherwise noted, quotes from Robinson are from this source.

6 For an analysis of the show's dynamics of looking through this episode, see Dana Heller, "How Does a Lesbian Look? Stendal's Syndrome and *The L Word*," in *Reading the L Word*, edited by Kim Akass and Janet McCabe (London: I. B. Tauris, 2006), 55–68.

7 Herman Gray, *Cultural Moves: African Americans and the Politics of Representation* (Berkeley: University of California Press, 2005), 86.

8 Gray, *Cultural Moves*, 88.

9 Angela Robinson, telephone interview with author, October 18, 2015.

10 Jenny Peters, "Female Directors on the Hunt for Work: Filmmakers Look Elsewhere for Employment," *Variety*, June 11, 2009, http://variety.com/2009/biz/news/female -directors-on-the-hunt-for-work-1118004830/.

11 Review of *D.E.B.S.*, *Variety*, January 21, 2004.

12 Femslash is fan fiction or video exploring the romantic and/or sexual relationship between two female characters on a particular show. Femslash is generally female-authored and geared toward women, many but not all of whom identify as lesbian. Examples are Captain Janeway–Seven of Nine on *Star Trek: Voyager* and Buffy-Faith on *Buffy the Vampire Slayer*. Pam-Tara is a "canon lesbian relationship" because the pair is already linked in the series; fanfic takes things further. See Julie Levin Russo, "Indiscreet Media: Femslash Fandom in the Era of Convergence," presentation at NCA, 2010, https://prezi.com/fm-37n7rrymo/indiscreet-media-femslash-fandom-in -the-era-of-convergence/.

Shine Louise Houston

An Interstice of Her Own Making

> Their sexual experiences are depicted, but often not by them, and if and when by the subject herself, often in the guise of vocal music, often in the self-contained accent and sheer romance of the blues.
> **—Hortense Spillers, "Interstices: A Small Drama of Words"**

> Was New Queer Cinema [NQC] an exclusively male, white and Anglo-American phenomenon? How was it influenced by, or influential for, lesbian film, Black queer work, or non-U.S. cinemas? . . . Through consideration of a range of narrative and national contexts, this part scrutinizes those troubling limitations that NQC, and its reception, initially enacted to provide a crucial but less visible trajectory of the evolution of New Queer Cinema.
> **—Anat Pick, "New Queer Cinema and Lesbian Film"**

> I know what the holes are in the market. I know there's a need for that. Fuck it, I wanna make it. I wanna make a porn. I'm gonna do it. And that was June of last year. June 2004. I was like, "I'm gonna start a porn company," and it was just a weird kind of half-thought. I'm gonna start a porn company! And a year later . . . I'm promoting my first film.
> **—Shine Louise Houston**

It is the twenty-first century, and there is a black lesbian director and producer making pornography! Porn, a genre of film and media that in the last quarter of the twentieth century many black feminist lesbians viewed as capable only of representing and manifesting violence, abuse, and shame. In this essay I examine one of the early works of the black lesbian filmmaker

Shine Louise Houston, *In Search of the Wild Kingdom* (2007), to explore how and why we have arrived at what is a transition from Blues Legacies and Black Feminisms to Pink and White Productions, and from New Queer Cinema to Porn for Pussies. Shine Louise Houston has made a name for herself by producing and directing what her website tags as "porn for pussies" and what others have called revolutionary lesbian porn.

Coming along more than a decade after the 1990s queer new wave of films that introduced audiences to the films of the groundbreaking director Cheryl Dunye, Houston released her first feature movie, *Crash Pad*, in 2005. She utilized the film festival circuit in the way pursued by numerous marginalized filmmakers before her. The difference was that she adamantly understood and marketed her work as pornography, and a very specific type that challenges the definition of pornography as well as the parameters of black and queer cinemas and black queer cinema. She quickly followed the success of her first film with *Superfreak* (2006), *In Search of the Wild Kingdom* (2007),[1] *Champion* (2008), several short films, an ongoing web-series based on *Crash Pad*, and a digital media forum entitled *Heavenlyspire* focused on masculine beauty, sexuality, and masculine appreciation. To date, most of the productions have received notable press and awards for what has been understood as a unique cinematic vision. Houston is an interstice, an interstice occupying multiple and simultaneous cultural trajectories. *Interstice* is defined as an interval of time or space, as well as a small or narrow space between parts of things uniformly organized. As a self-proclaimed porn auteur, Houston makes films that are no small drama of words. They inevitably reveal the false dichotomies between black feminist thought and antipornography and antisexual rhetoric, and cogently explore symbols, myths, and representations that early black lesbian filmmaking left alone—representations of interracial desire and intimacy, black butch and trans expressions—while also capturing the spirit of 1980s and 1990s black independent filmmaking.

Pink and White Production Company: Not So Much Black as Blue, Not So Much Lesbian as Queer

Though the pornography industry has been as much a part of California's economy as is Silicon Valley, its most successful productions are not often black, lesbian, or female ventures. In Hollywood too, despite successes of black, lesbian, or female films, the industry is slow to support and promote such productions on a consistent basis. Yet Houston emerges in the interval of each industry. Her move to pornography became a feasible option with black women's queer sexuality, and explicit representations thereof, no longer being relegated to a dying music genre too often tied to past generations of black womanhood and no longer being strategically contained by cinematic biopics and historical documentaries necessary for making visible invisible lives. However, my assessment of Houston and her porn production company is not a comparative analysis with blues music culture and visual media culture but rather a recognition that a new generation of black women cultural producers have located a cultural site outside of music and the romantic blues narrative, as well as outside the antiporn rhetoric of early black feminist and womanist ideology. Complicating representations of all women's sexuality, and thereby augmenting how black lesbian filmmakers might represent sexuality and desire for all races, genders, and sexualities, Houston emblematically represents an interstice of black women's collective drama around sexuality and pornography.

Hortense Spillers begins "Interstices: A Small Drama of Words" with a concern for intergenerational communication and discourses on sexuality, claiming, "I am interested here primarily in what we might call discursive and iconic fortunes and misfortunes, facilities, abuses, or plain absences that tend to travel from one generation of kinswomen to another, not unlike love and luck, or money and real estate."[2]

As I will demonstrate in my analysis of her third film, *In Search of the Wild Kingdom*, Houston chooses to acknowledge that which has been passed on by passing on them. That is, by understanding that generations of black women have inherited knowledge that black lesbians have been made invisible, that we know not how black lesbians have sex with each other, that sexual myths of black women exist, and that we have learned geometries of black (w)holes, she then moves toward a focus on what else has traveled from one generation to another.

Reading the work of Audre Lorde, Alice Walker, Patricia Hill Collins, Tracey A. Gardner, bell hooks, and other black feminists on porn, representation, and black women, it would appear that late twentieth-century black feminism and womanism could not imagine a twenty-first century that would make room for a Shine Louise Houston and Pink and White. In agreement with what Spillers articulates, hooks once suggested that "women are still struggling to find a sexual voice, to find places where our desires and fantasies can be articulated in all their strangeness and perversity."[3] However, I suggest that almost a decade later Houston's film would become the outlaw culture that hooks demanded in the 1990s, when she said, "We must change the way that we desire. We must not objectify."[4] Houston has expressed specific personal aspirations for herself and her work, admitting in one interview, "Hopefully part of my goal is to deliver something that the audience didn't even know that they wanted."[5] She has won several Feminist Porn Awards for her work, such acclaim suggesting that she is changing the way we desire.

Black lesbian filmmaking has been slowly but steadily increasing its presence on the Hollywood and independent filmmaking landscape. Films by Michelle Parkerson, Cheryl Dunye, Yvonne Welbon, Shari Frilot, Debra Wilson, and Tina Mabry have made it difficult to ignore, but it has continued to be marginalized even with the advent of what Anat Pick, in the anthology *New Queer Cinema: A Critical Reader*, discusses as the moment and movement during the 1990s when films focused on intimacy, desire, and sexualities of LGBT communities in the "discourses of post modernity."[6] But in this collection, like so many others, the stated project of questioning the whiteness and maleness of this cultural production fails since it only mentions rather than fully considers a tradition of black lesbian filmmaking, reducing black queer cinema to Marlon Riggs and Isaac Julien. As phenomenal black lesbian filmmakers such as Dee Rees continue to make visible strides outside of queer of color communities, as did Dunye before her, we should also find room to celebrate lesbian filmmakers working in alternative genres such as porn, who risk alienating and othering in order to bring us visions that could change the way we desire. From documentary and experimental to short and narrative feature films, little attention had been paid to black women filmmakers who direct and produce pornography, and certainly not lesbian filmmakers.

Houston's work challenges stereotypes and what black women can choose and not choose to depict, especially with regard to sexuality. It is important because it commits to not only being inclusive of sexual identity on screen but to the various ways to express such identity on screen. While the tagline for Houston's media empire is "porn for pussies," the stated mission of the company reflects more complexity and the key ingredients for her vision as a filmmaker: "Pink & White Productions creates adult entertainment that exposes the complexities of queer sexual desire. Taking inspiration from many different sources, Pink & White is dedicated to producing sexy and exciting images that reflect today's blurred gender lines and fluid sexualities."[7] Perhaps because of the ways lesbian criticism, filmmaking, and literature have been connected to black feminist agendas that have been antisex at the most, and race women–policing at the least, Houston's film production company

14.1 Promotional image of Shine Louise Houston. Pink and White Productions.

skips right over any configurations of itself as lesbian porn, choosing queer instead, even as its owner and director has identified as a black lesbian.

Mocking Invisibility, History, and Authentic Lesbians:
In Search of the Wild Kingdom

In "Shine Louise Houston Will Turn You On," Malinda Lo argues that Houston is someone who "knows the business and has plenty of ideas for making queer porn that's both hot and politically aware." The business is pornography, and if we buy Lo's words that Houston's work is hot and politically aware, does that mean we can change not only the way we desire but also how that changed desire will look? While any of Houston's films could be said to fulfill Lo's mandate, I focus here on Houston's third film, a mockumentary entitled *In Search of the Wild Kingdom*. Following in the tradition of Dunye's mockumentary *The Watermelon Woman* (1996), *In Search of the Wild Kingdom* fictitiously presents the quest of documentary filmmaker Georgia Mann to observe, record, and analyze authentic lesbian sex. Viewers follow Mann and her film crew as they hit the streets of San Francisco literally tagging and following their subjects into their "wild" environment.

Before any action or actors are presented to viewers, the film fades in from black to the following sentence: "Documentary filmmaker Georgia Mann came to San Francisco, May 2006, to film 'Real Lesbians of San Francisco.'" Frame 2 informs viewers, "Shine Louise Houston and crew followed the progress of Georgia's production to create the documentary 'In Search of the

Wild Kingdom.'" The final introductory frame continues with two separate statements situated in opposition. The first sentence, located at the top and center, completes a summary of what viewers of the reality show and the documentary of that reality show and film should expect: "The following is an assemblage of footage from both crew's brief five day expedition." The second sentence, attributed to the German philosopher Friedrich Nietzsche, "To become what one is, one must not have the faintest notion what one is," sits below the summary and serves as a dismantling of what came before: the notion of realism, reality, and authenticity implied by each legitimated and less illicit film and media genre. The last statement, directed toward lesbian subjects and spectators, encourages an active viewing experience of hard-core sexual expression.

From the onset Houston guides her film audience to challenge the perceptions of lesbian subjectivity that they might bring to the film. As Jill Dolan had argued more than a decade earlier, "Reconstructing a variable lesbian subject position . . . requires emptying lesbian references of imposed truths, whether those of the dominant culture or those of lesbian radical feminist communities which hold their own versions of truth. The remaining, complex, different referent, without truth, remains dependent on the materiality of actual lesbians who move in and out of dominant discourse in very different ways because of their positions within race, class, and variant expressions of their sexuality—dragging at the margins of structure and ideology."[8] By creating a plot in which we cannot ignore multiple gazes and the positions of those gazes, Houston refuses the very mechanisms that support misrepresentations and pretenses of real or monolithic truths about sexual communities. She says of herself as a filmmaker, "I do a lot of stuff with voyeurs and it's a big thing for me. It doesn't help that I have been reading a lot of Freud [*laughs*] and Linda Williams."[9] All of this is confirmed in the DVD bonus feature "The Mocking Of," in which Houston and her cast participate. In character, the "real" lesbians make comedic references to Georgia Mann's camera crew being especially adept at camouflage with their use of black clothes. As the actual film and the bonus features emphasize time and again, subjects in documentaries and reality TV and film become performers and actors by the very ways they attempt to ignore cameras and crews.

By aligning her film with existentialism and nihilism through Nietzsche, Houston as director demonstrates that the audience for this particular adult film might be different from the perceived audience for mainstream porn, where "there's definitely a set formula in mainstream that's like 'We want to see some oral, we want to see this, yadda yadda yadda.'"[10] Does anybody ever say "We want to see some Nietzsche" before mocking a documentary on lesbianism? Houston does. She constructs cinema that expects active and conscious viewers, not passive viewers. The Nietzsche epigraph succinctly corroborates my initial assessment about who Houston is as a filmmaker, why her films should be acknowledged, and how she is an interstice. There is no blueprint for black women who make pornography. There are no schools, film classes, books, or courses of action other than to do it the way one wants to do it. Though Nietzsche's sentiment is meant to situate viewers in the ethnographic quest of the film's protagonist, Georgia Mann, and her search for authentic and real lesbian lives and sex, it also underscores the methods Houston's films successfully employ to develop a unique vision that resists classification and labeling along the lines of race, gender, and sexuality.

Houston's decision to make *In Search of the Wild Kingdom*, a porn mockumentary, is meant to capture, Spillers argues, the various ways in which "sexuality is the locus of great drama, perhaps the fundamental one—and as we know, wherever there are actors, there are scripts, scenes, gestures, re-enactment, both enunciated and tacit."[11] Throughout the film Houston does an amazing job of using her pornographic creation to dismantle legitimate genres of filmmaking that represent sex on screen, specifically lesbian sex on screen, as well as other discursive mechanisms that produce sexual myths and misrepresentation. She takes aim at ethnographic and anthropological films, heterosexual soft-core films, and making-of documentaries.

Although Houston's films are never specifically about black queer communities alone, her third film signals the significant role documentary filmmaking has played in the lives of queer people of color, including her own. Matt Richardson provides a rich filmography of the black lesbian documentary that framed Dunye's previous attention to the documentary form in *Watermelon Woman*:

> Since the 1980s there has been a stream of documentaries made by people of various races, genders, and sexualities about black gender variance, lesbians, and bisexual women: *Stormé Lady of the Jewelbox* (Michelle Parkerson, 1987), *Tiny and Ruby: Hell Divin' Women* (Andrea Weiss, 1988), *Among Good Christian People* (Jacqueline Woodson, 1991), *B.D. Women* (Inge Blackman, 1994), *Frankie and Joice* (Jocelyn Taylor, 1994), *Black Nations/Queer Nations* (Shari Frilot, 1995), *A Litany for Survival: The Life of Audre Lorde* (Michelle Parkerson and Ada Gay Griffin, 1996), *Living With Pride:*

Ruth Ellis @ 100 (Yvonne Welbon, 1999), *Butch Mystique* (Debra Wilson, 2003), *The Edge of Each Others Battles: The Vision of Audre Lorde* (Jennifer Abod, 2004), *The Aggressives* (Daniel Peddle, 2005), *Still Black* (Kortney Ryan Ziegler, 2008) and *black.womyn.* (tiona.m., 2010).[12]

Dunye, who recently completed her own lesbian adult film, *Mommy Is Coming* (2012), certainly set an example for up-and-coming lesbian filmmakers on how to use the documentary form to engage questions of representation, spectacle, and gazes. As Laura Sullivan's "Chasing Fae: The Watermelon Woman and Black Lesbian Possibility" explains, the "film's technical qualities, such as the use of montage, talking-head interviews, segments that appear to be from early film news spots, and film footage with an archival look, lead viewers to perceive the text initially as based upon reality."[13] Houston, seemingly adopting an approach similar to Dunye's, enacts a different use of the documentary. Rather than using her adult films to show the possibilities of lesbian history, she exposes the process of such construction and its culpability in framing history and realities. She does so not only with Georgia Mann's faux-documentary but by also mocking another film genre important to lesbian representation on film, the short "making-of" film.

Two of the most influential documentaries of queer of color life, *Paris Is Burning* (Jennie Livingston, 1991) and *The Aggressives* (Daniel Peddle, 2005), were not directed by black filmmakers (Daniel Peddle and Jennie Livingston are white), and certainly viewers and critics alike have questioned how that shapes the film and representations therein. Shine's attention to this critique occurs in Georgia Mann, an individual incapable of taking on what Zora Neale Hurston expressed as the participant-observer role. Mann's crew might occupy such a space as they capture the interactions, but as she sits in a dark van watching on a computer screen, making comments that express titillation and awe in ways that her camera crew cannot, the ethics and purpose of such documentation come under fire. Houston's portrayal of Mann as a feminist filmmaker with questionable ethics peering into the lives of her lesbian subjects is meant to mock both the quest for and performance of authenticity and realism, as well as the purposeful construction of documentaries that would pretend to project a real subject. In one scene Mann speaks directly to the camera about true lesbians: "If we are ever going to know the true inner nature of ourselves, we must move past a clear understanding of heterosexuality and into the darkness of homosexuality. Lesbians are obviously different from women like myself. I am straight. I like men . . . no doubt about it, but what

14.2 Georgia Mann in *In Search of the Wild Kingdom*, directed by Shine Louise Houston, 2007.

I want to know is what makes them so different than me. I mean sex between two women must be completely different than normal heterosexual sex. By tracking their sexual behavior I hope to get the answers I want. There's something so fascinating about them. Many people have tried to get the true inner nature of lesbians before but their subjects were all too aware of the study."

Houston's character satirically appropriates the ethnocentric and Western voice of social science, while also playing with the issues of sexual validation, identity, and voyeurism. Her purpose is not to construct history, nor to imagine it from what is left over from the archives. Rather she critiques social science and cinematic discourses in general in ways that are mindful of critics' thinking, while still visibly representing lesbian sex and various bodies enacting that sex. Moreover Houston insists that since pornography is classified as a film genre inherently equated to the white masculine gaze, her mockumentary might also explode that myth and inform our pleasure and consciousness in the process. She does so by cleverly providing us with a visual rendering of the lesbian spectator for pornography. Mary Conway's "Spectatorship in Lesbian Porn: The Woman's Woman's Film" convincingly argues for new assessments of the lesbian subject: "As an unanticipated genre, lesbian produced porn promises to be a 'problem'; it illustrates viewing practices which diverge significantly from any theoretical understandings that precede it. New descriptions will have to fragment understandings of spectatorship by focusing on a spectator who was not anticipated by, and continues to pose problems for, gendered spectator theories. But the dearth of critique does not warrant attempts to fix a generalized lesbian spectator in any kind of rigid theoretical taxonomy."[14]

The female gaze represented by Mann, her all-female crew recording these lesbian experiences, coupled with the viewers' gaze on Mann and her subjects, all work toward every sexual subject having or coming to voice in the film. As Mann watches her subjects, viewers watch those same subjects, Mann, and her camera crew get turned on watching lesbian sex. None of these female spectators of sexuality are supposed to exist, so Houston's film creates them so that she can then also create the impossible lesbian spectator. Mann replaces the white male spectator and serves as a different type of viewer for film audiences, a conscious female heterosexual narrator whose gaze is not unmediated masculinity and patriarchy but who is still influenced by both. The combination of documentary and pornography draws our attention to the similarities and connections between these two models of filmmaking, one stigmatized and the other not but both capable of producing narratives important to how we understand sexuality, identity, and representation. We get to see the connection between different forms of media-making: the camera, the computer, and the producer and observer. Moreover the objective researcher, the camera crew, and the lesbians are all subjects for the lesbian spectator watching the film. We are constantly reminded that there are various ways to observe and participate, gaze and comprehend. Hence there is no singular lesbian spectator in the film or outside of it.

Houston's use of the mockumentary form allows her to signify on documentary filmmaking and the anthropological and ethnographic discourses that contribute to sexual knowledges; it also allows her to engage filmmaking discourses meant to cinematically depict lesbian sex outside of pornography, specifically behind the scenes, making-of shorts. Right after Mann suggests that people "have tried and failed to capture lesbian sex," the film cuts to and splices in what is supposed to be an excerpt from another documentary, *Lesbo Luv. No. 1*, conveniently directed by Richard Dickerson. The hypermasculine name with the double-phallus entendre is meant to underwrite the goal and audience of *Lesbo Luv. No 1*, a short that purports to be an excerpt from a making-of documentary about a soft-core lesbian film. It begins with two blond-haired, blue-eyed women engaging in dialogue such as "Your hair is very pretty, too, would you like to sit next to me?," before the lesbian sexual action ensues.

Houston's inclusion of the excerpt from the fake documentary answers Kelly Hankin's probing questions as to the purpose of making-of shorts for lesbian-themed film of any genre: "What [does] the lesbian making-of documentary's focus on the production of lesbian sex both [reveal] and [conceal]? What do we learn about the climate of lesbian feature filmmaking from these documentaries' emphases on the production of lesbian sex? And what does this emphasis on lesbian sex efface?" As Hankin also notes, making-of films concerned with heterosexual lives and culture seldom address sex on- or off-screen: "Despite the making-of video's increased attention to the minutiae of filmmaking, one of the areas that remains outside the purview of most Hollywood making-of documentaries is the production of sex. Discussions about the cinematic logistics of creating a sex scene—how, when, and with what resources—are usually not featured in making-of documentaries." Hankin notes that this paradigm shifts and changes when the film is explicitly centered on lesbian life and culture, arguing, "As several scholars have pointed out, Hollywood's representations of lesbians during and after the studio era, whether cartoonishly mannish or neurotic, were often desexualized, offering little in the way of sexual pleasure or fantasy. Representing sexualized images of lesbians would be left up to hard- and soft-core pornography as well as sexploitation films; though, as images meant to be consumed by men, both narratively and spectatorially, lesbian scenes in these cinema practices were often sculpted in a heterosexist and heteronormative manner. . . . As such, the representation of lesbian sex has become one of the central as well as one of the expected devices of lesbian feature filmmaking in the United States."[15]

The spliced-in excerpt from *Lesbo Luv* centers on white high-femme women with shaved underarm and pubic areas who simulate presumably what lesbian sex entails: moaning and slurping while genteelly patting, kissing, touching, and licking each other in an obvious performance for the camera. The actresses exaggeratedly position themselves and perform so that viewers might have unobstructed views of the sex. Viewers of Mann's documentary and Houston's film understand these as formulaic camera shots and positions of heterosexual porn that attempt and fail to visibly capture women's pleasure because the gaze they produce is too concerned with male pleasure in viewing women's pleasure. The actresses and their performance of lesbian sex are meant to be compared with the diverse groups of lesbians already seen in Mann's early sightings, highlighting Houston's unique presentation and vision of lesbian porn. Houston submits that these short films are yet another way lesbian sexuality is captured only and always through the voyeuristic hetero-normative gaze that Mann represents.

The making-of scene provides a nice juxtaposition to the opening scene of the Mann/Houston film in which we see "Beau-Flex," a thin, shapely Asian stud being aggressively undressed by "Courtney," a voluptuous red-haired woman who directs and orders her to strip. They too engage in kissing as foreplay, but safe sex practices are highlighted when the femme figure digitally penetrates and fucks Beau, and the scene ends with Courtney using a vibrator to pleasure Beau until she reaches orgasm. The scene with the two visibly hairy, racially and physically distinct female performers serves as a viable comparison to the timid petting, patting, and touching of the two blond lesbians who moan and perform while very aware of the camera. Later, viewers see a monogamous black couple, Papi Cocks and Wil Thustweel, two butches exemplifying the range of representations for black female masculinity, engage in a ménage à trois with Beau.[16] Papi is light-skinned, thin, with a close-tight haircut, while Wil is bigger and darker and sports a Mohawk with orange dreds. During sex all three women fluidly adapt and move from being penetrated to penetrating, as well as performing oral sex on each other.

Once again watching on a computer screen in the van, Mann vocally responds to Beau's presence in the couple's bedroom in a voice of surprise: "Wait a minute." Her words signal that another myth or expectation of lesbian sex, monogamy, has proven false. The modes of film genre reflect back on one another so as to consistently emphasize that Houston's pornographic culture intervenes anywhere and everywhere there is sex. Pink and White Productions employs queer people with all types of bodies, of various races and ethnicities, as well as diverse gender expressions of those bodies, sexualities, and races, and, as Houston explains, realness is not necessarily the main reason: "The core values are to stay true to my ideals of sex-positivity. . . . We have a mission to show different types of bodies: queer bodies, natural bodies."[17]

Here and elsewhere Houston avoids using the terms *real* or *authentic* within her mission statements, even as those who review her work do so. She does not engage in conversations about what is real or not real. Instead of replacing one configuration of realness with another, she simply advises that all impetuses to realness are someone's fabrication. Is it real black or real lesbian if it is directed and produced by someone who is not black or lesbian? In either case, are the considerations of race, class, gender, and sexuality addressed in ways that resist (neo)colonial practices? At the end of the Dickerson clip, the film cuts back to Mann, who proclaims, "I'm driven to find the absolute truth

about lesbians no matter what it takes." She continues on her ethically questionable quest, capturing all manner of lesbian sex along the way, and at the
end of her documentary she reports, "On the surface they seem so different,
but I've seen them engage in the same exact acts as heterosexuals. I mean they
have sex just like I do in a lot of ways. Maybe that's why I find it so hot [*shakes
her head*]. But if I can't make the distinction between these lesbian sexual
behaviors and my own then where do I draw the line between heterosexuals and homosexuals. What could this mean? I filmed the lesbians in hiding
so that I could capture them really being themselves. . . . I'm so confused." *In
Search of the Wild Kingdom* ends where it began: with the notion of what one
is. Houston uses her adult film to question categories and labels with regard
to women's sexuality, lesbian sex, and the validity or stigma of film genres. By
having little notion of what she is, she becomes what she could be: an interstice of her own making.

Notes

Epigraphs: Hortense Spillers, "Interstices: A Small Drama of Words," in *Pleasures and
Danger: Exploring Female Sexuality*, edited by Carol Vance (New York: Pandora / Harp-
erCollins, 1992), 74; Anat Pick, "New Queer Cinema and Lesbian Film," in *New Queer
Cinema: A Critical Reader*, edited by Michele Aaron (Edinburgh: Edinburgh University
Press, 2004), 101; Malinda Lo, "Shine Louise Houston Will Turn You On" (interview),
Curve 16.1 (2006), https://web.archive.org/web/20060506072624/http://www.curvemag
.com/Detailed/711.html.

1 The film has recently been retitled *In Search of the Wild*.
2 Spillers, "Interstices," 73.
3 bell hooks, "Good Girls Look the Other Way," in *Feminism and Pornography*, edited
   by Drucilla Cornell (New York: Oxford University Press, 2000), 83.
4 bell hooks, *Outlaw Culture: Resisting Representations* (1994; New York: Routledge,
   2006), 77.
5 Jill, "Let's Talk about Pornography: Interview with Shine Louise Houston," *Femi-
   niste*, April 7, 2009, http://www.feministe.us/blog/archives/2009/04/07/lets-talk
   -about-pornography-an-interview-with-shine-louise-houston/.
6 Pick, "New Queer Cinema and Lesbian Film," 104.
7 "About Pink and White Productions," Pink and White Productions, accessed
   August 24, 2017, http://pinkwhite.biz/about/.
8 Jill Dolan, " 'Lesbian' Subjectivity in Realism: Dragging at the Margins of
   Structure and Ideology," in *Performing Feminisms: Feminist Critical Theory and
   Theater*, edited by Sue-Ellen Case (Baltimore: Johns Hopkins University Press,
   1990), 53.
9 Lo, "Shine Louise Houston Will Turn You On."

10 Jill, "Let's Talk about Pornography."

11 Spillers, "Interstices," 74.

12 Matt Richardson, "Our Stories Have Never Been Told: Preliminary Thoughts on Black Lesbian Cultural Production as Historiography in *The Watermelon Woman*," *Black Camera* 2.2 (2011): 102.

13 Laura Sullivan, "Chasing Fae: *The Watermelon Woman* and Black Lesbian Possibility," *Callaloo* 23.1 (2000): 456–57.

14 Mary Conway, "Spectatorship in Lesbian Porn: The Woman's Woman's Film," *Wide Angle* 19.3 (1997): 93.

15 Kelly Hankin, "Lesbian 'Making-of' Documentaries and the Production of Lesbian Sex," *Velvet Light Trap* 53.1 (2004): 28, 26, 33.

16 A film placard or box on screen provides a summary before the scene begins.

17 Jill, "Let's Talk about Pornography."

From Rage to Resignation

Reading Tina Mabry's *Mississippi Damned* as a Post–Civil Rights Response to Nina Simone's "Mississippi Goddam"

All I want is equality / for my sister my brother my people and me.
—**Nina Simone, "Mississippi Goddam"**

If you really wanna help [us], then you go on and be what we couldn't be.
—**Anna, in *Mississippi Damned***

Much has been written about Nina Simone's song "Mississippi Goddam" because it lyrically achieves the political consciousness of the embattled community whose experiences and energy it intends to speak to, through, and for. With its curse words, impatient tone, and energetic rhythm, it could never be mistaken for the traditional, Christian-inflected civil rights dirge. "Alabama's got me so upset," the chorus complains. "Tennessee made me lose my rest, and," as if its atrocities need not be spelled out, "everybody knows about Mississippi, goddam!" The song was banned from radio airplay but still became part of the civil rights sound track; it was adopted as an anthem for college-age activists who participated in the 1964 Mississippi Freedom Summer, and Simone performed it at a concert organized by Harry Belafonte at the second fifty-four-mile march from Selma to Montgomery, Alabama, in March 1965. The crowd cheered when she adapted the verse to "Selma made me lose my rest."

Persistent interest in Simone's contributions to the history of African American activism and musical canon has generated copious scholarship. Using the insights wrought from some of those studies as my foundation, I will discuss how the musical narrative relates to another Mississippi-themed cultural product, the film *Mississippi Damned* (Tina Mabry, 2009). What intrigues me in particular is how these works can be read as a dialogue, in the call-and-response tradition, between black southern queer women, as they participate in the tradition of condemning the South through invocations of the Christian Hell. My goal is to demonstrate how their respective uses of the root word *damn* in their protest art also expresses a particular rhetorical and historical positioning for themselves as social beings. I propose that the tone and rhetorical purposes of "Mississippi Goddam" serve as a call that bespeaks defiance and self-determination from a politicized context of intensified threat and danger. And that forty years later, *Mississippi Damned* provides an equally emotional but distinctively pessimistic response from a post–civil rights generation that was experiencing a different kind of backlash to the struggle for inclusion and justice.[1]

To that end, the chapter is divided into three sections. The first section contextualizes Simone's "cursing" of Mississippi and relies on scholarship in performance studies, history, ethnomusicology, and culture studies to identify the song's social function and the artist's rhetorical project. Before moving into the comparative analysis, I spend time in the second section critiquing what I call the discourse of injured and injurious sexuality that undergirds the plot of *Mississippi Damned*. Last, I discuss the film's ethos of individual success as evidence of the neoliberal rhetoric that dominated the public discourse in the 1990s.[2]

Nina Simone's Call

Damn (dăm) *v. tr.* 1. To pronounce an adverse judgment upon. 2. To cause the failure of. 3. To condemn as harmful, illegal, or immoral. 4. *Theol.* To condemn to everlasting punishment.

Nina Simone, born Eunice Waymon, relates that 1963 marks the year of her transformation, wherein sadness and rage about the terrorist bombing of 16th Street Baptist Church in Birmingham, Alabama, precipitated an awakening in which "all the truths I had denied myself for so long rose up and slapped my face." Up until that point, although she was well aware of the ways racial boundaries circumscribed much of her life experiences, her upbringing dictated that she perceive racist encounters as her individual struggle, a struggle that was to be met with dignified stoicism. In her family silence was valued over confrontation. "The Waymon way was to turn away from prejudice and to live your life as best you could," Simone recalls, "as if acknowledging the existence of racism was in itself a kind of defeat." So the public spectacle created by activists engaged in collective acts of civil disobedience as a way to draw attention to oppressive systems would have been antithetical to her respectability politics. Further, she remembers that she did not feel connected to the black freedom struggle until her social circle began to include intellectuals whose political philosophy overtly informed their artistry. Namely, she credits James Baldwin, Langston Hughes, and especially Lorraine Hansberry for articulating how the fight for civil rights legislation was part of a broader social justice struggle. In *I Put a Spell on You*, Simone explains her awakening to ways her identity interacts with her social positioning: "Lorraine [Hansberry] started off my political education, and through her I started thinking of myself as a black person in a country run by white people and a woman in a country run by men. I realized I was ignorant and had much to learn, but my teachers from Lorraine onwards were the cream of the movement . . . most of whom I would never meet face to face but in their writings, speeches or just in their actions . . . they pointed the way forward."[3] Discussions with her activist friends and her awareness of recurring violence around the country made it clear that the societal structure, not interpersonal prejudices alone, created and perpetuated a racial double standard that many people did not want to see change. She began to see that "turning away from prejudice" was impossible because individual acts were components of a larger American machine that utilized various forms of violence against those who took a stand against the status quo.

The historical record shows that Simone's politicization occurred during a peak year of a protracted season of state-supported, antiblack extremism (1955–65) across the nation. Determined to maintain their control of and advantaged access to public resources, white Americans rose in mass resistance to various new desegregation laws handed down by the U.S. Supreme Court. For example, in 1957 nine high school students were chosen for a gradually phased desegregation program at Central High School in Little Rock, Arkansas, in accordance with the 1954 *Brown v. Board of Education* ruling. They were turned away by the Arkansas National Guard troops under orders from the governor. The students, collectively called the Little Rock Nine, were eventually allowed to attend classes when President Eisenhower used his executive powers to override the governor. But the resistance was rigid against change; the president had to send military soldiers to protect the children from the gesticulating mob of white parents that gathered on the campus, as well as from the white students who were relentlessly attempting to injure or

15.1 Nina Simone in *What Happened, Miss Simone?*, directed by Liz Garbus, 2015. Netflix.

intimidate them.[4] Shortly thereafter the Arkansas General Assembly enacted a law, approved by voters, to close all four of Little Rock's public high schools after the first phase of the integration (one academic year). The NAACP went to battle with the state in the courtroom to overturn the measure. Meanwhile black students bore the brunt of the violence of educational deprivation during that "lost" academic year.[5]

From the taxpayer-supported schoolyard to privately owned restaurant service, the white majority opposed change through violence, often with state support.

In 1960 organized sit-in campaigns in Greensboro, North Carolina, gained national media attention, and the tactic quickly spread across seven states. Racially diverse groups of college students occupied the whites-only service counters in restaurants and were often subjected to swift and violent retaliation by the opposition and carted away by police officers. In December that year the Supreme Court ruled in *Boynton v. Virginia* that racial discrimination against passengers was unconstitutional on interstate buses. Activists organized to test the ruling. The Freedom Riders, as they were called, were attacked by angry white mobs and encountered intimidating police tactics in Virginia, North Carolina, South Carolina, and most brutally in Jackson, Mississippi. A year later, in Oxford, Mississippi, Governor Ross Barnett refused to allow James Meredith, a twenty-nine-year-old Air Force veteran, the opportunity to enroll after being admitted to the University of Mississippi. White students rioted when Meredith finally registered, with the protection of federal marshals sent by Attorney General Robert Kennedy, and became the first African American to do so at their campus. All of these cases and incidents were prominent news stories that Nina Simone likely knew about but would not have connected with because of her passive attitude toward racial problems. But when she changed her viewpoint, the shift was rapid and radical.

Fast-forward to September 1963. Black America was still reeling from the murder the previous June of Medgar Evers, a field secretary for the Mississippi chapter of the NAACP. Evers was well known outside of Mississippi because he was James Meredith's advisor during the University of Mississippi confrontation. Simone realized that "the bombing of the little girls in Alabama and the murder of Medgar Evers were like the final pieces of a jigsaw that made no sense until you had fitted the whole thing together."[6] With this paradigm shift came a more clear-eyed determination to lend her art to the cause of progressive change.

She wrote "Mississippi Goddam," a show tune melody that floats atop a jovial and jaunty syncopation; however, the frustration and horror expressed in the lyrics belie the tune's merriment. The chorus builds, lyrically, toward the expletive, which captures the mounting tensions of the 1960s political environment. The incongruence between the upbeat feeling of the music and the dark, militant words is an innovation in the protest song tradition, which previously relied mostly on gospel music and spirituals for their form and content.[7] Scholars have identified the three major components of Simone's rhetorical project as the musical structure of the song, the narrative themes that emerge in the lyrics, and the additional function of the "curse" she heaps upon Mississippi. My discussion focuses on the latter two aspects and how symbolic elements, dialogue, and the ethos of Mabry's work overlap and diverge from them.

God/dam: To Curse and "Curse Out"

Even if Simone was not aware of the statistics, history has shown that Mississippi had earned its reputation as the state most overtly resistant to African Americans' quest for justice since emancipation. Charles Payne reports in *I've Got the Light of Freedom* that it had the highest rate of lynchings in the nation between the end of Reconstruction and the early 1960s. Neil McMillen also documents it as the most racially restrictive state in the South at the time because African Americans had the poorest quality education, fewest enforced rights, and no legal recourse against whites who acted criminally against them.[8] Nonetheless, as Ruth Feldstein points out, Simone rejects the notion that the South was unique in terms of discrimination when she declares in the song, "The whole country is full of lies."[9] It seems that this is the unsettling crux of Simone's alienation: what "everybody knows" is that there is no apparent sanctuary for black life; no school, no church, no community, and no elected official's office is free of antiblack sentiment. She voices discontent with the way black life is menaced, as James Baldwin often quipped, from every side.

Scholarship on the song also focuses on the alienation enacted by these lyrics from the internal politics of the civil rights movement. Alongside the work of calling out the "lies" of the American Dream and "melting pot" mythologies, the song breaks with gender and racial expectations of the mainstream movement. It does so by identifying the apparent failures of the middle-class respectability politics that her family had embraced, which was the movement's strategy of dignified stoicism under pressure. Marisa Chappell documents how respectability was an important component from the beginning of the modern freedom movement, as it served as a countermeasure to negative stereotypes that many believed could deter whites and middle-class blacks from sympathizing with the movement's tactics to attract publicity. Chappell explains:

> Even the most celebrated tactic to emerge during the [1955 Montgomery, Alabama,] boycott—nonviolent direct action—revealed black efforts to conform to ideals of middle class black respectability. Following the bombing of [Martin Luther] King's and [another movement leader's] homes, and again during the mass arrests under the state's anti-boycott law, [Montgomery Improvement Association] leaders demonstrated restraint and dignity in the face of extreme provocation which surprised white America and helped to sway opinion to their cause. The nonviolence of the protest, which a *Washington Post* account called "impeccably lawful, orderly, [and] dignified," belied pro-segregationist arguments that African Americans were purely instinctual beings, lacking the capacity for level-headed thought or restraint, and proved "especially gall[ing]" to white Montgomery. Restraint, order, and propriety were hallmarks of post-war middle-class respectability, and they proved powerful weapons for gaining public support.[10]

Part of the assimilationist approach was to submerge one's anger or indignation when one confronted those same emotions in whites. So the utterance of "goddam" in response to the bombings and murders, and in a public forum, was very "unladylike" and clearly the opposite of restraint. Along with that, the use of a curse word breaks with the religiosity of the protest song tradition, in that it entails a call for vengeance and condemnation rather than the "turn the other cheek" and "love thy enemy" ethos of Christianity.

When we couple this speech act with the lines, in the first verse, asking that "someone say a prayer" and, later, renouncing a belief in prayer altogether, the use of "goddam" becomes an ironic declaration that some rituals are less useful forms of intervention for harnessing spiritual forces against one's enemies.[11] It suggests a "fraught relationship with a God that she now rejects and yet simultaneously needs in order to fulfill her condemnation of the South."[12] Instead of calling on angels or God to protect the civil rights workers as they marched through the valley of the shadow of death, Simone demands that death's angels punish the South for its atrocities.

This reading is not inconsistent with Simone's interpretation of her role as performer. As Danielle Heard has demonstrated, Simone's performances were a type of spiritual work in which she would lead audiences into new perspectives.[13] Heard's views are gleaned from Simone's own words in *I Put a Spell on You*, wherein she describes her effect on audiences as "mass hypnosis," the "ability to make people feel on a deep level," and as "electricity hanging in the air." In addition to writing consciousness-raising lyrics, she defined her activism as the ability to hold audiences captive so they would become engaged listeners, as if at a sermon instead of a musical concert. Simone illustrates her conjure work thusly: "To cast a spell over an audience I would start with a song to create a certain mood . . . until I created a certain climax of feeling and by then they would be hypnotized. To check, I'd stop and do nothing for a moment and I'd hear absolute silence: I'd got them. It was always an uncanny moment."[14] So when the conjurer launches a curse upon the country, the South, and Mississippi in particular, the rhetoric functions to incite a "climax of [vindictive] feeling" against the wrongdoers.

I would add that Simone is also "cursing out" Mississippi, which is distinct from issuing a spiritual condemnation or a wish for failure. In African American idiom, "to curse somebody out" means to upbraid or to reprimand by way of hostile, disrespectful, attention-garnering language. It is a type of chastising that occurs in response to an emotional injury or some other perceived wrongdoing. Importantly, because cursing someone out can be an attempt to correct behavior, it sometimes reveals an investment in that person or relationship. That is to say, it is not necessarily an act of utter dismissal and alienation. Rather it is often a way to clarify or reinforce boundaries, claim one's authority in the situation, and shame the receiver for their misconduct. In this paradigm Simone curses out Mississippi because she wants to shame it into compliance with the new laws and the constitutional ideal of the right to life and liberty, and she does so on behalf of black Mississippians for whom the state is an ambivalent site of cultural traditions, nurturing, and wounding.

Overall, then, the "call" of 1963, in tone and text, is a brew of fury and discontentment but, ultimately, the voice of a defiant and empowered generation. The exclamation "goddam" functions rhetorically as a fire-and-brimstone condemnation, consciousness-raising conjure work, and truth-to-power upbraiding.[15] It is a black woman's fist shaking in the face of white terrorism, governmental apathy, and black respectability politics. As a voice of its generation, the musical text stakes a claim to collectivity ("All I want is equality for my sister my brother my people and me") and evinces a belief that progress is on the horizon. We will see that with a change in the title's modifying term from active to passive form, *Mississippi Damned* signifies on Simone's fist-waving "performance of rage."[16]

Tina Mabry's Response

Damned (dămd) *adjective*. 1. Condemned. 2. *Informal*. Detestable. 3. *Theol.* Souls doomed to eternal punishment.

A fictionalized account of Mabry's upbringing in Tupelo, *Mississippi Damned* centers on a working-class family constantly teetering on the edge of abject poverty.[17] Whereas Simone's narrator is an agent in the action, Mabry's title conveys that her characters are on the receiving end of it. The film "talks back" to the song with plot lines and outcomes that privilege self-improvement over collective progress and leave the audience with a sense of hand-wringing pessimism. A major focus of the film are the trajectories of three characters, Sammy, Leigh, and Kari, who are introduced as children and grow up over the course of the story. Viewers follow them as they "independently struggle to escape their circumstances and . . . [as they] decide whether to confront what's plagued their family for generations or succumb to the same crippling fate, forever damned in Mississippi."[18] The story takes place between 1986 and 1998 and has as its backdrop a town that has maintained the socioeconomic inequalities that were decried in the 1960s. If "Mississippi Goddam" represents the voice of a generation on the verge of impactful change by their

15.2 Paula (Jasmine Burke) and Leigh (Chasity Kershal Hammitte) in
Mississippi Damned, directed by Tina Mabry, 2009.

own doing, *Mississippi Damned* relays a message from the movement's ben-
eficiaries that overwhelmingly conveys disappointment and frustration with
promises unfulfilled.

The legislative changes that occurred in the years between the release of
the anthem and Mabry's birth in 1978 gave African Americans hope. The Civil
Rights Act of 1964 made it unlawful for an employer to discriminate in hiring
and workplace practices because of an individual's race, skin color, religion,
biological sex, or national origin; the Voting Rights Act of 1964 was passed to
overcome state and local legal barriers that had been put in place to prevent
African Americans from exercising their right to vote; and the Fair Housing
Act of 1968 expanded the protections of the previous acts to prohibit identity-
based discrimination in the sale, rental, and financing of housing. The decade of the 1970s saw the implementation of color- and gender-conscious
Affirmative Action programs and federal work programs that improved the
chances for many people to succeed, and increased the percentages of blacks
and whites who were able to steadily rise into a middle-class status. The government collected taxes to pay for programs that lifted people out of poverty,
trained youth for new jobs, and increased access to health, mental health, and
social services as well as child care, food, and housing.[19]

Unfortunately, as chronicled in the work of economic historians, the
gains wrought by these policies were constantly contested and, over time, reduced to their minimal effect. Particularly the backlash against federal- and

state-level antipoverty programs and other forms of economic justice led to an increasingly bifurcated black community in which one group represented middle-class success and the other an underclass "virtually unaffected" by the changes.[20] Mainstream resistance and governmental apathy peaked and have held sway since Ronald Reagan's tenure as president (1981–89). What is now known as "Reaganomics" was a set of policies that redistributed wealth from social programs for the poor in order to invest in building and concentrating wealth in the propertied classes.[21] This state of affairs is the context in which Mabry's characters exist. They are the working poor, an economic class made up of homeowners who struggle every month to meet their mortgage payments and monthly bills, renters on public assistance housing or in motels, and those living in shelters or on the streets, a large majority of whom regularly endure food insecurity.

Mississippi Damned focuses mainly on the children in an extended family who are "cursed" by an inability to escape the circumstances into which they were born. In keeping with the title, the characters encounter recurrent setbacks that trap the family in cycles of dysfunction, addiction, poverty, and overall underachievement—damned indeed. I am particularly interested in one of the central themes, the traumatic entry into sex during childhood, which ultimately constructs some sexual subjects as manifestations of injured-and-therefore-injurious behaviors. In other words, their sexuality is marred, or cursed, if you will, by the initial trauma and expressed through the repetition of it. This logic of the cursed body becomes a discursive minefield for Mabry as she attempts to avoid pathologizing her own sexuality in the story of her life.

The Problem of Injured and Injurious Sexuality in *Mississippi Damned*

The motif of injured and injurious sexuality begins with Sammy's story. As a young boy he is abused, and in each instance his victimization is tied to parental neglect or ineptitude. The first example occurs in a scene of sexual abuse. Sammy (Malcolm David Kelley / Michael Goodwin) is a talented high school basketball player whose mother, an employee at a local factory, cannot afford to buy him new athletic shoes or pay the $50 he needs to play in a tournament that would likely be attended by college and NBA scouts. Sammy's aspirations and his poverty make him an easy mark for Pumpkin (Eugene Long), the flashy-dressed pedophile who is also his uncle's friend. Pumpkin exploits his knowledge of Sammy's circumstances to coerce him into performing fellatio in exchange for the money he needs. When Sammy initially resists the solicitation, Pumpkin licks his lips and asks, "What you gone do with a drunk for a mama, huh Sammy? You got a goddam daddy that couldn't pick your ass out of a lineup, boy." Sammy, desperate for the opportunity to impress the sports scouts and undoubtedly feeling powerless, submits. This link between paternity, money, and violence is made again when his mother's boyfriend assaults Sammy in other ways. Willie Roy (Charles Parnell) is a tall, muscular, intimidating presence, yet Sammy rebelliously steals money from the sleeping man's wallet one morning when the refrigerator is empty. Upon his return from the grocery store with arms loaded with bags, Sammy is greeted at the door with a flurry of slaps and kicks that leave him and the food sprawled across the living room floor. Sammy's mother, Charlie (Jossie Harris Thacker), who was shown in the bed with Willie Roy earlier, is absent from the scene. It is implied throughout this story line of Sammy's dysfunctional home life that, although they are food-insecure, Sammy's mother insists on sharing the apartment with a man who does not respect her or contribute financially to the household.

Charlie's poor choices have a lasting and deep impact on her son. This is brought home when Sammy's role shifts from victim to perpetrator. Eventually Charlie is incarcerated for attacking Willie Roy's other lover with a knife. Although he moves in with his aunt and uncle, Sammy reaches out to his father in hopes of kindling their relationship; his father cancels their plans at the last minute. In his disappointment Sammy seeks company with his (approximately) six-year-old cousin, Kari, in her bedroom. With the light of the television flickering across their faces, she plants a sympathetic kiss on his cheek. Sammy's advanced sexual knowledge, or miseducation, leads him to respond to Kari's childish affection by raping her (off screen). If only he could have turned to his father at this pivotal moment in his life, the narrative suggests, the situation with Kari would never have happened.

So Sammy's traumatic history leads to actions that further negatively impact his own well-being, as well as Kari's and another teenage female victim, whom he sexually assaults when he is an adult. It is not my position that the logic of this trajectory is problematic. Sammy's outcome as a character aligns with decades-old studies in the behavioral sciences showing that victims of sexual abuse sometimes become abusers. Furthermore, according to the National Center for the Victims of Crime, most children are abused by someone they know and trust, although boys are more likely than girls to be abused outside of the family.[22] What I aim to show in this brief critique is how this framing, the motif of injured and injurious sexuality in the lives of the children, leads to a faulty parallel in Leigh's story and gaps or erasures in Kari's: Hers is the narrative that represents the writer-director's life.

In Leigh's case, the injurious sexuality is lesbian desire. Early in the film, Leigh (Chasity Kershal Hammitte) and Paula (Jasmine Burke)—whose ages and grade levels are unclear but who are older than Sammy—are revealed to be in a romantic relationship. During a family house party, the lovers steal away to a bedroom to indulge in each other's kisses as they flip through the pages of *Hustler* magazine. Later in the film they share in the stereotypical small-towner's dream of migrating to an urban center and making a life for themselves as a couple. Meanwhile, at the house party, Leigh's mother, Delores (Michael Hyatt), bursts into the room and, in her reaction, embodies the shaming gaze of heterosexist social forces that will inform the girls' individual choices and their trajectory as a couple. When Delores bursts into the bedroom, the kissing couple abruptly separates. As Paula attempts to leave the room, Delores, her face a mask of disapproval, fills the doorway with her body. Visibly intimidated, Paula squeaks, "Excuse me, Mrs. Peterson," as she tries again to escape. Delores does not move, so Paula is forced to crouch beneath Delores's armpit and squeeze her way through the doorframe. At this Delores turns her burning gaze to Leigh, the primary source of her irritation, and angrily instructs her to join the card game in the kitchen. Without vocalizing her opposition to the same-sex romance, Delores warns her daughter with a look in her eyes and body language. It is not until they get home that both of her parents confront Leigh about "bringing that dyke bullshit up in this house" and how they are not surprised that it's with Paula, who has turned out "just like that no good mama of hers." For the rest of the film Leigh's sexual nonconformity is constructed as a central problem in her life; her attraction to Paula is framed as a symptom of her addictive personality and malformed emotional development.

Leigh's injured and injurious sexuality is forged in the loss of Paula's companionship when she ends the relationship abruptly. Leigh's reaction to the emotional rupture evokes what Ann Cheng describes in another context as a "melancholic response." Cheng's discussion proceeds from "Mourning and Melancholia," in which Freud posits that the difference between these emotional states is in the time a person spends in the throes of grief. Mourning is "a healthy response to loss; it is finite in character and accepts substitution (that is, the lost object can be relinquished and eventually replaced)." Melancholia, in contrast, is an unhealthy pathological response in which "the melancholic is psychically stuck" in a cycle that refuses any substitution that would fill the void. Cheng goes on to explain that the melancholic constantly feeds on the memory of loss, which in itself is a type of nurturance, until that individual is defined by it; this is self-making through loss and denigration.[23] It is also an accurate description of Leigh in *Mississippi Damned*, for her lesbian subjectivity is defined by loss, denigration, and injurious desire.

The narrative creates parallels between Leigh's material instability and her melancholic behavior, a staging that ties her outcome to the disease of addiction (a predisposition inherited from her father). Twelve years after her breakup with Paula, Leigh epitomizes the "constant feeding on the memory of loss." Paula has settled into the stability of a traditional, respectable heteronormative existence in marriage, motherhood, and a home. Leigh, in her early thirties by this time, has allowed the dream of escape with Paula to the big city to become a melancholic haunting. Perpetually single and struggling to maintain payments on a rented trailer, she regularly drives past Paula's home or parks across the street in hopes of catching a glimpse of her. When Leigh's gambling addiction leads to eviction and homelessness, Kari finds her parked in Paula's driveway, staring dejectedly, hair uncombed, and surrounded by all of the possessions she could pack into the car. At that point the material and emotional losses intersect and Leigh is metaphorically, literally, and psychically stuck just outside the realm of (what she must imagine is) Paula's domestic bliss. Her existence is reduced to a type of "ambulatory despair" defined by unrequited longing.[24] "She'll probably call the police again," Leigh thinks aloud, confirming that Paula views this attachment as a threat. Also this is stalking behavior, a criminal violation of Paula's personal space and private property. When considered in the larger symbolic scheme, homosexual attachment is excessive; it is analogous to a gambling addiction *and* Sammy's learned pedophilic behavior. To drive this point home, the film carries this parallel through to its logical conclusion when Sammy commits suicide and Leigh is institutionalized, which is a social death. In her final scene Leigh's face is expressionless and her demeanor unnervingly subdued beneath the hospital gown. The lesbian menace is contained at last, a point that leads me to the last child character to grow into adulthood over the course of the film, Kari (Kylee Russell / Tessa Thompson).

Mabry has spoken often in interviews about the autobiographical nature of the film (it is also stated in the credits). She has explained that Kari, with a few creative adjustments, is herself: the exception to the rule in her family of unsuccessful attempts to climb out of the fray. This is important because Mabry is also a lesbian who is public about her marriage to her producer and editor, Morgan Stiff, and she considers her art a sociopolitical tool against the marginalization of nonwhite and nonmainstream stories, homophobia, and ignorance. So it is disappointing that Kari's exceptionalism is not also represented by the development of a healthier queer subjectivity. I concede that time-saving editorial decisions must be made in a story chock full of complex characters and complicated circumstances that are designed so that audiences will identify with Kari's desire for escape and change.[25] Nonetheless Kari's story leaves something to be desired. She has no romantic experiences, no pursuers, no burning desire other than to study music in New York City.[26] She works hard, saves her money, and is in constant search of a financial lifesaver through scholarship and loan options. We, the audience, worry: Will she be accepted into the school of her choice? If so, will she be able to afford the costs to travel and live in the city? Will she have to give up her savings to help her parents? That is not to say that Kari is a flat character; rather, she is underwritten. While her childhood trauma and its effects are made evident, her characterization is underdeveloped in comparison to her counterparts'.

The effects of the rape on Kari are dramatized by her silence, fear, and guilt. When Sammy returns to Mississippi as a recently injured ex-NBA player, Kari is afraid to accept his offer to contribute to her tuition with a personal loan. When he seems perplexed by the rejection, she does not explain that she fears her acceptance would be mistaken as a gesture of forgiveness. Also, like many victims of sexual assault, she did not discuss the experience with anyone but her sister. The choice to remain silent (in the family and community) about his offense creates guilt for Kari when Sammy rapes the young sister of Kari's friend. "Leigh said he's done this shit before. Has he?" Omar (Michael Pagan) demands to know when he learns of the crime. As the tears trickle down her face, Kari confirms as much but cannot speak her truth any further. Her inner life is complicated, and her silences speak volumes about her pain. With all of this, it would be politically dangerous for a black, out lesbian filmmaker to represent Kari's burgeoning sexuality in a story about people whose sexual-emotional adulthood is evidence of suffering in their early lives. Accordingly Mabry chose not to leave it open for interpretation.

Kari's sexual-emotional solitariness seems the only solution to the dilemma of black lesbian self-representation in a narrative that relies on the logic of trauma to underwrite all of the characters' motivations. When we consider that Leigh's addictive behavior as a gambler and forlorn lover is attributed to entrenched poverty, limited life options, and a homophobic environment, and that Sammy's acts of sexual violation are reverberations of the violence of

15.3 Morgan Stiff and Tina Mabry at the 2009 Zurich Film Festival.

poverty, abuse, and neglect he suffered in his youth, it follows that the muting of Kari's sexuality would be a strategic silence to avoid any suggestion that lesbian desire is the result of a traumatic heterosexual encounter. This silence could very well be Mabry's refusal to lend her work, even unintentionally, to discourses of self-loathing and internalized homophobia. The transformation of disrupted lesbian desire into melancholic stagnation (in Leigh's plotline), although still a pathologizing perspective, is not quite the same as defining a lesbian identity as trauma-induced evasion of men.

Mississippi Be Damned: The Ethos of Individual Success

In regard to the film's sociopolitical ethos, the cultural politics evident in the resolution represent the shift in dominant racial discourses from a spirit of collective progress, Simone's "myself, my brother, and me" of 1963, to the 1990s neoliberal self-help ideology of independent success. Unlike Simone's theme of social collective progress through collective processes, Mabry's portrayal defines progress as individual change through escape—the collective be damned. This is because, as I have stated, during the 1980s the strong mainstream support of Affirmative Action laws and policies garnered during the civil rights era steadily waned. Laws crafted to remedy the effects of centuries of institutionalized racial and gender exclusions stirred racial resentments and provoked cries of "reverse racism" from many whites, which consequently triggered renouncements by some conservative-leaning blacks as an unearned advantage. Such conservatives, including Ward Connerly Jr., Armstrong Williams, and Supreme Court Judge Clarence Thomas, rose to prominence during this period and made the case that black people should feel insulted by any racially conscious criteria that would facilitate their entry into previously closed doors. Black success, according to this rationale, would be marred by a nagging doubt that could be avoided by an equally competitive "color-blind" playing field. Moreover many white Americans felt that ongoing efforts to create an egalitarian society had gone on too long and began to insist on making a distinction between "equal rights" (every citizen is the same under the law) and what they considered "special rights" (oversight and accountability provisions in hiring, housing, and education). So by the time the character Kari was applying to college in 1998, lawsuits against educational institutions' use of Affirmative Action strategies were being filed and negative campaigns against antipoverty programs had facilitated the erosion of the social safety net by Presidents Reagan, G. H. W. Bush, and Clinton.[27]

Of course the turn in mainstream ideology was not really a new direction; it was the resurgence of the nineteenth-century definition of success made in the Horatio Alger image of the self-made, self-contained man who earned material gains through luck and pluck, a white male-authored fairy tale of American meritocracy. The political vision of social transformation through publicly funded initiatives was eventually eclipsed by a neoliberal narrative of individualism that was advanced in popular culture by perspectives that relegated the problem of "real racism" to a distant past.[28] As Jeffrey Dudas explains, "Indirectly, this understanding of contemporary American politics leads to a preferred explanation for why African Americans, for example, disproportionately work at lower-paying jobs, live in worse housing conditions, and possess less income than whites: they have refused or otherwise failed to take advantage of the equal opportunities afforded them."[29] Hence the deserving are rewarded and the undeserving marked by their low station in society. To be clear: It is not my contention that *Mississippi Damned* argues against the kind of social justice called for in the civil rights era. My position is that Mabry's art is a reflection of and response to the dominant neoliberal discourse of her generation and, in comparison to the foremother's "call," indicates a shrunken sense of empowerment in the face of such social resentment and governmental defaulting on its contracts with historically disadvantaged groups.

As the film nears its end, a spirit of resignation hovers, like swollen gray clouds, over Kari as she mulls over her remaining possibilities to pay for college should she be accepted. Her aunt Anna (Simbi Khali Williams) discourages Kari's idea to defer college in order to continue financially supporting her ailing mother and recently laid-off father. She had already turned her savings over to them to keep their mortgage payments afloat, and her scholarship application, even if approved, would not be enough to cover a year of tuition and expenses. She is also concerned about Anna, to whom she is very close and whose health is visibly deteriorating. These decisions and anxieties reflect the ambivalent ways in which the place, for her, is not just about distress and struggle. It is home, a site of highly honored bonds and the deeply planted roots that provide necessary emotional and spiritual succor. Opposite and, sometimes, concurrent with the painful moments were those filled with nurturing, loving, and protective expressions. For Kari, the choice is not between family and self but between the immediate and distant futures.

However, as Kari cleans and straightens her aunt's living room, Anna warns her about the quicksand of dreams deferred in a statement that sets Kari's needs apart from the family's. "Don't you let this mess we got going on stop you," Anna insists. Their dialogue then pursues the we/you binary in a way that refuses traditional gender expectations that tether daughters to their dead or dying mother's households or demand that, if they do find fruitful opportunities, they "get set up and send for the rest of us." Anna uses the conversation to disabuse Kari of such self-sacrificial thinking with advice that captures the cadences of the neoliberal discourses that govern their circumstances. As she does so, Kari's mother interrupts, literally embodying the competing narrative of domestic obligation:

ANNA: The only thing about getting old is you can see twenty-twenty. . . . You can see options where you thought you ain't had none. And since you ain't old and gray, I'm gon be your sight. Ima tell you, if you don't leave now, you ain't gon never leave. You gon be sitting here, just like me: old and alone and with nothing to show for your life . . .

KARI [interrupts]: I can stay here and I can help y'all out.

[ANNA]: By helping yourself, you helping us. You see that? By helping yourself . . .

> [Phone rings. Kari answers, has a brief exchange, hangs up.
> Her mother has summoned her.]

Kari seems to have shaken off her aunt's words and begins to walk out of the room. Anna calls her back and reiterates the point with straight-faced conviction: "If you really wanna help, you go on and be what we couldn't be." The unspoken directive, "and to do so, you must go where we cannot," lingers in the kitchen when Kari closes the door behind her.

As it was for Nina Simone, Mabry's relationship to Mississippi is ambiguous. Family members find ways to support each other but can never find a way to rise above mere existence to a place where they can thrive. The advice from Anna, and the final scene in which Kari waves good-bye to her proud but debilitated family, community, and home state, illustrates that the tribulations in and of Mississippi are heartbreakingly overwhelming. This resolution, along with Sammy's literal death and Leigh's symbolic one, suggests that those who remain there do so at their own peril. So there is also resignation to the irreparable and irredeemable nature of the South, for which Mississippi is a symbol.

As Kari's northern migration follows the freedom-chasing route of millions of African Americans before her, the camera flashes across a sign bearing the state's motto: "Welcome to Mississippi. It's like coming home." Ironically, as she is "coming home" to her dreams, she travels away from everything familiar. Not shaking a righteous fist of solidarity. Waving a solitary, ambivalent gesture of good-bye.

Notes

1 The "post–civil rights era" refers to the decades following the passage of the Civil Rights and Voting Rights Acts in the 1960s, when the black freedom struggle encountered new challenges stemming from political leaders' declining commitment to racial equality and the erroneous belief that racism no longer existed. The term is used synonymously with "after 1965." Greta de Jong, *Invisible Enemy: The African American Freedom Struggle after 1965* (Sussex, UK: Wiley-Blackwell, 2010), 6.

2 Though I will provide some necessary historical contextualization, it is beyond the scope and intent of this chapter to outline all of the changes in the American sociopolitical landscape in the decades between "Mississippi Goddam" and *Mississippi Damned* or to pinpoint the images and dialogue in the film that may correlate to civil rights discourses.

3 Nina Simone and Stephen Clearly, *I Put a Spell on You: The Autobiography of Nina Simone* (New York: Da Capo, 1992), 89, 86, 87.

4 Melba Patillo Beals, a member of the Little Rock Nine, details the violence they endured from other students in her memoir *Warriors Don't Cry* (New York: Simon & Schuster, 1994).

5 According to Sondra Gordy, while 93 percent of white students found some form of alternative schooling, only 37 percent of displaced black students found public

schools in Arkansas to attend. Some located parochial schooling, others found out-of-state public and private schooling, and some entered college early. However, 50 percent of displaced black students found no replacement educational situation. Sondra Gordy, "Lost Year," in *The Encyclopedia of Arkansas History and Culture*, accessed March 10, 2013, http://www.encyclopediaofarkansas.net/encyclopedia/entry -detail.aspx?entryID=737.

6 Simone and Clearly, *I Put a Spell on You*, 89.

7 Tammy L. Kernodle, "'I Wish I Knew How It Would Feel to Be Free': Nina Simone and the Redefining of the Freedom Song in the 1960s," *Journal of the Society for American Music* 2.3 (2008): 295.

8 Neil McMillen, *Dark Journey: Black Mississippians in the Age of Jim Crow* (Urbana: University of Illinois Press, 1997), 9.

9 Ruth Feldstein, "I Don't Trust You Anymore: Nina Simone, Culture, and Black Activism in the 1960s," *Journal of American History* 91 (March 2005): 1349.

10 Marisa Chappell, Jenny Hutchinson, and Brian Ward, "'Dress Moderately, Neatly . . . as If You Were Going to Church': Respectability, Class, and Gender in the Montgomery Bus Boycott and the Early Civil Rights Movement," in *Gender and the Civil Rights Movement*, edited by Peter J. Ling and Sharon Monteith (New Brunswick, NJ: Rutgers University Press, 2004), 92.

11 Civil rights demonstrators often prayed in public spaces for inspiration, to demonstrate their belief that God was on their side, and as a form of moral suasion for onlookers and antagonizing forces. See Coretta Scott King's foreword to Schomburg Center for Research in Black Culture, *Standing in the Need of Prayer* (New York: Simon & Schuster, 2003). Relatedly, in "'I Wish I Knew How It Would Feel to Be Free,'" Tammy Kernodle argues that Simone's lyrics in this period represent the growing presence of more militant and secular factions of the movement that would not rely on moral arguments to make their case for inclusion and equality. She further argues that this song redefines the protest song and ushers in socially conscious lyrics in R&B music, such as "People Get Ready" by Curtis Mayfield.

12 Daphne A. Brooks, "Nina Simone's Triple Play," *Callaloo* 34.1 (2011): 188.

13 Danielle Heard, "'Don't Let Me Be Misunderstood': Nina Simone's Theater of Invisibility," *Callaloo* 35.4 (2012): 1065.

14 Simone and Clearly, *I Put a Spell on You*, 93.

15 Brooks, "Nina Simone's Triple Play," 189; Heard, "'Don't Let Me Be Misunderstood,'" 1065–66.

16 Feldstein, "I Don't Trust You Anymore," 1366.

17 Cast members include Michael Hyatt (*The Wire, Nightcrawler*), Tonea Stewart (*A Time to Kill, Girls Trip*), Tessa Thompson (*Creed, Dear White People*), and D. B. Woodside (*24, Lucifer*).

18 *Mississippi Damned*, "About," accessed August 24, 2017, www.mississippidamned .com/about/.

19 Mimi Abramovitz, "Welfare Reform in the United States: Gender, Race, and Class Matters," *Critical Social Policy* 26.2 (2006): 348.

20 Roopali Mukherjee, *The Racial Order of Things: Cultural Imaginaries of the Post-Soul Era* (Minneapolis: University of Minnesota Press, 2006), 12.

21 President Reagan's free market agenda imposed particular hardships on African Americans. One-third of the nation's black citizens lived below the poverty line in the 1980s, and they suffered greatly from the weakening of the social safety net. De Jong, *Invisible Enemy*, 49–50.

22 A National Center for the Victims of Crime study in three states found 96 percent of reported rape survivors under age twelve knew the attacker; 4 percent of the offenders were strangers, 20 percent were fathers, 16 percent were other relatives, and 50 percent were acquaintances or friends.

23 Anne Cheng, *Melancholy of Race* (Oxford: Oxford University Press, 2001), 7, 8.

24 Cheng, *Melancholy of Race*, 23.

25 Mabry and Stiff discuss the activist aspects of their work in an interview with *AfterEllen* on August 10, 2009. In addition, I asked Mabry about the absence of Kari's sexuality in an interview, and she replied that she had written the character as a lesbian but that it made the movie too long. See "From a Real Place and Real People: Interview with *Mississippi Damned* Writer/Director Tina Mabry," *Black Camera* 2.2 (2011): 130–37.

26 I acknowledge that Kari could also be read as a person on the asexual spectrum, were it not for Mabry's express claims that she is telling her own story through this character and that Kari's sexual or romantic attractions were edited out of the film (see note 25).

27 Jeffery R. Dudas, "In the Name of Equal Rights: 'Special' Rights and the Politics of Resentment in Post–Civil Rights America," *Law and Society Review* 39.4 (2005): 725; Robert M. Collins, *Transforming America: Politics and Culture in the Reagan Years* (New York: Columbia University Press, 2007), 131–33; de Jong, *Invisible Enemy*, 70–74; Mukherjee, *The Racial Order of Things*, 207–14.

28 Mukherjee analyzes the function of the civil rights nostalgia in 1990s Hollywood films in the third chapter of *The Racial Order of Things*.

29 Dudas, "In the Name of Equal Rights," 729.

The Circuitous Route of Presenting Black Butch
The Travels of Dee Rees's *Pariah*

At the 2012 Golden Globe awards, during her acceptance speech for the Best Actress award for her performance in *The Iron Lady* (Phyllida Lloyd, 2012), Meryl Streep gave a shout-out to Adepero Oduye for her role as Alike in Dee Rees's feature film *Pariah* (2011). The sentiment behind this esteemed acknowledgment was that brilliant performances in important independent films were overlooked and deserved recognition. Streep would go on to win the Best Actress Oscar for her portrayal of Britain's first woman prime minister, the ultraconservative Margaret Thatcher. Ironically Streep was championing Oduye's performance as the young queer black woman at the center of *Pariah* while accepting an award for embodying the neoliberal Iron Lady whose eleven-year reign deepened racial animosity, decimated support for the working class, and ushered in an Act of Local Government that prohibited the promotion of homosexuality.[1] Streep uttering Oduye's name on national television may have been the first time some viewers heard the name Adepero Oduye or learned of the film *Pariah*, but for some viewers, this author included, the expression of adoration was both surprising and heartwarming.

Those privileged enough to catch a screening of the short film *Pariah* (2007) were able to experience a rare cinematic moment in viewing a lyrical and emotionally stirring film about a young black lesbian struggling to embrace her sexuality. The arrival of the feature film version in theaters around the country brought the director Dee Rees and her film into the mainstream. *Pariah*'s presence in cinema houses nationwide allowed those who might not frequent film festivals to have access to the cinematic experience of feeling represented by Rees's rich and captivating depiction of black butch pleasure, pain, and intimacy on the big screen. The nod from Hollywood royalty put *Pariah* on the map for potential viewers who overlooked this coming-of-age film about a black lesbian teen from Brooklyn.

Although *Pariah* is not the first feature film to visualize the life of a black lesbian, cinematic narratives about black queer women have made few appearances in popular culture. Fifteen years before *Pariah* was released, Cheryl Dunye was credited with making the first black lesbian feature film, *The Watermelon Woman* (1996). The field has expanded in the years since Dunye's documentary-style narrative made its debut in theaters. In more recent years Lee Daniels's 2009 film *Precious* infused this cinematic adaptation of Sapphire's novel *Push* (1996) with a queer subplot by giving the lead character's mentor and teacher a lesbian life. Dee Rees's *Pariah* is the second feature film made by an out black lesbian director to have a national theatrical release in the United States. With *Pariah* the new millennium has a feature-length film dedicated to visualizing a critical, vulnerable moment in the life of a black queer teenager coming into her own.[2]

By exploring the narrative differences that emerge between the award-winning short film and the feature-length version of *Pariah*, my analysis attends to the industry demands required for an independent film about black queer adolescence to be viable in mainstream media. The undeniable success of the short film on the festival circuit, coupled with the feature film's presence in mainstream media, agitates conceptions of blackness that presume black heterosexuality.[3] This discussion of Rees's film addresses the manner in which the representation of black lesbian identity, and the familial discord set in motion by a black teenager's declaration of her queerness, visualizes an array of tensions produced within black families and religious communities around sexuality, authenticity, and national belonging. Through queer of color critique, I address the deep-rooted homophobia that courses through *Pariah* by offering a discussion of the relationship between heteronormativity, queerness, and blackness.[4] The chapter comes to a close with analysis of the visual representation of the black mother figure in which I raise questions about the marketing strategy used to garner mainstream appeal for the feature film version of *Pariah* and examine narrative changes that tap into historical characterizations of overly aggressive, pathological black motherhood.

Pariah: From Short to Feature

By tracking the cinematic journey of *Pariah* from short to feature, I attend to notions of universality that are used to market the visualization of black queer women's sexuality for a mass audience.[5] Of all the groundbreaking accomplishments a short film can generate, making a profit is usually not an expectation. The narrative modifications made for *Pariah*, the feature, are indicative of film industry demands for universal appeal in the capital-generating venture of Hollywood filmmaking. *Pariah*'s transition from a short film that spoke powerfully to a so-called niche market to a feature film expected to deliver universal appeal seems to have required a broadening of narrative scope and a shift in casting. Its nationwide theatrical release was monumental; no other narrative feature film dedicated to exploring the intricate dynamics of a black family grappling with the repercussions of having a lesbian daughter has been able to emerge in mainstream cinema. Yet the narrative demands placed upon the feature-length version of *Pariah* to attract a wider audience disrupted some of the poignancy and quiet tenderness captured in the short film—which makes that version stand alone as one of the most important pieces of film dedicated to visualizing black queer sexuality in the United States.

Rees has described the trajectory of the *Pariah* narrative as beginning with a feature-length script written during her time as a student at NYU Film School. For her thesis film project Rees excerpted the first act of her screenplay to make the short film version of *Pariah*.[6] The goal for Rees and her producer Nekisa Cooper with the short was to generate enough interest and capital to fund the feature. This approach worked. After the success of the short film version of *Pariah* on the festival circuit, Rees was approached by film industry insiders who were interested in reading a feature-length draft of the screenplay. Rees rewrote the script and casting changes were made.[7] Given the possibility that this kind of film would not generate a huge box office success, financial backing came from investors who were admittedly more interested in this story being told than in a large profit margin, though a profit was anticipated.[8] The narrative that captivated audiences, studio executives, and financial backers tells a heartbreaking story of a young woman trying desperately to be herself.

Pariah is a film about an African American teenage girl, Alike (pronounced Ah-Lee-Kay), who is learning to embrace her sexuality. She is already aware that she is a lesbian but has not had a girlfriend or even a first kiss. Alike is embracing her masculinity and working to find comfort and build confidence in her own gender identity.[9] She lives at home with her parents and her sister. They have a religious home, not overly deistic, but Christianity is the guiding force for the system of values that govern their household. Alike's best friend, Laura, is an out lesbian and could be read as butch or aggressive.[10]

16.1 Dee Rees with crew on the set of the feature film *Pariah*, 2011.

Laura shepherds Alike through an exploration of her gender expression by dressing her, giving her advice about finally getting that first kiss, and even supplying her with a strap-on dildo, albeit a white one.[11] Laura is estranged from her mother and has dropped out of high school yet manages to maintain her friendship with Alike. Alike lives a double life: she hides her sexuality and gender identity at home but changes into more masculine clothes once she gets to school. Her mother begins to worry that she is too much of a tomboy and becomes relentless about Alike behaving more like a lady. The narrative reaches a climax when Alike is literally backed into a corner by her mother and father and blurts out that she is a lesbian. She suffers an act of violence at this moment from which the family may never recover.

The changes between the short film narrative and the feature-length narrative are significant and have historical resonances. The two most striking narrative developments in the feature film center around Alike's fraught relationship with her mother, Audrey, and Alike's sexual encounter with Bina, who happens to be both a schoolmate and a member of the same church. Alike's mother forces her to befriend Bina because, unlike Laura who is unabashedly queer, aesthetically Bina reads as a straight young woman and Audrey thinks that she will be a good influence for Alike. Of course Alike resists a friendship with Bina out of what appears to be nothing more than defiance toward her mother. After spending time together, Bina and Alike become drawn to one another through music and poetry. One night, on a seemingly casual sleepover, Alike finds herself in Bina's bed and finally has her first kiss,

16.2 Alike (Adepero Oduye) in *Pariah*, directed by Dee Rees, 2011.

which turns into her first sexual experience with a woman. The next morning Bina is distant and tells Alike that she is not gay, that what happened between them was nothing serious and will never happen again. Alike is devastated, heartbroken, but this well of intense emotions gives her the courage to reveal her sexuality to her parents.

In the short film version of *Pariah* Alike's father, Arthur, reacts with violence when he learns that she is a lesbian and repeatedly strikes her.[12] In the feature film Alike's father is the more compassionate of her parents, and when Alike confirms that she is not a tomboy going through a phase but is in fact gay, her mother becomes violent. After the act of violence in both the short and the feature version of the film, Alike runs to Laura's apartment, where her best friend nurses her physical and emotional wounds. Alike's father finds her there and attempts to reconcile with her, encouraging her to come home.[13] The short film ends on this ambiguous note. In the feature Alike breaks the news to her father that she has been accepted into an early admission program at UC Berkeley and plans to leave immediately to begin her college education. Before she travels by bus from Brooklyn to the Bay Area, Alike visits her mother at work to say good-bye. She expresses her love for her mother, who refuses to return the sentiment. Heartbroken but undeterred, Alike boards the bus and heads west into a life that is of her own making. The analysis that follows works to contextualize the relationship between black families, the church, and heteronormativity in order to historically situate the homophobia that fuels Audrey's rejection of Alike.

Homosexuality and the Black Church in *Pariah*

Unlike the interracial love story that is at the center of Dunye's *The Water-melon Woman*—the first and only other feature film made by a black lesbian director featuring black queer women characters to garner a national release—*Pariah*'s narrative foregrounds sexual attraction between black women from strong churchgoing black families. The issues of authenticity and belonging in the black community that are visualized in Rees's narrative are undergirded in part by the conception that black queer sexuality is not authentic to blackness. Though visibility can be an oppressive regime in which black queer and trans people are policed and regulated, representing black lesbian sexuality on the big screen can also work to dismantle the mutual exclusivity of blackness and queerness.[14] With *Pariah* Rees offers us the cinematic presence of black lesbians loving who do not lose their blackness, even if they may be threatened with losing their families. Rees's visualization of sensuality between two young black women, whose mothers know each other from church, is provocative as these images challenge notions of black authenticity and implicate the black church in sanctioning homophobia.

While discussions of homophobia in black families and in the black church run the risk of perpetuating essentialist notions of black sexuality, it is important to address this tension given that homophobia in this black family is an integral component of the narrative of *Pariah*.[15] In my discussion of the impact that religion and homophobia have on Alike's family, I address the conservative ideology at work in Alike's mother's life and make sense of the religious crisis that erupts for her. The particular church that Alike's family belongs to is not made explicit in the film, beyond it being a predominantly black and Christian fellowship. The presence of religion and the black church emerges in the narrative when Alike sneaks in past her curfew. Audrey catches Alike tiptoeing to her bedroom and scolds her by telling her to wrap her head up so that her hair will look nice at church the next day; in this scene it becomes evident that this family actively participates in a religious community. The next morning Audrey expresses her disapproval of Alike's outfit and demands that she change into a more feminine top to wear to church, which makes Alike miserable. Throughout the last scene that Audrey and Alike share, when Alike visits her mother at work to say good-bye, Audrey holds her Bible close to her chest while refusing to reconcile with her daughter, making painfully clear that religious dogma has severed their relationship. Rees's depiction of the kind of black religiosity that foments homophobia unflinchingly represents the irrevocable ruptures that tear through families and break queer hearts. Without a doubt, inclusive black churches exist and black religious families do contend with dogmatic contradictions and embrace and love their LGBT children unconditionally— but this is not the narrative thrust of *Pariah*. Rees's film animates the conservative social connection between this black family and their church then dramatizes the horrendous act of violence and familial unraveling that occur as a result. In order to attend to this narrative conflict I offer some context for Audrey's deeply felt resistance to Alike's sexuality.

Black religious communities have historically been a nexus for fellowship and belonging for African American families, whether they vigorously embrace religious tenets or simply accept them as part of the fabric of the community space.[16] For generations black churches have served as centers for mobilizing resistance to racial and class oppression. In the struggle to achieve racial, economic, and social equality, the logic of impeccable moral standing was expected of black church members in order to be regarded as upstanding members of the community.[17] This produced an understanding that homosexuality had to be rooted out of black families and could not be accepted in black social networks. The black feminist scholar Patricia Hill Collins contends, "One reason the black church has seemed so resistant to change is that it has long worried about protecting the community's image within the broader society and has resisted *any* hints of black sexual deviance, straight and gay alike."[18] Within a hegemonic and white supremacist national climate, homophobia in the black community can become a way to resist racism and promote upward mobility in the eyes of a church and its members. With this logic, freedom from oppression is directly linked to heterosexuality.[19] To be sure, not all black churches and not all black families reject their queer children, relatives, and congregation members simply because of their sexuality and gender identity. Yet the perception of categorical homophobia within the black community persists. In fact the perception that black communities are decidedly antigay was exploited during the 2008 presidential election, in which black voters' increased presence at the polls was blamed for the passage of the anti–gay marriage bill, Proposition 8, in California, the election in which Barack Obama defeated John McCain. What was much less popularized and much more influential for the passage of Prop 8 than the increased black voter turnout was the funding of Prop 8 by the Mormon Church. The perception of deep-rooted black homophobia stoked anger and resentment in the LGBT community that was exacted against the black community, and in the process produced a conflict that erased black queer experiences, LGBT allies in the black community, as well as antiracist, nonblack members of the LGBT community.[20] The rhetoric surrounding Prop 8 that pitted the LGBT community against the black community exemplifies the damage wrought by the perception that black communities are homophobic, and yet this is the social and racial landscape through which *Pariah* treads.

While *Pariah* does relentlessly contend with black religious homophobia through Alike and Audrey's relationship, Rees also includes a representation of black queer love and kinship in scenes that capture Alike and her community of friends. *Pariah* opens with a lush and titillating scene in a black lesbian nightclub, which captures a sexiness that is palpable as well as the vulnerable awkwardness of our protagonist, which is quite endearing. A scene at the pier shows Laura and Alike with their extended group of friends, who hang out late into the night. We are witness to the tenor of this crew of queer kids who are coupled up, who tease and joke and make each other laugh, and who also look out for one another when they need a couch to sleep on for the night. Though he does not explicitly state this, Alike's father, Arthur, appears to be accepting of Alike's sexuality; he is the one who finds her at Laura's house after she runs away and asks her to come back home.

Rees's visualization of the multiplicity that exists within queer communities of color works to destabilize the imposed political divisions and essentializing conceptions of blackness that obfuscate black queerness and reinforce the notion that black communities are inherently homophobic. Homophobia exists in black communities as it does in differently racialized and nonracialized communities throughout this country, and its representation in this film may be the filmmaker's way of working through a personal experience as well. In a frank discussion about her own coming-out story, Rees recalls that she came out at the relatively older age of twenty-seven. When she told her parents that she was a lesbian, ostensibly with the making of her short film *Pariah*, they were terribly concerned. They flew from Tennessee to New York to circumvent the direction toward which her sexuality was heading.[21] The intervention was to no avail, but this point demonstrates the stakes of embracing queer sexuality for some members of black families. Rees's personal story is illustrative of the complexity of being a member of a racially, sexually, socially, and economically oppressed group in the United States working to protect and love each other while inevitably being impacted by the ways in which dominant groups have historically and contemporarily perceived, denied the value of, and stolen the lives of black people for simply existing, let alone being queer.

Visibility, Silence, and the Desire for Black Heteronormativity

The visibility of black women's sexuality, black queerness, and black trans identity has historically been threatening to black aspirations for equality within dominant society. The images of tragic black butchness presented in *Pariah* alongside the resistance by religious mother characters and hyper-masculine black male characters in the film create a cartography of violence that Alike, and her friends, must navigate at great peril. The strident opposition to black women embracing their sexuality in Rees's film is terrain that has been traversed by black women for generations. The long history of exploitation and repression paradoxically existing as concomitantly hypervisible and invisible is theorized in Evelynn Hammonds's "Black (W)holes and the Geometry of Black Female Sexuality." Hammonds contextualizes this contradiction by asserting, "Historically, black women have reacted to this repressive force of the hegemonic discourses on race and sex with silence, secrecy, and a partially self-chosen invisibility."[22] Black women reformers during Reconstruction developed methods to counter the damaging stereotypes that cast black women as overly sexual and wanton, constructions that were used to justify the sexual violence and terror that black women suffered during slavery and well after its abolition.[23]

The politics of silence was a set of strategies black women reformers used to protect black women during this perilous era that also required black women to be silent about their sexuality. Reformers embraced Victorian moral codes in an effort to dismantle the construction of black women as immoral.[24] The culture of dissemblance works in concert with the politics of silence to protect black women from violence and to improve, to borrow Gramsci's term, common sense understandings of black womanhood as sexually promiscuous, inherently rapable, and truly immoral.[25] As Hammonds asserts, this strategy failed because the culture of dissemblance that was produced through the politics of silence developed a seemingly earnest expression of morality, but in actuality the culture of dissemblance continued to make black women's sexuality invisible and limited the ways that black women could express their own sexuality. This strategy became a classed project in which middle-class black women policed black women lower on the socioeconomic scale, insisting that they adhere to strict Victorian morality as a method of uplifting the entire race.[26]

The culture of dissemblance and the politics of silence, which circumvent black women's articulation of their own sexuality, have had a far-reaching effect on black women's sexuality. There has been a cloaking of the wide and varied sexual expression in black communities, which interrupts the kind of healthy sexual atmosphere that would aid in recovering from historic sexual violence and negative stereotypes. But the impetus for these strategies must be kept in mind. The culture of dissemblance and the politics of silence were devised to mitigate the violence black women faced by advising them to hold fast to staunch sexual morality and quietude in order to disaggregate their sexuality from depravity. The expectation that black women had to negate their sexuality in an effort to reduce the threat of sexual violence in their everyday lives extends to the pressure faced by black families to be regarded as normative, morally upright, and politically conservative.

The fact of black families' blackness keeps them perpetually on the margins of heteronormativity.[27] Alike's mother (in the feature) and her father (in the short) are unable to accept her as a lesbian. This inability to accept her, while not articulated in the film, is laden with a history of black families being excluded from heteronormativity despite their proper "ideals and practices."[28] The American studies scholar Roderick Ferguson discusses African American culture and the constructs of heteronormativity that work to marginalize black families in his groundbreaking text, *Aberrations in Black: Toward a Queer of Color Critique*. Ferguson contends, "African American culture has historically been deemed contrary to the norms of heterosexuality and patriarchy. As its embodiment in whiteness attests, heteronormativity is not simply articulated through intergender relations, but also through the racialized body. . . . African Americans' only way to counter being deemed pathological is approximat[ing] heteronormative ideals and practices embodied in whiteness and ennobled in American citizenship."[29] Ferguson's assertion that heteronormativity remains within the domain of whiteness situates black families outside of heteronormativity, even though they may have familial elements that could constitute a heteronormative household.

In order to further explicate the fragile relationship between blackness and heteronormativity it is necessary to discuss a document that is commonly known as the *Moynihan Report*. In 1965 *The Negro Family: The Case for National Action* was published, in which Daniel Patrick Moynihan studied the "problem" of "negroes" not assimilating into heteronormativity after the passage of the 1964 Civil Rights Act. The sociologist found that the family structure was the fundamental problem with the Negro family, and the female-headed household was the outstanding culprit. Ferguson summarizes, "As a familial formation that 'retards progress' because of its nonheteronormative conformity, the female-headed household impedes the march of civil rights."[30] The *Moynihan Report* shifted the blame for this apparent lack of progress from racism, capitalism, and patriarchy onto the shoulders of black women. *Pariah* represents a black family that is ascending toward heteronormativity in terms of family structure, homeownership, religious practices, education, and freedom from dependency on social welfare resources—all of which are expected of black normativity. As is indicative of the racialization of heteronormativity, this black family's relationship to heteronormativity is tenuous and perpetually out of reach, which makes their daughter's lesbian sexuality a shocking threat to their attainment of it, despite all of the jobs, church-going Sundays, and family dinners.

Pariah's narrative poignantly represents the tension that a young queer black woman withstands when she begins to express her sexual desire at home, facing the conservative restrictions of her parents. While aspirations of heteronormativity are rooted in and given credence by the black church, dominant society maintains the belief that black families are not heteronormative no matter what configuration they assume. This raises the stakes for Alike's sexuality. Ferguson discusses dominant society's construction and proliferation of black families being deemed deviant because black women, wives, and mothers are overly aggressive and depose black men, husbands, and fathers from their rightful place as head of the household.[31] The black family as a unit has been critiqued as hopelessly nonheteronormative and as a result finds itself regimented by nationalistic concerns and religious tenets that protect the rule of the father in the household. Queer identities come under severe attack in this kind of societal and familial environment; the black church and the black family become the venues through which homophobia, heterosexism, and sexism are used as necessary elements in the "normalization" of black family structures.[32]

In the short film version of *Pariah*, when Alike's father beats her to the ground, yelling, "So you want to be gay, huh?," he is not simply trying to beat the gay out of her. He is also trying to beat back the racism that has oppressed him during his life. He is trying to beat back the deviance Alike possesses that will ostracize the family from their community and dashing any hopes of their assimilating into heteronormativity. The control he exerts over his daughter who cries for him to stop punching her and the power he displays over his wife when she begs him to stop beating their child demonstrate the violence that black queer children have to endure because racist and religious tenets have constructed authentic blackness as heterosexual.

Religiosity and the black church have served as vectors through which the dinge of sexual deviancy becomes absolved. The act of violence visualized in *Pariah* is a cinematic eruption that captures the sorrow and the stakes of not belonging and the pain that queer youth suffer when they are not interested in muting and contorting themselves to belong, despite the emotional and physical cost. Arthur's rage is indicative of the loss of all that he has worked for because his daughter "wants to be gay." This family is doing everything to achieve heteronormativity: the mother and father are married, they are both employed, they go to church, and they provide a good home for their children. This family is dispelling the belief that black families are inherently pathological. Arthur beats Alike as if she is stealing the normalcy he is rightfully entitled to as a black man who lives at home with his family as the head of the household. Alike's gayness tears that dream of normalcy down to the ground, so he beats her and beats her while his wife screams for him to stop. He screams back at her and blames her for their daughter's "affliction." He beats Alike with his fists and verbally abuses her and his wife in order to establish the law of the father that heteronormativity depends upon, that is slipping through his fingers. Alike is being blamed for destroying a heteronormativity that their family aspired to but never could actually achieve, even if their daughter was not gay.

In the feature film Rees rewrote this scene to have the mother be the violent parent. In an interview with Ernest Hardy for the *LA Weekly*, Rees explains, "Yeah, when I first wrote the feature script it was the dad who committed the violence. It was coming from a place of surprise, of him feeling betrayed that his best friend [his daughter] hadn't been honest with him. But as I workshopped it, it just didn't feel right. I realized that Arthur wouldn't be capable of this. I realized that it's Audrey who's not being listened to. It's Audrey who everybody's pushing away, so she's the one who's isolated. She's the one who's gonna be able to [commit an act of violence] and just lose herself." While Rees's explanation of her narrative choice is clear, Audrey's scorn of Alike and Laura has deeper historical resonances that reach back to the politics of silence and the culture of dissemblance.

Laura does not attempt to hide her sexuality or her masculinity. Her unapologetic butchness subverts the silence and dissemblance that respectable black women are expected to maintain about their sexual lives, which bolsters Audrey's justification of her contempt for Laura. Before Audrey ever lays a hand on Alike her disdain for homosexuality is made evident through her interactions with Laura. Laura is a young queer black woman who, while still in high school (in the short) and getting her GED (in the feature), lives on her own (in the short) and with her sister (in the feature) and holds a job stocking a grocery store warehouse. In the feature film Laura successfully studies and receives her GED. She brings the notification of this achievement to her mother, who, like Alike's mother, refuses to even engage her in conversation, let alone share in the joy of her academic success. The motherly disgust for Laura is expressed in the short film as well, but only through Alike's mother, whose disdain for Laura permeates the room whenever the two meet.

Throughout the film Audrey struggles with her husband over decisions about how to handle Alike's gender presentation as well as his behavior and overall presence in their marriage. Audrey does engage in struggles for power with Arthur yet always seems to defer to him in the end. Arthur tolerates Audrey's anxiety over Alike's self-expression while not sharing her concern.[33] The intimacy has drained from Audrey and Arthur's love life. Audrey is angry and lonely and silenced by her husband's dominance in the home. Her character occupies the space of the black mother who challenges the father's decisions, struggles for control of family matters, and in the process drives a wedge through her family unit. This character's overbearing and overly religious approach to her family pushes her husband away and apparently into another woman's arms. (The feature film alludes to Arthur's having an affair.) Audrey, as the villain of the story, is left to carry the burden of the failures in her marriage and in her home, while Arthur's affair is left uninterrogated and his character is able to hold the space of the understanding and tolerant father. Audrey is enacting the Negro problem outlined in the *Moynihan Report*, whose struggle to make decisions in the family enacts the failure of black heteronormativity. The multiple sources of loss and anxiety that plague Audrey are directed toward her desire to control Alike. As a black mother, Audrey is caught in a bind in which ascending toward black heteronormativity requires that she acquiesce to her husband while demanding that her child comply, though she may never enjoy the privileges of heteronormativity.

The scene in which Audrey strikes Alike is much less ferocious than in the short film but nevertheless unforgivably violent. The lyrics of the song Rees chose to include in the scene in which Alike, beaten and bruised, shows up at Laura's house, are "someday, some way, I'm going to bring all of me." These lyrics communicate the kinds of choices that queer youth have to make when contending with people, systems, and institutions that censure their sexuality and restrict their expression of gender. This scene visualizes the strength of the LGBT community and the reality that many gay youth and adults can rely only on their friends for support and love, friends who become their family. Laura's and Alike's mothers' refusal of motherly love and compassion for their masculine lesbian daughters is striking. Bearing in mind Rees's narrative explanation, along with the history of the pathologization of black mothers in the *Moynihan Report* and the representation of black mother figures who refuse to mother their lesbian daughters in *Pariah*, the following analysis raises questions about the relationship between the notion of universality, capital, and the commodification of difference embodied in the figure of the abject black mother.

The Rhetoric of Universality and *Pariah*

The rhetoric of universality is employed by Rees in the marketing of *Pariah*. In interviews in *LA Weekly*, *Italian Vogue*, and elsewhere, Rees frames the film as being about identity, "not checking a box," and being true to oneself, to which everyone can presumably relate.[34] While the impetus to reach all kinds of people with this film is clearly genuine, the rhetoric of universality has an indelible relationship to capital and to the commodification of difference that must be addressed. My critical engagement with *Pariah* explores the tension between the concept of universality used to market the feature film and the visualization of a specifically racialized, sexualized, and gendered group of black and brown lesbian, aggressive, gender queer, and butch women represented in *Pariah*. Because the short film did not have the same pressure to reach a mass audience and earn capital as did the feature film, the return on investment for the short film was attention to the filmmaker and her team and an appreciation for the story. The demand to earn a profit impacts the marketing of *Pariah* as a feature film and creates a bind between the rhetoric of universality and the particularities found within *Pariah*'s narrative. The relationship between blackness and queerness, as discussed previously, is fraught and complex, and this history raises the stakes for telling a story about a black lesbian teenager finding her way and owning her sexuality. The concept of universality as a selling point for marketing the film has a history within dominant Hollywood cinema and its roots in capital. Universality is not incidental but an integral element of capital that presents itself, through cultural texts, as liberal democratic benevolence.[35]

Grace Kyungwon Hong's theorization of the convergence of racialized gendered oppression in what she calls the national phase of U.S. capitalism is key to this analysis of the rhetoric of universalism employed to market this black lesbian coming-of-age film.[36] Hong levies a critique of capital through a women-of-color feminist framework that ties the burgeoning movement from the 1970s and 1980s to the contemporary moment using a discussion of racialized immigrant women's culture. I build on Hong's theorization of the propertied subject and possessive individualism by expanding the scope of her analysis from the literary canon to film. Through the realm of culture, differently racialized and gendered bodies were incorporated into or expelled from citizenship. In her analysis of *Huck Finn*, Hong critiques the manner in which racialized subjects are treated with benevolence by liberal white masculinist figures who demonstrate possessive individualism and are subsequently lauded for treating particular racialized bodies with respect rather than critiquing the entire system of racialized oppression and slavery. Focus Features in some ways occupies the space of the benevolent entity whose choice to distribute *Pariah* secures their brand as fearlessly liberal, obscuring a larger critique of the film industry that markets this "niche" film by subsuming difference under the guise of universality. On the relationship between culture and universality Hong asserts, "Culture is not an innocent category, but one that has been constituted by struggles around national identity. U.S. narratives of development produce an abstract, ostensibly universally attainable subject by narrating the transcendence of social constraints through the exercise of will. The subject of this narrative moves from his embeddedness in the particularity of his social situation to become a mature self-determining subject who is the master of his own fate."[37]

The discourse of universality that is meant to draw in viewers who may not relate to a black lesbian teenager also abstracts the very particularities of gender and sexuality that are being centralized in *Pariah*'s narrative. The concept of transcending difference rather than celebrating it becomes a tacit theme in the marketing strategy of the feature film. In her analysis Hong draws upon the concept of the propertied subject as one who has the ability and capacity to own. Not only does the propertied subject have possession of objects, but the ability to maintain possession of one's self, the ability or inability to own at all, determines one's relationship to the state.[38] The notion that everyone has the right to own property creates the illusion of achieving equality through capital and property rights. The liberal democratic benevolence of a white masculinist property owner, in this discussion Focus Features, to racialized bodies such as Alike, Laura, and their families, champions the discourse of universality in order to abstract the specificity of a black, lesbian coming-of-age story to garner appeal to wider audiences.

With the paradoxical logic of universality and difference in mind, let the figure of the black mother enter the discussion. Given the history of the pathologized black mother who has shouldered the blame for impeding the progress of black assimilation and civic integration with her aggression and divisiveness, the relationship between the unloving black mothers in the feature film version of *Pariah* and the rhetoric of universality that frames the marketing of the film must be explored. The demand that capital makes of a product, such as the feature film *Pariah*, to earn a profit or at least achieve critical acclaim that can be used to leverage a future profit, uses the familiar trope of the pathological black mother to reach a mass audience. In order to offset the niche nature of the black lesbian narrative, the recognizable historical icon—the abject black mother—finds her way into the story. The history of forced silence and dissemblance and the paradox of hypervisibility and invisibility that the abject black mother represents on screen in concert with Audrey's shaming, shunning, and beating of Alike situate Audrey as both perpetrator and victim of racialized, gendered violence. *Pariah* becomes universal through the trope of the unloving, overbearing black mother, reminiscent of the kind of black woman deployed in the *Moynihan Report*, albeit with a homophobic twist. The familiarity of the abject black mother trope in popular culture, along with trope of the exceptional black character who transcends difficulty and reaches success—Alike receiving a scholarship to a prestigious university and matriculating before she even graduates from high school—produces a narrative of universality that can be packaged and sold to mass audiences.

This kind of narrative is consistent with what Hong describes as a narrative of development: "Developmental narratives produce identification with the abstract propertied citizen of the U.S. nation-state, the possessive individual, subordinating difference by positing this subject formation as universal."[39] The rhetoric of universality in *Pariah* affords Alike possession of herself while making her mother lose possession of what she seems to hold most dear: her family. Even though the notion of transcendence has the potential to be uplifting, what becomes threatened with erasure in the narrative ascent are the identificatory particularities that make Alike's struggle real and palpable to queer people of color. The logic of universality that works through abstraction insists that difference can be overcome through tenacity. Alike's name also reads as *alike* and as such suggests similarities, commonalities between this character, those around her, and those who are watching her on screen. Finding the similarities between Alike's character, audience members, and the characters that populate the film is not problematic, but transcending her differences in order to achieve universality subverts some of the power that Rees harnessed in her short film.

Alike's hard work in school provides a gateway for her to escape her abusive, homophobic mother and sets her on a path toward a bright future. Despite her sexuality, her race, her gender, and her "pathological" mother, she finds a way to be herself through her intellect and academic achievements. As the universal subject who transcends her difference, Alike becomes the abstract citizen who has possession of herself, which is rendered in a poignant cinematic moment when Alike takes her leave from home, yet she is alone, singular, the exception. The closing images of the film poetically place Alike on a cross-country bus heading west, with Laura and her father left behind, in the past. This scene is solemn and pregnant with possibility. The problematic component of this dénouement is the exceptionalism that grants Alike her place on that bus, her ticket to her future, her self-possession. She becomes an anomaly in the group of black and brown lesbians who appear in *Pariah*, many of whom are estranged from their families and at least one of whom is homeless. Alike is coming into her own, but she is also becoming her own. She is a possessive individual and she is on her own. Alone. She is a visual anomaly. She is the exception who has transcended her difference.

Alike rescued herself and became a universal subject. While she may be an exceptional student who is able to escape a difficult family dynamic, becoming a universal subject is not the only way out. She could keep all of her intersecting identity boxes checked and not transcend difference but possess herself and the differences that she represents in dominant society. The rhetoric of universality and the insatiable desire of capital forces an abstraction of difference and a reliance on tropes that is not necessary and actually undermines the brilliance of Rees's narrative, which offers the world a rare and beautiful cinematic journey with a black lesbian character who embraces herself without mollifying her contradictions or apologizing for her sexuality.

The price of universal appeal paid to bring *Pariah* to theaters, to have Meryl Streep acknowledge this film's significance and champion the talent of its lead actor, Adepero Oduye, at one of the world's most prestigious film and television award ceremonies, is balanced by the projection of black lesbian, gender queer, butch, femme, and trans images on the big screen. *Pariah* may not have won a Golden Globe or been nominated for an Oscar, but it did win a Gotham award, a GLAAD award, an Image award, and an Independent Spirit award.[40] Accolades aside, visualizing black and brown lesbian, masculine of center, and gender queer people and enabling members of this community to experience the pleasure of being represented with integrity is valuable, though whether it is worth industry demands for universal appeal can and should be debated. Perhaps *Pariah* is pointing us toward a future in which this equation does not have to exist, this trade of niche narratives for universal box office appeal does not have to be made. As a black queer woman filmmaker, Rees has made cinematic history with the epic feat of turning her award-winning short film into an award-winning feature film that had a nationwide theatrical release. The pleasure of watching *Pariah* grow from a short to a feature film and rooting for Rees and her cast and crew to be recognized for their accomplishments inspires hope that *Pariah* will not exist as an anomaly of the new millennium but that this film will be joined by other cinematic works of this caliber that are able to capture the mood, the timbre, the sensuality, the precariousness, the charm, the complexities, the sorrow, and the luster of black lesbian, masculine of center, gender queer, and femme lives and represent them on the big screen without compromise.[41]

I have worked to be both critical and mindful in my analysis of *Pariah* and to account for the long history of racialized and gendered exploitation that emerges in Rees's cinematic representation of black motherhood, black religiosity, masculine black womanhood, and queer sexuality and gender. My analysis of black motherhood and critique of the rhetoric of universality are meant to lay bare the relationship between capital and the commodification of difference rather than undermine the rarefied significance of this film and the extraordinary contribution to black popular culture, queer cinema, and independent film that is delivered with Rees's first feature.

16.3 Alike (Adepero Oduye) in *Pariah*, directed by Dee Rees, 2011.

The national release of *Pariah* changed the cinematic landscape. This film's presence in popular culture makes the visualization of black lesbian sexuality and erotics part of a productive national conversation. *Pariah* has made a crucial impact in black popular culture by taking on the challenge of visualizing black women engaging in complicated love relationships with one another. Despite the repackaging and narrative changes with *Pariah* the feature, its presence in theaters across the country cleared the path for dialogue to take place about the tensions between blackness and queerness on a much larger scale than a short film with limited accessibility is capable of generating. Rees's successful helming of a feature-length Hollywood film promises more films on the national stage from this black queer woman director and also opens the door a bit wider for the next black queer or trans directors of black queer and trans films to appear on the big screen in less than the fifteen years that lapsed between the theatrical release of *The Watermelon Woman* and *Pariah*. Your audience awaits.

Notes

1 In 1988 Margaret Thatcher passed section 28 of the Local Government Act, which prohibited teaching or publishing any materials that promote homosexuality. In 2003 this section of the act was voted out.

2 Since *Pariah*'s release two more films about black lesbian sexuality have been produced and screened internationally: Cheryl Dunye's hard-core lesbian porn shot in Germany, *Mommy Is Coming* (2012), and the black British filmmaker Campbell X's queer buddy pic and romantic dramedy *Stud Life* (2012).

3 For a variety of perspectives and critical discussions about queer, gay, and lesbian sexuality, see Roderick A. Ferguson, *Aberrations in Black: Toward a Queer of Color Critique* (Minneapolis: University of Minnesota Press, 2004); Evelynn M. Hammonds, "Black (W)holes and the Geometry of Black Female Sexuality," in *Feminism Meets Queer Theory*, edited by Elizabeth Weed and Naomi Schor (Bloomington: Indiana University Press, 1997); Combahee River Collective, "A Black Feminist Statement," in *All of the Women Are White, All of the Blacks Are Men, but Some of Us Are Brave*, edited by Gloria T. Hull, Patricia Bell Scott, and Barbara Smith (New York: The Feminist Press, 1982).

4 The term *queer of color critique* was coined by Ferguson in his seminal text, *Aberrations in Black*.

5 My use of *queer* refers to a wide range of sexualities and genders that are non-normative. *Queer* also indexes resistance to the limits of normalization and can be understood as, but is not limited to, a political position, a way of being that binds a community or resists normative expectations of time and family, and can describe a collection of loved ones that forms a kinship structure.

6 Director Spike Lee was a mentor for Rees and supported her during the process of making *Pariah*.

7 The casting changes made for the feature version added a love interest played by Aasha Davis, of *Friday Night Lights* fame. Alike's parents were recast; Kim Wayans replaced Gameela Wright as Alike's mother, and Charles Parnell replaced Wendell Pierce as Alike's father.

8 In interviews with Richard Peña at Lincoln Center and with *Italian Vogue*, Dee Rees discusses the genesis of the film from the original script to the feature film. "Q&A with Dee Rees, 'Pariah,'" posted by Film Society Lincoln Center, March 9, 2012, YouTube, https://youtu.be/i_Zrh7epH98; Susanna Cappellaro, "Dee Rees," *Vogue Italia*, June 2, 2012, http://www.vogue.it/vogue-black/spotlight-on/2012/02/dee -rees#ad-image160964.

9 For a compelling critical discussion of black lesbian homonormativity in popular culture, see Kara Keeling's *The Witch's Flight: The Cinematic, the Black Femme, and the Image of Common Sense* (Durham, NC: Duke University Press, 2007). My discussion of the dichotomy between femme and butch in *Pariah* is not meant to exclude the spectrum of queer sexual expressions and gender identities but rather to describe the narrative tension in this film.

10 I am using the terms *butch* and *aggressive* here as they mark gender expression and queer masculinity. The 2005 documentary film *The Aggressives*, directed by Daniel Peddle, offers a representation of the lives of queer people of color who identify as aggressive.

11 See Judith [Jack] Halberstam's *Female Masculinity* (Durham, NC: Duke University Press, 1998) for a critical and historical exploration of masculinity in women's bodies through key pieces of visual culture and literary texts.

12 The character Bina and the story line surrounding Alike's relationship with her are not included in the short film version of *Pariah*.

13 Interestingly several scenes from the short film are incorporated into the feature-length version, including the scene in which Laura consoles Alike after she suffers the parental beating.

14 Keeling's *The Witch's Flight* offers a critical engagement with the politics of black lesbian visibility in cinema.

15 The controversy over marriage equality has provided a platform for black church leaders across the country to express their views on gay marriage. Chicago area leaders in black churches and communities are divided on the issue; some oppose marriage equality, while others, such as Rev. Richard Tolliver, support gay marriage and argue that this is a civil rights issue and not a religious concern. American Civil Liberties Union, "African-American Clergy Urge Immediate Passage of Marriage Equality Legislation in Illinois," ACLU, April 4, 2013, http://www.aclu-il.org/african -american-clergy-urge-immediate-passage-of-marriage-equality-legislation-in -illinois/.

16 My discussion of homophobia in the black church is informed by the black feminist scholar Patricia Hill Collins's analysis of the relationship between antigay senti-ments in the black church that has historically been a hub for black families for religious and community purposes in *Black Sexual Politics: African Americans, Gender, and the New Racism* (New York: Routledge, 2005), 107–14. Johnetta B. Cole and Beverly Guy-Sheftall discuss the prevalence of and offer historical context for homophobia and privileging of black men leaders in black churches in *Gender Talk: The Struggle of Women's Equality in African American Communities* (New York: Bal-lantine, 2003), 114–17, 160–76.

17 This tension between religion and black sexuality is also discussed in Candice Jenkins's *Private Lives, Proper Relations: Regulating Black Intimacy* (Minneapolis: Minnesota University Press, 2007), in which she defines the "salvific wish" in uplift ideology as a pledge for salvation from the pathologizing discourse of black sexual-ity. She argues that ideologies of upward mobility and the salvific wish encourage silence and denial about sexuality.

18 Collins, *Black Sexual Politics*, 107.

19 Later I discuss black nonheteronormativity and queerness by engaging with Fergu-son's discussion of black nonheteronormativity in *Aberrations in Black*.

20 Proposition 8 was overturned by a Supreme Court ruling in 2013, ending the ban on gay marriage in California.

21 Dee Rees discusses her coming out in an interview with *Vogue Italia*. Cappellaro, "Dee Rees."

22 Hammonds, "Black (W)holes and the Geometry of Black Female Sexuality," 263. Hammonds accounts for three historical themes that conspire around black women's sexuality. The first is that black women are essentially sexual, invisible, and ulti-mately all that white womanhood is expected not to be. The second is a theme of resistance to the construction of black womanhood as a hypersexual void and one that recognizes material effects that negative stereotypes engender. The third theme describes "the evolution of a culture of dissemblance and a 'politics of silence' by

black women on the issue of their sexuality" (263). The concept of "the politics of silence" is explained and critically engaged by Evelyn Brooks Higginbotham in her article "African-American Women's History and the Metalanguage of Race," *Signs* 17.2 (1992): 251–74. Higginbotham also discusses "the politics of respectability" in *Righteous Discontent: The Women's Movement in the Black Church, 1880–1920* (Cambridge, MA: Harvard University Press, 1994). "The culture of dissemblance" is discussed by Darlene Clark Hine in "Rape and the Inner Lives of Black Women: Thoughts on the Culture of Dissemblance," in her book *Hine Sight: Black Women and the Reconstruction of American History* (Bloomington: Indiana University Press, 1994).

23 Hammonds, "Black (W)holes and the Geometry of Black Female Sexuality," 263.

24 Hammonds, "Black (W)holes and the Geometry of Black Female Sexuality," 263.

25 In *The Prison Notebooks* the Italian theorist Antonio Gramsci outlines elements of hegemony, which include the notion of common sense. Common sense is an axiomatic understanding of the ways things are or should be that is part of the hegemonic process of coercion and consent that exacts power over subordinate people and communities. This concept is an integral part of Keeling's theoretical framework that supports her discussion of black lesbian visibility in *The Witch's Flight*.

26 Hammonds, "Black (W)holes and the Geometry of Black Female Sexuality," 264.

27 In a footnote in their foundational queer theory article "Sex in Public," Lauren Berlant and Michael Warner offer a definition of heteronormativity that is helpful for this discussion: "By heteronormativity we mean the institutions, structures of understanding practical orientations that make heterosexuality seem not only coherent—that is, organized as a sexuality—but also privileged. Its coherence is always provisional, and its privilege can take several (sometimes contradictory) forms: unmarked, as the basic idiom of the personal and the social; or marked as a natural state; or projected as an ideal or moral accomplishment. It consists less of norms that could be summarized as a body of doctrine than of a sense of rightness produced in contradictory manifestations—often unconscious, immanent to practice or to institutions. Contexts that have little visible relation to sex practice, such as life narrative and generational identity, can be heteronormative in this sense, while in other contexts forms of sex between men and women might not be heteronormative. Heteronormativity is thus a concept distinct from heterosexuality." Lauren Berlant and Michael Warner, "Sex in Public," *Critical Inquiry* 24.2 (1998): 547–66.

28 Ferguson, *Aberrations in Black*, 21.

29 Ferguson, *Aberrations in Black*, 20–21.

30 Ferguson, *Aberrations in Black*, 119, 122.

31 Despite the categorical lambasting that the black family suffered with the findings of the *Moynihan Report*, black power movement organizations used the rhetoric found in the report as evidence to reinstate black men as the head of the household and ultimately reinforce sexist roles that subjugated black women in the home (Ferguson, *Aberrations in Black*, 115–16). This increased the pressure for black women in the home to withstand succumbing to rules and orders based on gender, physical

violence, and emotional abuse from the man of the house in the name of black empowerment. Leaders of black power movements, namely Eldridge Cleaver, used the report to denounce homosexuality (122).

32 In "There Is No Hierarchy of Oppressions," Audre Lorde offers a definition of sexism and heterosexism that supports my discussion here: "I have learned that sexism (a belief in the inherent superiority of one sex over all others and thereby its right to dominance) and heterosexism (a belief in the inherent superiority of one pattern of loving over all others and thereby its right to dominance) both arise from the same source as racism—a belief in the inherent superiority of one race over all others and thereby its right to dominance." Lorde begins her chapter "Scratching the Surface: Some Notes on Barriers to Women and Loving" in her collection of essays *Sister Outsider: Essays and Speeches* (Trumansburg, NY: Crossing Press, 1984), 45, with these definitions:

> Racism: The belief in the inherent superiority of one race over all others and thereby the right to dominance.
> Sexism: The belief in the inherent superiority of one sex and thereby the right to dominance.
> Heterosexism: The belief in the inherent superiority of one pattern of loving and thereby its right to dominance.
> Homophobia: The fear of feelings of love for members of one's own sex and therefore the hatred of those feelings in others.

Though homophobia is commonly understood as disdain, hatred, and disgust for those who are gay and lesbian, in Lorde's definition she is addressing an underlying reason why someone would feel this way.

33 Critical analysis of the role of Alike's father, though not within the scope of this chapter, would be a productive contribution to the discourse surrounding Rees's feature film.

34 This quote was taken from Rees's interview on CBC. "Interview: Dee Rees," *George Stroumboulopoulos Tonight*, January 10, 2012, http://www.cbc.ca/strombo/videos /guest-interview/dee-rees-1/P552.

35 Grace Kyungwon Hong, *The Ruptures of American Capital: Women of Color, Feminism, and the Culture of Immigrant Labor* (Minneapolis: University of Minnesota Press, 2006), 12.

36 Universality is a central theme in Hong's *The Ruptures of American Capital*.

37 Hong, *The Ruptures of American Capital*, xvi–xvii, 3–4, 12–13, 8.

38 Hong, *The Ruptures of American Capital*, 10–11.

39 Hong, *The Ruptures of American Capital*, xxvi.

40 In 2011 *Pariah* won a GLAAD Media Award for Outstanding Film with a Limited Release, Best U.S. Feature Film in the Mill Valley Film Festival, National Board of Review Freedom of Expression Award, and the Cinematography Award in the Dramatic Competition in the Sundance Film Festival. In 2012 Adepero Oduye was awarded a Black Reel Award for Best Breakthrough Performance for her

performance in *Pariah*, and *Pariah* won an Image Award for Outstanding Motion Picture. *Pariah* was nominated for a host of other awards in 2011 and 2012. "*Pariah*: Awards," IMDb, accessed August 24, 2017, http://www.imdb.com/title/tt1233334/awards.

41 During the time that I have been writing this article, several films about black queer and trans life have entered the market, including the very impressive *Major!* (2015), *Tangerine* (2015), *Free CeCe* (2016), and *Kiki* (2016).

Creating the World Anew
Black Lesbian Legacies and Queer Film Futures

> The plan is two words: global domination. That is the strategic plan. There need to be as many Queer Women of Color filmmakers around the world as possible so that we are not telling anybody's stories because they have the skills to tell their own stories.
> **—Kebo Drew, Queer Women of Color Media Arts Project**

> What if we can create the world anew? We can create the world anew by amplifying our stories through media and art, connecting people to their passionate work and one another and sharing knowledge and information.
> **—Julia Roxanne Wallace (also known as Sangodare Akinwale), Queer Renaissance and Black Feminist Film School**

Deeply grounded in the legacy of Black lesbian artists, writers, and filmmakers, current Black lesbian filmmakers are helping to build infrastructure for a transformed future using deeply interconnected methods to transform the whole world and (while we're at it) the meaning of life. This chapter looks at two projects, the established and evolving Queer Women of Color Media Arts Project based in San Francisco and the emerging Queer Renaissance and Black Feminist Film School Project based in Durham, North Carolina, as examples of the robust future of Black lesbian filmmaking as a transformative community-building practice.

The Queer Women of Color Media Arts Project (QWOCMAP) was founded in 2000 as a space to train queer women of color to make their own films and to screen those films for a diverse local community. The core creators and sustainers of the project are the artist-organizers Madeline Kim, Kebo Drew, and Liliana Hueso, but the staff is supported by a large number of volunteers, donors, and local organizations. Over the sixteen years of their existence, QWOCMAP has trained hundreds of new filmmakers and taught technical skills to many women of color who have been able to mobilize their creative and technology-based training to support many aspects of the activist and arts communities. Every year QWOCMAP conducts free trainings for the community and has hosted multiple dedicated trainings for queer women of African descent. They also host themed film festivals to showcase the work of their students and to impact the discourse in their multiple communities.

Black Feminist Film School (BFFS) is the newest project of Queer Renaissance, in collaboration with Eternal Summer of the Black Feminist Mind, and is an educational and production-based initiative in Durham. The initiative kicked off in 2012–13 with a year of free screenings, discussions, workshops, and panels and engaged a collaborative filmmaking process to generate their first film, *When We Free*, a narrative historical film that imagines the first camp-meeting revival after emancipation, with the aim of growing autonomous filmmaking skills in the queer community of color in Durham. BFFS sees QWOCMAP as an all-star example and a resource for brilliance, and I assert that both projects exist as different manifestations of the same legacy and an aligned vision.

These two projects exist among many other contemporary inspiring media projects led or cocreated by Black lesbians, Black queer womyn, and Black genderqueer media makers, including (but not limited to) the Sistah Sinema Project, Harriet's Gun Media, and Q-Roc.TV, which are grounded in powerful intergenerational legacies of filmmaking and emphasize the role of continued transformative media-making in the creation of moments of presence and an abundant future where the bodies, ideas, art, and communities of Black LGBTQ people are surrounded in sustainable love. (I am a participant witness.) This chapter looks closely at the roots, visions, and strategies of QWOCMAP and BFFS to provide insight into this broad and growing futuristic movement.

To be transparent, I write these words as a deeply invested beneficiary and longtime fan of QWOCMAP and a collaborator directly involved in cocreating BFFS. Yvonne Welbon, the editor and initiator of this book, and other contributors have participated in the activities of both or one of these projects, and this is as it should be. The future of Black lesbian filmmaking is not something about which we can be objective; it is something we do. It *is* our lives, and it saves our lives. It is our tangible practice for representing and creating the world. Therefore it is important for us to theorize and examine it with creativity, urgency, hope, and love.

Rooted

On multiple levels both QWOCMAP and BFFS have strong and explicit ties to Black lesbian herstory. In addition to being influenced by Black lesbian filmmakers, the founders of these projects are also grounded in even longer legacies of Black lesbian art and activism and Black feminist resistance, and they are also rooted in current collaborations with intergenerational organizations that serve Black lesbians of multiple ages. The accountability to the dead, the living, the filmic, the otherwise epic, and those yet to come distinguishes and clarifies the work and their standards for measuring success.

In a recent interview, Kebo Drew explained part of the project's origin story. QWOCMAP emerged at the very beginning of the twenty-first century and was influenced by the third world cinema and Black feminist cinema circles that Madeline Lim participated in as a filmmaker and dedicated viewer. Lim (referred to as "Mad" by Drew in this piece and by the QWOCMAP family more broadly) was traveling to film festivals with her own film when she met Aishah Simmons and Yvonne Welbon. Simmons made the film *NO!*, a rape documentary, in a rigorous eleven-year process with a crew composed entirely of women of color, mostly LGBTQ; Welbon was touring with *Living with Pride*, her crucial documentary about the Black Detroit-based lesbian elder Ruth Ellis at age one hundred. Though QWOCMAP was founded for and is accountable to women of color from many backgrounds, Drew emphasizes the influence of Black feminist lesbian and gay filmmakers and poets on the film conversation that inspired Mad in her films and in her vision for QWOC-MAP: "There is something really interesting about Mad and her influence, like in dance you know the teachers of your teachers and their teachers, and she was really influenced by Marlon Riggs, Isaac Julien, and Pratibha Parmar, what they were doing even before Cheryl Dunye. Mad was also paying attention to Yvonne and Trin Min-ha. Those filmmakers were pulling on the legacies of Black lesbians like Audre Lorde and Pat Parker. They were pulling it into film, combining dance, poetry, visual arts, and all those things that are important. . . . Filmmakers in that legacy, Aishah and Yvonne, Michelle Parkerson, and also being inspired by Yvonne with the Ruth Ellis project and running into each other with VHS tapes in their bags."[1] Drew emphasizes, "Mad is a mastermind." Mad's initial vision to create QWOCMAP as a space to train and incubate queer women of color filmmakers was a crucial turning point in the actualization of the collective visions that shaped the messaging radical lesbian and gay filmmakers of color expressed in their films. The institutional focus and nurturing of consistent space for queer women of color filmmakers to collaborate on expressing their visions and growing their skills has had an irreversible impact. The timing of this work, just at the cusp of the digital revolution in the way films are made, has made, possible a completely transformative future in film.

Drew explains that while these roots, and in particular filmmakers who were influenced by Black lesbian feminist writers, flow through everything that QWOCMAP does, the accountability to Black queer women's filmmaking in particular has also resulted in specific programming for women of African descent: "In 2006 there was a specific African-descent class created, and that has had an influence on who has been doing work since in California to open the door wider for Black women filmmakers. It also allows other Black people to still claim the space. This is the legacy, and this is how we challenge that legacy. There are many people who have been through QWOCMAP, like Melinda James and Sarah Beth Harris, who went off to film school afterwards. We do those classes so that people can access that legacy into the future." Like QWOCMAP, BFFS values the legacy and has a futuristic vision. BFFS screens films made by Black women who are self-identified womanists, feminists, and lesbians, and those who are not in order to create a countercanon out of which a contemporary discourse of Black feminist filmmaking can emerge. One of the primary goals of the BFFS screening series is to watch films by and about Black women in order to ask the question "What is a Black feminist film?" Since many films by Black women have not been widely distributed and remain inaccessible, BFFS partnered with the Sallie Bingham Archive of Women's History at Duke University to find and purchase rare films in order to screen them in community settings where emerging Black feminist filmmakers and community members in general can see the films, discuss them, and ground their own films in the context of a larger filmic conversation.

Many of the first films BFFS screened in its opening year (including Michelle Parkerson and Ada Griffin's *A Litany for Survival*, Julie Dash's *Praise House*, Camille Billops's *Suzanne, Suzanne*, Barbara McCullough's *Water Ritual #1*) shared the theme of intergenerational healing. The participants in the screening process have been able to explore these films for insights into their own intergenerational healing processes and also to envision how their work

Black Feminist ⟨ *bffs* ⟩ **Film School**

Friday, June 6th at 6:15pm
Summer Session Opening Intensive

screening

free and open to the public
blackfeministfilmschool.wordpress.com

for more info email:
blackfeministfilmschool@gmail.com

Join us as we screen films in process and titles from the bffs
library. We will also be welcoming this summer's fellows.

Hosted at: Center For Documentary Studies @ Duke
Auditorium
1317 W. Pettigrew Street
Durham, NC 27705

17.1 Black Feminist Film School flyer, 2012. Courtesy of
cofounder Alexis Pauline Gumbs.

as artists and filmmakers adds to and challenges this vital intergenerational conversation.

In her lecture at the inaugural BFFS event, cofounder Julia Roxanne Wallace (Sangodare Akinwale) outlines a possible definition of Black feminist film that draws on the cultural practices of Black women starting long before film technologies were widely available. She opened by quoting Alice Walker and honoring the unnamed ancestors who, according to Walker, "dreamed dreams that no one knew—not even themselves, in any coherent fashion—and saw visions no one could understand . . . [who] waited for a day when the unknown thing that was in them would be made known; but guessed, somehow in their darkness, that on the day of their revelation they would be long dead."[2] So from its inception BFFS has invited and valued a multitude of ancestors as audience and collaborators. In Wallace's opening words you can see a version of the practice that Drew describes in the inception of QWOCMAP, where Black feminist practices of literacy and creativity form the conditions of possibility for imagining a libratory relationship to filmmaking. More than a decade after QWOCMAP was founded Wallace said:

> (I want to engage the "what is" a Black Feminist Film/Filmmaker question by talking about the image of Black Feminist Filmmaking that I am walking in and toward, even as I am creating it)
>
> I make myself a filmmaker like **Milla Granson** was a teacher. She was a slave who learned to read from the children of her owner. She taught 12 students at a time, also slaves, to read in her midnight school. Once they learned she dismissed them and taught 12 more. Over the years, she taught hundreds of slaves to read and write and many of them used that tool to gain their freedom. . . .
>
> **I make myself a filmmaker** in the legacy of the Combahee River Collective's Statement, which is a foundational text for any Black Feminist. They agreed,
>
> *"If Black women were free, it would mean that everyone would have to be free since our freedom would necessitate the destruction of all systems of oppression."*
>
> **I make myself a filmmaker** knowing that we can create the world anew; a world we deserve to have if we choose to do so.
>
> Finally, **I make myself a filmmaker** in the spirit tradition of specific directors who have created films that are for me canonical; filmmakers such as Julie Dash with *Daughters of the Dust*, Euzhan Palcy with *Sugar Cane Alley*, Camille Billops with *Suzanne Suzanne* and even contemporary filmmaker Kortney Ryan Ziegler in his film, *Still Back: A Portrait of Black Transmen.*[3]

And just like Welbon was present for Mad with VHS tapes and film festival stories to share, she spoke at the first BFFS event, teaching the history of Black feminist filmmaking and providing a context for the collaborative and transformative process through which the films we screened and others were created. In light of those collaborative roots and histories of practice it becomes clear that the question of what it means for a queer Black feminist filmmaking practice to be rooted is not only a question of naming the correct ancestors, influences, or referents but also a question of *how* the work

17.2 Black Feminist Film School on location shooting *When We Free*, directed by Julia Roxanne Wallace, 2015. Photo courtesy Alexis Pauline Gumbs.

happens and how it is or is not connected to the wider community of Black women, Black lesbians, and Black queer people.

In 2014 BFFS launched its production curriculum with the BFFS Production Summer workshops for the first class of Fellows funded by a community fundraiser. Ladan Siad of that first class became the assistant director for the film *When We Free*. The Fellows created three short films each during the summer intensive and learned skills about camera use, storyboarding, lighting, and storytelling that they are now able to apply to their community-based projects that focus on masculine of center black queer visibility, people of color as leaders in design, sustainable farming, and more.

QWOCMAP has modeled this form of rootedness in the Bay Area by creating and screening films in specific partnerships with intergenerational Black lesbian organizations. Drew explains how her work early on to build relationships with Black women's organizations not only set the standard for how QWOCMAP partners with community organizations in general but also had an impact on the access of existing Black lesbian organizations to each other and their own futures: "I got a fellowship from the Horizons Foundation to build the relationship with Black women's organizations. That also formed the model for how the community partnership model and the grassroots fundraising [have] developed since. Working with Black lesbian organizations was the model."

If we say that Black lesbian feminist filmmaking and Black queer filmmaking are rooted in the lived experiences and organizing culture of Black lesbians, that means not only do the films we make draw resources (audiences, actors, crew, funding) from Black lesbians and the organizations that we have created, but they also replenish the soil by bringing people together, increasing visibility, and providing a vehicle for necessary conversations in our community.

Transformative

Black lesbian and queer filmmaking as practiced by QWOCMAP and envisioned by BFFS is a holistically transformative experience. The measures for success in these contexts are whether the process of making the film positively transforms the artists involved, the view on an individual level, and the community on a collective level. Drew explains how transformative it was for her to be able to work on her artistic vision in the rigorous transformative space of the QWOCMAP workshops: "There was something about sitting together in the lobby of this tiny black box theater in the Red Stone building on Sixteenth Street. I had this story in my head . . . all these exercises were about getting it closer to a screenplay. The story was about surrogacy and mammies because some people in my family were domestics. So I started to write this screenplay, and I had had these experiences in the past of being the only Black queer anything in the room."

She continues, "The difference at QWOCMAP was that everyone got what I was talking about. Everyone knew why the mammy story was important. To be able to sit in a room with people who came from our community who understood why I would want to tell Black women's stories over and over again, there are just no words for how it felt, how it shifted my work, how validating it was." Importantly, Drew explains that the transformation she experienced was not limited to the safe space of the QWOCMAP workshops. She and other QWOCMAP participants have also been able to bring the affirmation of that safe space into more mainstream spaces as a transformative force.

In order to more effectively transform themselves, each other, and the world they move in, QWOCMAP is also in a continual state of institutional transformation. As the participants and staff are transformed, they are able to see new ways to improve the transformative space they have created and to make transformation more powerful and sustainable for themselves and future participants. According to Drew, "We have a working agreement statement where we talk about how our views of race and class impact how we treat each other. What assumptions do you make? We are trying to bring those things out to have nonviolent, nondefensive communication when sexism has taught us not to communicate about these things. How can this bring us together instead of shutting us down and polarizing us? How do you create a space where people come together and leave *together*?"

The work it takes to transform and grow from conflict as an institution is worthwhile because of the transformative impact that participating in a transformative institution has on the participants and also because of the impact the collective practice can have on society as a whole. Drew explains:

That's why we spend so much time nurturing Black lesbian and queer Black women filmmakers. We say, "We believe in your story. We know the community desperately needs your story." People need it for their own survival, their own affirmation, to see themselves. We got this letter from this mom who thanked us in Spanish, who said, "I don't know what I was thinking before about LGBTQ people, but now I know so much more about how I can love and how I can value people." If no one but queer and trans people of color made films for the next hundred years it wouldn't counter all that has been done.

It is important because our community needs our films so bad. As many of us need to tell our stories as possible. Jewelle Gomez [a Black lesbian feminist author, activist, and philanthropy genius] was saying learning how to make a film is as important as learning how to organize a protest. She has such an amazing history, and she just knows that the production of our own media is becoming more crucial than ever. We have to make the film and organize the march and organize the meditation circle.

The American arts grants are also asking folks to put a number on it. After doing all the math our budget is less than $250,000 a year, but the investment we put into the workshops alone is like half a million dollars every year, and who puts that resource in our community? And what does it do to create jobs in our community? This is an investment we are making in our community and saying, "I challenge you to put that much money to us."

Many queer Black women filmmakers, scholars, and artists have benefited from QWOCMAP's investment in community. Beatrice Sullivan, an artist, dancer, and activist, participated in the 2006 QWOCMAP workshop that was specifically for queer women of African descent. Her filmmaking process unfolded at the same time that I was in Durham strategizing with other women of color, survivors of sexual violence, and allies about how to respond to the verbal and ideological violence launched at the bodies and spirits of women of color and sex workers in the wake of the Duke Lacrosse rape scandal. Sullivan's video and the space that allowed her to envision it informed and affirmed that work.

Sullivan participated in QWOCMAP as a recent college graduate, and the lessons she learned in the program have impacted and will continue to impact her approach to her healing creative work. In Sullivan's words, "My project was about body image and movement for me as a Black queer woman. It was an unscripted movement video. It helped me to come to terms with the image of my body on screen and how I want to be seen versus how I'm perceived. Finding words for what would be a script were challenging; I could only come up with camera angles and movements. It became clear to me that visualizing the film came easier than communicating the message behind the images. I think this lesson helped me rethink how I use words to communicate in life."[4]

Jennifer Brody participated in QWOCMAP in 2012. At a very different moment in her career than Sullivan, Brody participated in the workshop as a tenured professor with years of Black feminist cultural and literary criticism and participation in Black feminist filmmaking community under her belt as a way to build community after moving to a new city. She said:

> I think I have a *much* greater appreciation for what it takes for queer women of color to make a film, even with the shift to newer digital technologies. I had worked as a consultant and crew member on Cheryl Dunye's first film, *Janine*, when I was in graduate school in the early 1990s in Philadelphia and was loosely a member of a larger group of Black queer filmmakers. I love that the mode of production was made available to this group and would only hope that fundraising will keep the organization moving forward.
>
> Among the most memorable experiences in the program were the community fellowship and friendship forged in the program. Many of us commuted together—I was designated driver—and learned to work together through the group assignments. Simply being and working together several hours every week for sixteen weeks helped to foster a sense of belong-

ing. I loved that the diversity of the queer "women" in the group were FTM, younger, older, differently abled, bi, queer, lesbian, Black, butch, femme, Filipina, Chicano, from the East Bay, the city, and the Peninsula, from couch surfers to homeowners. It was an affirmation of becoming a collective.[5]

These experiences, shared by only two of the hundreds of queer Black women whom QWOCMAP has impacted, emphasize QWOCMAP as a space that enables the Black feminist practices of embodied healing, community building, and transformation.

Necessary

When the blatant racism of the world of filmmaking is as apparent as it has ever been, the futures that QWOCMAP and BFFS envision and enable are urgently necessary. At a moment when digital access and movement building have made the glaring white male–centric limitations of the mainstream film industry very visible, and where videos and interviews circulate with prestigious well-funded white filmmakers saying that there don't need to be any people of color behind the scenes on the film set, or with white women complaining that Viola Davis should not quote Harriet Tubman or speak about race at the Emmy awards, it is no longer enough for Black lesbian and queer filmmakers to simply soldier through a racist field one heartbreak and one victory at a time.

As many of the chapters in this book make clear, visionary Black lesbian filmmakers have made heroic achievements against the odds in a film industry designed to push them out. Those achievements are an important part of what make the worldviews of QWOCMAP and BFFS possible, but QWOCMAP and BFFS also share the view that we are past the time of notable exceptions and are entering the era of critical mass and a world that represents Black women in all of their complexity and nuance, where the representation is so thick it moves beyond representation into transformation. As Drew explains, "This is the power of a group coming at you as filmmakers. We have like a hundred films about queer Black women, so there is no way you can say we're all the same. We can show this whole breadth of this community, a beautiful tide of possibilities. Cheryl Dunye has come in and done workshops. Shine [Louise Houston] from the Crash Pad series has come and done stuff. Come look at all of us and all the films we have. It is going to take more than just one of us having a really good career or being noticed. It is going to have to be like, 'Oh, there are five hundred of you.'"

From its inception, Hollywood has played a major role in teaching the nation and the world what is possible by constructing images that reflect the ideologies of the white male privileged filmmakers who have held the bulk of power in that field. The impact of a Black feminist worldview, a worldview informed by queer women of color, is dangerous to the status quo. Also the nuance and depth that black women filmmakers have been forced to use in order to counteract the stereotypes blasted for generations through the dominant media lead to what Drew calls "simply better writing" where the bulk of character development (or lack thereof) in mainstream films has been "lazy."

BFFS brought together a community to create *When We Free* with high cinematic standards and rich interactive character development for five thousand crowdfunded dollars. QWOCMAP is in the midst of training women of color survivors and other disenfranchised artists all over the world in the techniques of making quality films from their own crucial perspectives. The impact of QWOCMAP and BFFS is that the stereotype-slinging white male worldview that has dominated contemporary image making can never again be secure that an alternative will remain on the margins and that even the marginalized people will have to see themselves through the ignorant and superficial representational practices of the privileged. Never again will we be dealing with a world where there is one of us at a time. We are creating a queer reality and a Black feminist film future where the world as we know it will never look, feel, or sound the same again.

Notes

An expanded version of this essay can be found on the website www.sistersinthelife.com.

1 Kebo Drew, interview by Alexis Pauline Gumbs, August 1–8, 2013. Subsequent quotations of Drew come from this interview.
2 Alice Walker, "In Search of Our Mothers' Gardens," in *In Search of Our Mothers' Gardens* (New York: Harcourt Brace Jovanovich, 1983), 232–33.
3 Formatting is Wallace's, as reproduced in "Create Anew: Black Feminist Film School. Black Feminist Filmmaking as Spiritual Leadership," Black Feminist Film School, accessed August 24, 2017, https://blackfeministfilmschool.wordpress.com/about/bffs-rationale/.
4 Beatrice Sullivan, interview by Alexis Pauline Gumbs, July 30, 2013.
5 Jennifer Brody, interview by Alexis Pauline Gumbs, June 7, 2013.

Acknowledgments

First and foremost, I would like to thank Alex Juhasz. This is my first book. She has written many. When I asked her to co-edit this volume with me, she said yes, without hesitation. And from that moment on, what once was just an idea began to take form and shape. Thank you, Alex, for taking a leap!

There are so many other people to thank for their support. First, the writers who contributed the essays in this book. Their individual pieces of scholarship are the heart and soul of this volume. I am grateful for their willingness to stay the course over the years it took to bring this volume to print. Their contributions during the development phase of the project informed, inspired, and helped to guide us.

I wish to thank the directors who are featured within this book for making media and for making history. Thank you for answering the calls from the writers who interviewed you. Thank you for sharing materials and assisting the writers as they wrote your stories.

In Alexis Pauline Gumbs's essay, she states that I spoke at the first Black Feminist Film School event at Duke University. What she doesn't say is that it was there that I met an audience member. Jade Brooks told me that she worked at Duke University Press and invited me to lunch to discuss the *Sisters in the Life* book project. At the end of that meal she invited me to submit a proposal. She continued supporting the project and working with us over the years, further shaping the book to the version that you are reading. There are no words to adequately express how grateful I am for her contributions to this project.

Mellon grants and fellowships enabled me to develop this project and to conduct research. They include the Mellon Future of Minority Studies Post-doctoral Mentoring Fellowship for HBCU Faculty, the Mellon Foundation Summer Residency Fellowship at Duke University with William "Sandy" Darity, and the Humanities Writ Large Visiting Faculty Fellowship at Duke

University, where I was hosted for an academic year by the Women's Studies Department. There I had the opportunity to participate in "Pre-print," a seminar that allowed me to workshop the introduction to the book. The Duke University community of faculty, fellows, and staff who participated provided critical mentorship, guidance, and critique. Support from Bennett College provided time and resources for me to write.

For their crucial help in getting the manuscript into print, I am grateful to my sister, Anita Welbon, who joined our team as our copyeditor, and to the entire team at Duke University Press.

Throughout the long process of this project, I have received encouragement from many friends and relatives. I thank each of you for your kind words, inspiration, and ongoing unconditional love and support.

Dear reader, we wrote this book for you. Thank you for participating in this project of creating greater visibility for Sisters in the Life media makers. Please join us as we continue the conversation online at www.sistersinthelife.com.

Your Sister in Cinema,
Yvonne
AUGUST 2017

Selected Bibliography

Aaron, Michele. "Overview." In *New Queer Cinema: A Critical Reader*, edited by Michele Aaron. Edinburgh: Edinburgh University Press, 2004.

Abramovitz, Mimi. "Welfare Reform in the United States: Gender, Race and Class Matter." *Critical Social Policy* 26.2 (2006): 336–64.

Baldwin, James. *Nobody Knows My Name*. New York: Dell, 1961.

Brick, Neil D. "How Childhood Sexual Abuse Affects Interpersonal Relationships." SMART *Ritual Abuse Pages*, 2005. https://ritualabuse.us/research/sexual-abuse/how -childhood-sexual-abuse-affects-interpersonal-relationships/.

Brooks, Daphne A. "Nina Simone's Triple Play." *Callaloo* 34.1 (2011): 176–97.

Bruzzi, Stella. *New Documentary: A Critical Introduction*. London: Routledge, 2000.

Chappell, Marisa, Jenny Hutchinson, and Brian Ward. " 'Dress Moderately, Neatly . . . as If You Were Going to Church': Respectability, Class, and Gender in the Montgomery Bus Boycott and the Early Civil Rights Movement." In *Gender and the Civil Rights Movement*, edited by Peter John Ling and Sharon Monteith. Piscataway, NJ: Rutgers University Press, 2004.

Cheng, Anne. *Melancholy of Race*. Oxford: Oxford University Press, 2001.

Cole, Johnnetta B., and Beverly Guy-Sheftall. *Gender Talk: The Struggle for Women's Equality in African American Communities*. New York: Ballantine, 2003.

Collins, Patricia Hill. *Black Sexual Politics: African Americans, Gender, and the New Racism*. New York: Routledge, 2005.

Collins, Robert M. *Transforming America: Politics and Culture in the Reagan Years*. New York: Columbia University Press, 2007.

Conway, Mary. "Spectatorship in Lesbian Porn: The Woman's Woman's Film." *Wide Angle* 19.3 (1997): 91–113.

Cvetkovich, Ann. *An Archive of Feelings: Trauma, Sexuality, and Lesbian Public Cultures*. Durham, NC: Duke University Press, 2003.

"Dee Rees on CBC." *Focus Features*. Posted January 11, 2012. http://focusstaging .bronsonhq.com/pariah/news.

"Dee Rees Speaks with Richard Peña at Lincoln Center." *Focus Features*. Posted December 8, 2011. http://focusstaging.bronsonhq.com/pariah/news?bid=dee_rees _speaks_with_richard_pe__a_at_lincoln_center.

"Dee Rees Talks to *Italian Vogue*." *Focus Features*. Posted February 6, 2012. http://focusstaging.bronsonhq.com/pariah/news.

Dent, Gina, ed. *Black Popular Culture*. New York: New Press, 1989.

Dolan, Jill. "'Lesbian' Subjectivity in Realism: Dragging at the Margins of Structure and Ideology." In *Performing Feminisms: Feminist Critical Theory and Theater*, edited by Sue-Ellen Case. Baltimore: Johns Hopkins University Press, 1990.

Dudas, Jeffrey R. "In the Name of Equal Rights: 'Special' Rights and the Politics of Resentment in Post–Civil Rights America." *Law & Society Review* 39.4 (2005): 723–57.

Dunye, Cheryl, and Zoe Leonard. *The Fae Richards Photo Archive*. San Francisco: Artspace Books, 1996.

Experian Simmons. "The 2012 LGBT Report: Demographic Spotlight." Accessed August 24, 2017. http://www.experian.com/assets/simmons-research/white-papers/simmons-2012-lgbt-demographic-report.pdf.

Feldstein, Ruth. "I Don't Trust You Anymore: Nina Simone, Culture, and Black Activism in the 1960s." *Journal of American History* 91 (March 2005): 1349–79.

Ferguson, Roderick A. *Aberrations in Black: Toward a Queer of Color Critique*. Minneapolis: University of Minnesota Press, 2004.

Ferrera-Balanquet, Raúl, Shari Frilot, Leah Gilliam, Thomas Allen Harris, Brent Hill, Charles Lofton, Alfonso Moret, Dawn Suggs, Jocelyn Taylor, and Yvonne Welbon. "Narrating Our History: A Dialogue among Queer Media Artists from the African Diaspora." In *XII Black International Cinema Anthology*. Berlin, 1997.

"Film Company Expanding." *Billboard*, January 28, 1922, 104.

Forgacs, David, ed. *The Antonio Gramsci Reader: Selected Writings, 1916–1935*. New York: New York University Press, 2000.

"Freedom Summer: Three CORE Members Murdered in Mississippi." *CORE—Congress of Racial Equality*. Accessed January 26, 2013. http://www.core-online.org/History/freedom_summer.htm.

Gates, Henry Louis. "An Interview with Josephine Baker and James Baldwin" (1973). Edited by Quincy Troupe. In *James Baldwin: The Legacy*. New York: Simon & Schuster Touchstone Books, 1989.

Gordy, Sondra. "Lost Year." In *The Encyclopedia of Arkansas History and Culture*. Accessed March 10, 2013. http://www.encyclopediaofarkansas.net/encyclopedia/entry-detail.aspx?entryID=737.

Halberstam, Judith [Jack]. *Female Masculinity*. Durham, NC: Duke University Press, 1998.

Hammonds, Evelynn M. "Black (W)holes and the Geometry of Black Female Sexuality." In *Feminism Meets Queer Theory*, edited by Elizabeth Weed and Naomi Schor. Bloomington: Indiana University Press, 1997.

Hankin, Kelly. "Lesbian 'Making-of' Documentaries and the Production of Lesbian Sex." *Velvet Light Trap* 53.1 (2004): 26–39.

Heard, Danielle C. "'Don't Let Me Be Misunderstood': Nina Simone's Theater of Invisibility." *Callaloo* 35.4 (2012): 1056–84.

Higginbotham, Evelyn Brooks. "African-American Women's History and the Metalanguage of Race." *Signs* 17.2 (1992): 251–74.

Hine, Darlene Clark. *Hine Sight: Black Women and the Reconstruction of American History*. Bloomington: Indiana University Press, 1994.

Hong, Grace Kyungwon. *The Ruptures of American Capital: Women of Color, Feminism, and the Culture of Immigrant Labor*. Minneapolis: University of Minnesota Press, 2006.

hooks, bell. "Good Girls Look the Other Way." In *Feminism and Pornography*, edited by Drucilla Cornell. New York: Oxford University Press, 2000.

———. *Outlaw Culture: Resisting Representations*. New York: Routledge, 2006. Orig. pub. 1994.

Houston, Shine, director. *In Search of the Wild Kingdom*. Blowfish Video, 2007.

Hull, Gloria T., Patricia Bell Scott, and Barbara Smith. *All the Women Are White, All the Blacks Are Men, but Some of Us Are Brave*. Old Westbury, CT: Feminist Press, 1982.

Jenkins, Candice M. *Private Lives, Proper Relations: Regulating Black Intimacy*. Minneapolis: University of Minnesota Press, 2007.

Johnson, Patrick E. " 'Quare' Studies, or (Almost) Everything I Know about Queer Studies I Learned from My Grandmother." *Text and Performance Quarterly* 21.1 (2001): 1–15.

Jong, Erica. *Invisible Enemy: The African American Freedom Struggle after 1965*. Sussex, UK: Wiley-Blackwell, 2010.

Keeling, Kara. *The Witch's Flight: The Cinematic, the Black Femme, and the Image of Common Sense*. Durham, NC: Duke University Press, 2007.

Kernodle, Tammy L. " 'I Wish I Knew How It Would Feel to Be Free': Nina Simone and the Redefining of the Freedom Song in the 1960s." *Journal of the Society for American Music* 2.3 (2008): 295–317.

Kregloe, Karman. "Interview with 'Mississippi Damned' Filmmakers Tina Mabry and Morgan Stiff." *AfterEllen*, August 10, 2009. http://www.afterellen.com/movies/56451 -interview-with-mississippi-damned-filmmakers-tina-mabry-and-morgan-stiff.

Lo, Malinda. "Shine Louise Houston Will Turn You On." *Curve Magazine* 16.1 (2006). https://web.archive.org/web/20060506072624/http://www.curvemag.com/Detailed /711.html.

Loren, Arielle. "Black Feminist Pornography: Reshaping the Future of Adult." *Clutch Magazine Online*, April 20, 2011. http://www.clutchmagonline.com/2011/04/black -feminist-pornography-reshaping-the-future-of-adult-entertainment/.

Lune, Sadie. "Interview: Shine Louise Houston." *Bend Over Magazine*, no. 4. Accessed August 24, 2017. https://web.archive.org/web/20120415092932/http://www .bendovermagazine.com:80/articles/57-shine-louise-houston-interview.html.

Mayer, Vicki. *Below the Line: Producers and Production Studies in the New Television Economy*. Durham, NC: Duke University Press, 2011.

McMillen, Neil. *Dark Journey: Black Mississippians in the Age of Jim Crow*. Urbana: University of Illinois Press, 1997.

Miller, Joshua L. "The Discovery of What It Means to Be a Witness: James Baldwin's Dialectics of Distance." In *James Baldwin Now*, edited by Dwight A. McBride. New York: New York University Press, 1999.

Mississippi Damned. "About." Accessed August 24, 2017. www.mississippidamned.com /about/.

Moore, Marlon Rachquel, and Tina Mabry. "From a Real Place and Real People: An Interview with *Mississippi Damned* Writer/Director Tina Mabry." *Black Camera* 2.2 (2011): 130–37.

Muhammad, Erika. "Black Hi-Tech Documents." In *Struggles for Representation: African American Documentary Film and Video*, edited by Phyllis Rauch Klotman and Janet K. Cutler. Bloomington: Indiana University Press, 1999.

Mukherjee, Roopali. *The Racial Order of Things: Cultural Imaginaries of the Post-Soul Era*. Minneapolis: University of Minnesota Press, 2006.

Mumin, Nijla. "A Dark Warmth: A Review of *Mississippi Damned*." *Post No Ills Magazine*, October 12, 2009. http://www.postnoills.com/main/?p=115.

Muñoz, José Esteban. *Disidentifications: Queers of Color and the Performance of Politics*. Minneapolis: University of Minnesota Press, 1999.

Payne, Charles M. *I've Got the Light of Freedom: The Organizing Tradition and the Mississippi Freedom Struggle*. Berkeley: University of California Press, 1995.

Pick, Anat. "New Queer Cinema and Lesbian Film." In *New Queer Cinema: A Critical Reader*, edited by Michele Aaron. Edinburgh: Edinburgh University Press, 2004.

Rachal, John R. "'The Long, Hot Summer': The Mississippi Response to Freedom Summer, 1964." *Journal of Negro History* 84.4 (1999): 315–39.

Rees, Dee, director. *Pariah*. Focus Features, 2011.

Rhyne, Raga. "Pink Dollars: Gay and Lesbian Film Festivals and the Economy of Visibility." PhD dissertation. New York University, 2007.

Richardson, Matt. "Our Stories Have Never Been Told: Preliminary Thoughts on Black Lesbian Cultural Production as Historiography in *The Watermelon Woman*." *Black Camera* 2.2 (2011): 100–113.

Sesko, A. K., and M. Biernat. "Prototypes of Race and Gender: The Invisibility of Black Women." *Journal of Experimental Social Psychology* 46 (2010): 356–60.

Simone, Nina, and Stephen Clearly. *I Put a Spell on You: The Autobiography of Nina Simone*. New York: Da Capo, 1992.

16th Street Baptist Church. "A Brief History of the 16th Street Baptist Church." Accessed August 24, 2017. http://www.16thstreetbaptist.org/brief-history%2C-part-1 .html.

Sobchack, Vivian. "The Scene and the Screen: Envisioning Photographic, Cinematic, and Electronic Presence." In *Carnal Thoughts: Embodiment and Moving Image Culture*. Berkeley: University of California Press, 2004.

Spillers, Hortense J. *Black, White, and in Color: Essays on American Literature and Culture*. Chicago: University of Chicago Press, 2003.

———. "Interstices: A Small Drama of Words." In *Pleasure and Danger: Exploring Female Sexuality*, edited by Carol Vance. New York: Pandora / HarperCollins, 1992.

Springer, Claudia. "Black Women Filmmakers." *Jump Cut*, no. 29 (February 1984): 34–37.

Stewart, Jacqueline. *Migrating to the Movies: Cinema and Black Urban Modernity.* Berkeley: University of California Press, 2005.

Stone, Allucquère Rosanna. *The War of Desire and Technology at the Close of the Mechanical Age.* Cambridge, MA: MIT Press, 1995.

Sullivan, Laura. "Chasing Fae: *The Watermelon Woman* and Black Lesbian Possibility." *Callaloo* 23.1 (2000): 448–60.

Voss-Hubbard, Anke. " 'No Document—No History': Mary Ritter Beard and the Early History of Women's Archives." *American Archivist* 58.1 (1955): 16–30.

Wallenberg, Louise. "New Black Queer Cinema." In *New Queer Cinema: A Critical Reader,* edited by Michele Aaron. Edinburgh: Edinburgh University Press, 2004.

Watson, Bruce. *Freedom Summer: The Savage Season That Made Mississippi Burn and Made America a Democracy.* New York: Viking Press, 2010.

Welbon, Yvonne. "Sisters in Cinema: Case Studies of Three First-Time Achievements Made by African American Women Feature Film Directors in the 1990s." PhD dissertation, Northwestern University, 2001.

Winokur, Mark. "Body and Soul: Identifying with the Black Lesbian Body in Cheryl Dunye's *Watermelon Woman.*" In *Recovering the Black Female Body: Self-Representations by African-American Women,* edited by Michael Bennett and Vanessa D. Dickerson. New Brunswick, NJ: Rutgers University Press, 2001.

Contributors

Jennifer DeVere Brody is a professor of cultural studies, African American literature, and performance studies at Stanford University. Her books, *Impossible Purities* (Duke University Press, 1998) and *Punctuation: Art, Politics and Play* (Duke University Press, 2008), discuss relations among and between sexuality, gender, racialization, visual studies, and performance.

Jennifer DeClue is an assistant professor in the study of women and gender at Smith College. Her research interests include queer studies, black feminism, visual studies, cultural studies, diasporic loss, histories of segregation and miscegenation in the United States, the afterlife of chattel slavery, and the construction, production, and reproduction of blackness in the United States.

Raúl Ferrera-Balanquet is a prominent Cuban American artist, writer, curator, and Fulbright scholar from the Mariel Generation. He holds a PhD from Duke University and an MFA from the University of Iowa. He has exhibited at the Museum of Latin American Art, Long Beach; the Whitney Museum of American Art, New York; the Museum of Contemporary Art, Chicago; and Centro de Cultura Contemporanea, Barcelona, among others.

Alexis Pauline Gumbs is the founder of Eternal Summer of the Black Feminist Mind and the co-creator of the Queer Black Mobile Homecoming Project. She has a PhD in English, Africana Studies, and Women's Studies from Duke University and is the author of *Spill: Scenes of Black Feminist Fugitivity* (Duke University Press, 2016).

Thomas Allen Harris is the founder and president of Chimpanzee Productions, a company dedicated to producing unique audiovisual experiences that illuminate the human condition and the search for identity, family, and spirituality. His films include *Through a Lens Darkly* (2014), *Twelve Disciples of Nelson Mandela* (2005), and *É a Minha Cara / That's My Face* (2001).

Devorah Heitner founded Raising Digital Natives for parents and educators seeking advice on how to help children thrive in a world of digital connectedness. She is the author of *Screenwise: Helping Digital Kids Thrive (and Survive) in Their Digital World*

(Duke University Press, 2016) and *Black Power TV* (Duke University Press, 2013), a book on black public affairs television.

Pamela L. Jennings has used creative problem solving through computational thinking, creativity, and technology as key drivers of her creative, academic, research, policy, philanthropic, and entrepreneurial activities. She has held leadership positions in corporate research think tanks and research universities and art schools. She ran the National Science Foundation CreativeIT program and continues to be summoned as a leader and advocate of integrative creative, research, and pedagogical practice for national policy development.

Alexandra Juhasz is a director and producer who has made more than fifteen documentaries on feminist and lesbian issues from AIDS to women's films and teen pregnancy, including the features *Scale* (2008), *Video Remains* (2005), *Dear Gabe* (2002), and *Women of Vision* (1998). She also produced the acclaimed narrative features *The Owls* (2010) and *The Watermelon Woman* (1996). She is chair of the Department of Film at Brooklyn College and the author of critical writings about alternative media.

Kara Keeling is an associate professor in the Division of Critical Studies in the School of Cinematic Arts and in the Department of American Studies and Ethnicity at the University of Southern California and the author of *The Witch's Flight: The Cinematic, the Black Femme, and the Image of Common Sense* (Duke University Press, 2007). Her research has focused on African American film, theories of race, sexuality, and gender in cinema, critical theory, and cultural studies.

Candace Moore is an assistant professor at the University of Michigan, where her work focuses on queer representation in film and television. Moore's articles have appeared in *Cinema Journal*, GLQ, *Production Studies: Cultural Studies of Media Industries*, *Televising Queer Women*, *Reading the L Word: Outing Contemporary Television*, and *Third Wave Feminism and Television*.

Marlon Rachquel Moore is an assistant professor of English at the United States Naval Academy and the author of *In the Life and in the Spirit: Homoerotic Spirituality in African American Literature* (2015). Her current research focuses on the intertwined themes of spirituality, homosexuality, and racial identity in African American literature.

Michelle Parkerson is a writer, filmmaker, and educator from Washington, DC, and has served on the faculties of Northwestern University, Howard University, and Temple University. Her award-winning films include *Gotta Make This Journey: Sweet Honey in the Rock* (1983); *A Litany for Survival: The Life and Work of Audre Lorde* (codirected with Ada Gay Griffin, 1995); and *Stormé: The Lady of the Jewel Box* (1987). She is currently scripting *Lifted*, a 1920s action adventure about the first black woman pilot, Bessie Coleman.

Roya Rastegar is a curator, producer, and writer. She is a producer of the Netflix documentary *Gaga: Five Foot Two* (2017) and writer of the magical realist documentary *Wildness* (2011), which premiered at MoMA's Documentary Fortnight and won a Grand Jury Prize at Outfest. She is currently on the programming team at the Sundance Film Festival, focused on US fiction features and virtual reality content. She was previously a visiting professor at Bryn Mawr College, the director of programming at the LA Film Festival, and a programmer at the Tribeca Film Festival. Roya's writing on gender, race, and popular culture can be found in *Wired*, *The Nation*, and the *Huffington Post*.

L. H. Stallings is an associate professor of women's studies at the University of Maryland. She is the author of *Funk the Erotic: Transaesthetics and Black Sexual Cultures* (2015) and *Mutha Is Half a Word! Intersections of Folklore, Vernacular, Myth, and Queerness in Black Female Culture* (2015).

Yvonne Welbon is the founder of the Chicago-based nonprofit Sisters in Cinema, the senior creative consultant at Chicken & Egg Pictures, and an award-winning independent filmmaker. She has produced over two dozen films, including *Living with Pride: Ruth Ellis @ 100* (1999), *Sisters in Cinema* (2003), *The New Black* (2013), and *Sisters in the Life* (2018).

Patricia White is a professor of film and media studies at Swarthmore College. She is the author of *Uninvited: Classical Hollywood Cinema and Lesbian Representability* (1999) and is completing a book on global women's feature filmmaking in the twenty-first century.

Karin D. Wimbley is an assistant professor of English at DePauw University. Her research interests focus on African American cultural production across aesthetic registers and canons, especially African American literature, film, and visual culture.

Index